The Magic of Merrythought
— A Collector's Encyclopedia

by John Axe

The Merrythought Teddy Bear, used in many catalog illustrations.

Published By **HOBBY HOUSE PRESS, INC.**
Cumberland, Maryland 21502

Acknowledgments

One of the greatest experiences of my life was my trip to Ironbridge, Shorpshire, England, to research the production of Merrythought Limited for this book. While I was there I fell in love with the Merrythought toys and with the people of Shropshire. Now when I think of Merrythought I will also think of the people of Shropshire, who are so friendly and helpful. I hope that they like this book.

Of all the people to whom I am deeply indebted, the first is Mr. B.T. Holmes (Trayton), Merrythought's Chairman. I have never met a toy manufacturer who is as honest, sincere and obliging.

Oliver Holmes, Merrythought's Managing Director, is worthy of his heritage and of Merrythought and he is a super hot air balloon pilot.

Linda K. Smith of Tide-Rider, Inc., is gracious, lovely and very astute, and always a great help.

I could not have managed without these persons from Shropshire and Merrythought: Carol and John Baker, Sheila and Pepe Bakkioui, Edith Boden, Fanny Elizabeth Davis, Connie and Ken Downing, Elsie Duddell, Dorothy Guest, John Harrington, Jimmy Matthews, Doris Morris, Martin Oliver, Stephanie Owens, John Parkes, Jacqueline Revitt, Phyllis Taylor, Esther and Denis Walters, Marjorie Wilde and Irene Yates.

Some other generous friends helped with pictures, Merrythought collectibles and sound advice: Kay Bransky, Wanda Lodwick, Jane Holmes Rowan, and Glenn and Helen Sieverling.

Proofreading all these Merrythought numbers would have been impossible without the help of my sister, Patricia E. Axe.

I am fortunate to have my good friend, Donna H. Felger, as Editor.

Gary R. Ruddell, Publisher of Hobby House Press, Inc., put the whole project together.

I thank them all.

John Axe

Additional Copies of this Book may be Purchased at $19.95
from
Hobby House Press, Inc.
900 Frederick Street
Cumberland, Maryland 21502
or from your favorite bookstore or dealer.
Please add $1.75 per copy for postage.

© 1986 by Hobby House Press, Inc.

All rights reserved. No part of this book may be reproduced or utilized in any form or by any means, electronic or mechanical, including photocopying, recording, or by any information storage and retrieval system, without permission in writing from the publisher. Inquiries should be addressed to Hobby House Press, Inc., 900 Frederick Street, Cumberland, Maryland 21502.
Printed in the United States of America

ISBN: 0-87588-274-9

Table of Contents

Chapter I	Merrythought Limited	7
Chapter II	Teddy Bears, Polar Bears, Pandas, Koalas	23
Chapter III	Dogs	51
Chapter IV	Cats	70
Chapter V	Rabbits	76
Chapter VI	Domestic Animals	84
Chapter VII	Wild Animals	91
Chapter VIII	Jungle Animals	105
Chapter IX	Fantastic Animals	111
Chapter X	Birds and Insects	112
Chapter XI	Dolls	116
Chapter XII	Walt Disney Designs	126
Chapter XIII	Famous Artists' Designs	147
Chapter XIV	Movie, Television and Cartoon Characters	156
Chapter XV	Toys	163
Chapter XVI	Nightdress Cases	186
Chapter XVII	Miscellaneous	196
Appendix	A Preview of 1986	198

A collection of 1984 Merrythought dogs.

B. T. (Trayton) Holmes, Merrythought's Chairman, with his son, Oliver, Merrythought's Managing Director.

B.T. Holmes, Merrythought's Chairman; John Axe; and Oliver Holmes, Managing Director of Merrythought.

MERRYTHOUGHT
LIMITED
Est. 1930

Manufacturers of Britain's finest
Soft Toys & Night-dress Cases

Reg. Office & Factory:
Ironbridge, Telford,
Shropshire TF8 7NJ,
England.
Phone 095245-3116

Your Ref:

Our Ref: WOTH/JM

August 23, 1985

Gary Ruddell Esq.
HOBBY HOUSE PRESS INC.
900 Frederick Street
Cumberland, Maryland 21502
U.S.A.

Dear Gary:

In order to write this book, John Axe has spent a considerable time here in Ironbridge researching all our original archival material and talking to our staff. Three of the ladies that he talked to were in fact here at the beginning in 1930, and hence were able to add their own first-hand experiences.

We were very pleased to allow John Axe the exclusive use of our records because we knew that with his previous experience as an author he would make this book the first class job that it is. We are also most grateful to John for turning up all the information which was "new" to us and most probably would have been lost forever without his diligent work.

Our sincere thanks go to Gary Ruddell and Hobby House Press for making this book possible and for producing what is, in our opinion, a very careful and accurate history of Merrythought Limited, and its products.

Yours sincerely,
for MERRYTHOUGHT LIMITED

W. O. T. Holmes
(Director)

Trayton Holmes
(Chairman)

London Showroom: 2nd Floor, 52-54 Southwark Street, London SE1 1UA. Telephone 01-407-6682/3

Registered No. 250646 (England). Directors: F. E. Davies, J. H. Matthews, J. A. Parkes, A. W. Holmes, B. T. Holmes, W. O. T. Holmes.

ABOVE LEFT: Jacqueline Revitt, who has designed all Merrythought products since she began with the company in 1970.

ABOVE RIGHT: John Parkes, a Merrythought Director.

LEFT: Charles, the Prince of Wales, presented with a Merrythought Lion when he visited Ironbridge on July 4, 1979.

I. MERRYTHOUGHT LIMITED

Merrythought Teddy Bears, cats, dogs, other animals, dolls, and toys are all products of Shropshire, England, and have perhaps the most interesting history of all soft toys.

Shropshire is a county in west central England, on the Welsh border. It is mainly agricultural and about 80% of the area is farmland. It has been populated since pre-historic times and during the 1st century a Roman legion fortress existed in Viroconium, which was one of the largest towns in Britain. Shropshire is crossed by the Severn River, which divides the hilly south and west from the rolling plains of the north and east. Several small industries developed along the valley of the Severn in the 1700s and today this area is called the "Cradle of the Industrial Revolution."

In 1709 in a small brick building, still preserved, Abraham Darby was the first to smelt iron ore with coke, processed from the coal of nearby mines. This little iron foundry made the village of Coalbrookdale the greatest iron-producing region in the world. The first iron wheels, the first iron rails and the first steam locomotive were made there. The greatest of all the iron building achievements occurred in 1779, when Abraham Darby III built an iron bridge across the Severn. The world's first iron bridge was hailed as its "eighth wonder" and visitors came to marvel at it. This was the first large-scale structural use of cast iron in the world. The first iron bridge still stands over the Severn and the village around it is now called Ironbridge.

Other industries developed in Coalbrookdale and Ironbridge. There were iron foundries, tile and brick making factories and china factories, the most famous being Coalport China, which relocated at Stoke-on-Trent in 1927. The old factories at Coalbrookdale (about a mile from Ironbridge) closed years ago and the Severn gorge near the world's first iron bridge has been a museum to early industry since 1973, attracting tourists from all over the world.

In 1930 Merrythought Toys opened a factory at Coalbrookdale (now Ironbridge) in one of the foundry buildings of the Coalbrookdale Co., which built the first iron bridge in 1779. The beginning of Merrythought was in 1919 when W.G. Holmes went into partnership with G.H. Laxton and opened a small spinning mill in Yorkshire to make mohair yarns from raw mohair imported from Turkey, South Africa and other places. In the 1920s the demand for mohair fabric was declining because of the invention of synthetic fibers.

A customer of the yarns from Holmes and Laxton and Co. was Dyson Hall and Co., Ltd., in Huddersfield, a plush weaving factory, which also suffered loss of business during the 1920s. The plush weaving factory was bought out by Holmes and Laxton and then they had to find something to do with their mohair yarns and mohair cloth. The sales director of the now combined companies knew Mr. C.J. Rendle, who was in charge of toy production at Chad Valley, and Mr. A.C. Janisch, who was in charge of sales at J.K. Farnell, also a maker of soft toys. Both Rendle and Janisch were ready to leave their respective positions; Holmes and Laxton needed an outlet for their mohair yarns. Holmes and Laxton hired Rendle and Janisch as directors, rented space from the Coalbrookdale Co. and began producing Merrythought Toys.

Merrythought is the old English term for a wishbone, the breastbone of a fowl. According to superstition, when two persons pull a wishbone apart, the one getting the largest portion will have his wish granted. Nobody remembers why, but Merrythought Limited became the name of the new company that would produce toys made of mohair cloth.

Mr. Rendle brought some other workers with him from Chad Valley and they moved into the former social room of the Coalbrookdale Co. in Ironbridge, which was rented by Holmes and Laxton in September of 1930.

One of these former Chad Valley employees was Florence Atwood, who worked under designer Norah Wellings. (Norah Wellings later left Chad Valley to found her own soft toy company.) Florence Atwood, a deaf mute, learned designing at the "Deaf and Dumb School" in Manchester, which she attended with Mr. Rendle's daughter. She produced the entire range of toys for the first Merrythought line of 1931 and some of these items are still in production. She made toys of her own creations and translated into toys the drawings of well-known artists, such as Cloé (Chlöe) Preston (*Dinkie, the dog*), G.E. Studdy *(Bonzo)*, Lawson Wood (monkeys), and from MGM Studios in Hollywood, *Jerry Mouse*. (Note: In the early years MGM was happy to have Merrythought produce animals of the company's cartoon characters because it gave publicity to the characters. By the 1960s MGM wanted higher and higher royalties for the use of its copyrighted animal characters and this cost had to be included in the price of the item, forcing such popular characters as *Tom* and *Jerry* out of production.) Until 1949, when she died from cancer, Florence Atwood was the chief designer for Merrythought.

In early 1931 more space was rented from the former iron foundry. Trees, which were growing up to 20 feet high from the earth floor, had to be cleared out of the inside of the buildings, central heat was installed, other updating of the plant was completed, and more workers were hired to produce Merrythought Toys. Over the years the Merrythought factory facilities, which were purchased from the Coalbrookdale Co. in 1956, have been improved and new buildings added,

ABOVE: In the center is Fanny Elizabeth Davis, who began with Merrythought in its beginning as the bookkeeper and later became company secretary and now is a director of the company. At the left is Dorothy Guest who began with Merrythought in 1931 as a machinist and retired in 1975 as a manageress. At the right of Mrs. Davis is Phyllis Taylor, Mrs. Guest's sister, who began with Merrythought as a finisher at age 14. Mrs. Taylor has also retired from Merrythought.

LEFT: Martin Oliver, Merrythought's Works Manager.

but the main portion of the factory is still the large brick building that was built by the iron foundry in 1898.

World War II began when Germany invaded Poland on the first day of September 1939 and Britain and France declared war on Germany on September 3. On 5 September 1939, C.J. Rendle, Merrythought's Managing Director, issued a letter to the company's clients:

"We are compelled to make [new] arrangements now owing to the higher costs which have occurred. Further, there are difficulties in connection with raw materials. We shall do all we possibly can to maintain the standard quality of our goods, but we cannot guarantee maintenance of standard either as to quality or type of raw materials which were applying to our goods previous to this date. We must reserve the right to substitute the nearest and best quality we have at the time of making.

"With regard to delivery dates, we cannot undertake to deliver at any specified date. We shall do our best to accommodate our customers in every way, but it must be realized that our making capacity will be seriously affected as soon as the dark evenings come. It is not our intention to keep this factory open and working during the black-out hours. We consider it far too dangerous for our workpeople [sic] and staff to go on to [sic] the roads to return to their homes after work during the black-out hours."

By 1939 about 200 persons worked at Merrythought. Eight of those who began in the early 1930s are still with the company. One of them is Mrs. Fanny Elizabeth Davis, a lively and sparkling 80-year-old, who was hired to do costings of products and bookkeeping; later she became the company secretary; now she is a director of the company. Mrs. Davis told of what happened to Merrythought during World War II:

"The British Admiralty took over our buildings for storing plywood and for map making. Admiralty charts that were used for the war were made at Ironbridge and stored there in case the other map making sites were bombed. One bomb was dropped near the factory at Ironbridge but it did not do much damage. Merrythought rented space in nearby Wellington and with about eight people who did not leave for war work, we continued to make some toys. Then at the request of the government we began to produce things for the war: chevrons (sleeve badges that denote rank in the armed forces), linings for helmets, tiny ignitor bags, gas mask bags, covers for hot water bottles for hospitals, and other items from gaberdine and velour.

"In March of 1946 we started up production again in Ironbridge and hired and trained new workers. We fetched all our stuff back and got it on the floor when the flood hit. When the Severn flooded in 1946, we lost all the old samples of our toys made before the war, and a great deal of our supplies."

Other notable aspects of the early years of Merrythought are that in 1949 Mr. B.T. (Trayton) Holmes, the son of one of the founders, came to the factory, and in 1952 Dean and Son Ltd. began to represent Merrythought.

Under Trayton Holmes' management, Merrythought began to expand again. In 1955 an automatic stuffing machine was brought from the United States to fill soft animals, although hand stuffing was not abandoned. In 1956 the factory facilities were purchased from the Coalbrookdale Co. The original foundry building was improved again, a new design and showroom building was erected and an office block was built on the grounds. In 1958 Merrythought showed its products at the Toy Fair in Nürnberg, Germany, which is one of Europe's most important trade shows.

Trayton Holmes is a true native of Yorkshire, whose people are genuinely friendly and hospitable. He still runs his large sheep farm near the village of Clun, which has been famous for the high grade of its wool since the 13th century, and he has continued to manage the company on a basis that permitted it to retain its "family" character instead of automating and entering mass-production, as all other soft toy producers have done.

Mr. Holmes told of his background and his philosophy of what Merrythought is and will be:

"In my youth I was brought up as a mohair spinner and my goal was never to become rich, but to have a successful small business. My intention was to keep Merrythought small and exclusive and to keep it busy all year round with no 'stop-go,' as many toy companies have. Merrythought Toys are a quality product and we never wanted them in every shop. If I can tell a bloke that we are all sold out, it is the best advert we can have. The place was all disorganized when I came to the factory and with some luck I have turned it around."

Before the War the mohair for Merrythought Teddy Bears and animals came from the factory that Mr. Holmes' father and his partner purchased and from other mills in Yorkshire. There are two types of plush used in Merrythought animals. One is plush that is woven on a loom. The other is a knitted process. The best woven plush is now imported; knitted plush comes from various sources in Britain.

Because of the lack of supplies in England after World War II, Merrythought had to allocate their products to customers. In time orders began to "dry up" because of the allocation system. When more supplies to make toys and animals were available, Holmes needed an agent to represent him. This is when he obtained the representative services of Jimmy Matthews of Dean and Son Ltd. Mr. Matthews was attuned to the soft toy market and he was always trusted to suggest improvements in the products and in the lines of production.

Jimmy Matthews from Dean and Son Ltd. began as a salesman for the company's children's books and worked his way up to the position of Managing Director. He traveled all around the world showing Dean's products, and in 1952 he also began to represent Merrythought. He said, "We have taken Merrythought to the top of the tree, beginning with a big order from Selfridge's in London." (Merrythought Toys had never made a profit before 1941.)

Merrythought Toys are recognized in England as the best there is. The products of Merrythought are only sold in the better stores in England and about 80%

of production is for the home market; the remaining 20% is for export to other countries. The Merrythought factory has never been able to produce all the soft toys that they had the potential of selling.

Jimmy Matthews explained why:

"High quality merchandise can't be mass-produced on a large scale. There is a high element of hand-work in each Merrythought animal and we have been too well-respected in the trade for too long to change that and begin to mass-produce. Another aspect of all the hand-production is that no two animals of a Merrythought design are exactly identical."

After years of traveling the world representing Dean's books and Merrythought's toys, Mr. Matthews retired in 1976. He is still a consultant and Sales Director for Merrythought.

Holmes says, "Merrythought animals should always be appealing looking and they should be near-replicas of real animals or humanized animals. They should always be bed-worthy."

In 1972 Oliver Holmes, Trayton Holmes' son, came to the company after training as an engineer. He is now the Managing Director of Merrythought; Trayton Holmes is Chairman of the Board. But neither gentleman has become officious, as happens to many directors of successful toy companies.

Oliver Holmes says of Merrythought:

"It is a traditional private British Company. It is family-owned and I hope it always will be. We like to think that we provide quality, value and service. If one of our animals makes one smile, then it is a successful toy."

Since 1982 Merrythought's line of traditional Teddy Bears for collectors has been represented in the United States by Tide-Rider, Inc. of Baldwin, New York. Oliver Holmes asserts of these Merrythought collectibles:

"We strive to make our collectible products more interesting. We still use old skills and traditional techniques. As long as I am involved with Merrythought, we will strive to continue manufacturing traditional teddy bears with embroidered noses and classic designs. There will be no compromise in the production of the British Bears!"

Tide-Rider, Inc. says of the Merrythought products:

"Merrythought Ltd. is one of England's oldest established toy manufacturers. For over 50 years their careful selection of materials, diligent work and traditional craftsmanship have earned their toys the highest reputation for quality."

Merrythought Limited is a pleasant place to work. Doris Morris has been happily stuffing animals since 1931 and her speciality is the larger ones. She tells that the method has not changed at all since she began and that it takes about an hour to stuff an average size animal and about two hours for the larger ones. Carol Baker is a machinist (sewing machine operator) and she likes the products so well that she has a special room in her home that is exclusively for the display of Merrythought animals.

Elsie Duddell began as a machinist in 1936 at age 14. She reported the Merrythought tradition best of all when she said,

"It was more like a production line when I began; now the work on animals is more individual. I am never working on the same thing all the time. The name Merrythought speaks for itself and I like working for a company that has a high reputation. I've always been quite happy with my work. I like doing teddy bears best of all."

Dorothy Guest, who retired in 1975, still comes back to the factory to visit regularly. She began as a machinist in 1931 at age 15 and about her work she said, "I enjoyed every minute of it." Her sister, Phyllis Taylor, began a little later, at age 14, as a finisher — doing noses, ears and claws by hand. This is the way they are still done at Merrythought under the strict supervision of Esther Walters and Marjorie Wilde, who both began as youngsters with the company.

Jacqueline Revitt, who began with the company in 1970, is the current designer of all Merrythought animals. Mrs. Revitt trained as a clothing designer and pattern cutter and practiced these arts before accepting her current assignment with Merrythought. She receives suggestions from other principals in the company, who may also request that certain animal designs be added to the company's line of products. She then has full license to design from her conception of what the finished animal will be.

To create a pattern for a specific animal, Revitt draws a picture of the animal in profile and then engineers the joining parts to create patterns from which the design can be cut in mohair or plush cloth. The pattern "anatomy" has to be rendered in such a way that it will be machinable and practical to make and retain the realism of the envisoned animal when it is complete. Jacqueline Revitt gets her inspiration from observing real animals in action and from seeing them in films and on television.

After a pattern is created, Mrs. Revitt and her assistant produce a factory model which is studied and approved — or rejected — by the Directors of the company. Revitt also designs the costumes that some of the anthropomorphic animals wear. Once new designs have been accepted and they become part of the Merrythought line, Mrs. Revitt checks the production work to make sure that the animals being produced are up to the standards of the prototype model.

MERRYTHOUGHT DESIGNERS	
1930-1949	Florence Atwood
1953-1965	Jean Barber
1965-1967	various designers
1967-1969	Jackie Harper
1970-1977	Jacqueline Revitt
1977-1982	Pam Ford
1983-	Jacqueline Revitt

Jacqueline Revitt said,

"I think that the most successful and best accepted of my designs are the lions and tigers that I introduced to Merrythought production in the late 1970s. I always enjoy doing realistic animals best, as I like them better than animals that are caricatures."

All Merrythought animals are produced "by hand," although for convenience more than for cost-cutting, some facets of the operation are done by machine, such as an automatic cutter that can stamp out several pieces of plush pile at a time. The 1931 catalog showed about 150 styles of animals; the 1985 catalog has about 200 different styles. None of the animals from Merrythought over these 53 years were produced in extremely high numbers because of the company's avoidance of "mass-production." Both in England and abroad they were always retailed in the "better" stores, usually large department stores, who placed special orders with the company for the exact pieces they wanted before they were made.

Merrythought Production, 1930-1985

In 1930 Florence Atwood, Merrythought's first designer, entered 32 patterns in the pattern book, which is still in the company's archives. The first company catalog, which incorporated these designs, was issued in 1931. The first animal shown in the first catalog was *Greyfriars Bobby*. *Bobby* was inspired by the celebrated Skye Terrier who accompanied his master, John Gray, to Edinburgh from northern Scotland in 1858. John Gray died the day after his arrival in Edinburgh and he was buried in the churchyard of Greyfriars. Bobby, who was two years old, was discovered lying on his master's grave the next day. He stayed there for 14 years and when he died, he was buried in Greyfriars Churchyard also, near to his master's grave. Realistic and very appealing dogs became one of Merrythought's staple lines over the years.

The 1931 Merrythought catalog also introduced the company's fabulous line of Teddy Bears. The bears came in many different sizes with a wide selection of colors and materials. These 1930 designs, which have become classics, are still in production.

Other cute and charming animals, such as bunnies, lambs and ducks, were also offered. By the second catalog, 1932, the line had been expanded to include other domestic animals, like the *Black Cat;* farm animals; jungle animals; wild animals; animals on wheels; and even dressed animals, like *Toby,* a "Movie Toy," that could be placed in many different positions and hold them.

In 1933 dolls were added to production. At first the dolls were simple toys for babies, but by 1937 they were fully-articulated felt "art dolls," similar to the production of Lenci of Italy and Chad Valley of England.

Also in 1933 large riding toys were added to the line. These continue to be part of present Merrythought production.

By the 1950s dolls were not as important a part of production. In these years production of pyjama cases of dogs and other animals became more prominent in the line, as did designs by famous artists, including the designs of Walt Disney from cartoon films.

During the 1960s and 1970s Merrythought increased production of animals made of softer fabrics that were filled with lighter weight materials to meet consumer demand. Each year saw new items introduced, which increased the range of various types of animals without compromising quality in either fabrication or design.

1982 was another important year for Merrythought production when Tide-Rider, Inc. of Baldwin, New York, began to import traditional mohair Teddy Bears to meet collector demand in the United States. Since that time Merrythought has continued to produce traditional and original designs for Tide-Rider using traditional standards to address the needs of collectors.

Dating Merrythought Collectibles

As with the production of most companies who manufactured mohair and plush toys, the dating of collectibles cannot always be an exact science. If an item was made for a limited and specified time, the dating can be more accurate. For toys that have been manufactured over a long period of time, it is often impossible to determine if the item came from the early production stages or if it was from the later years. Some generalizations can be made about the dating of Merrythought toys:

— Pewter buttons in the ears — late 1930s.
— Woven cloth tags attached to the animal that read:
   MERRYTHOUGHT
   HYGENIC TOYS
   MADE IN ENGLAND   — before World War II
— Printed cloth tags attached to the animal that read:
   MERRYTHOUGHT
   IRONBRIDGE, SHROPS.
   MADE IN ENGLAND   — after World War II

The following chart shows the stock numbers used for the Merrythought toys over the years. This guide is based on the year the toy was designed, not the year it was placed in production. Some items may have been redesigned; some items have been renumbered; some items were never put into production; and some items were specials for certain shops and were never put into any of the company catalogs.

Stock Numbers

Years	Toys	Nightdress Cases
1930-1955	1000-2010	
1956	2011-2070	
1957	2071-2106	
1958	2107-2138	
1959	2139-	
(renumbered)	100-189	900
1960	190-232	↓
1961	233-282	to
1962	283-300	↓
1963	301-344	943
1964	345-395	944-960
1965	396-436	961
1966	437-462	962-984
1967	463-539	985-993

Stock Numbers		
Years	Toys	Nightdress Cases
1968	540-561	994-X1
1969	562-607	X2-X17
1970	608-632	X18-X30
1971	633-699	X31-X43
1972	700-743	X44-X59
1973	744-794	X60-X65
1974	795-839	X66-X71
1975	840-A12	X72-X78
1976	A13-A59	X79-X85
1977	A60-A84	X86-X92
1978	A85-B14	X93-X98
1979	B15-B42	X99-Y19
1980	B43-B72	Y20-Y37
1981	B73-C26	Y38-Y61
1982	C27-C62	Y62-Y70
1983	C63-D13	Y71-Y82
1984	D14-D64	Y83
1985	D65+	Y84+

Catalog Numbers and Sizes

The catalog numbers for an animal correspond to the size of an animal. Some catalog numbers are the actual sizes; others show the size differential.

Baby Lamb from 1935 catalog:

S1326/5½	Smallest Size	5½ inches (14cm) tall
S1326/6½		6½ inches (16.5cm) tall
S1326/7½		7½ inches (19.1cm) tall
S1326/8½		8½ inches (21.6cm) tall
S1326/9½		9½ inches (24.2cm) tall
S1326/11	Largest Size	11 inches (27.9cm) tall

Frog from 1984 catalog:

C28/1	Smallest Size	8 inches (20.3cm) tall
C28/2	Middle Size	10 inches (25.4cm) tall
C28/3	Largest Size	12 inches (30.5cm) tall

(Prefix letters, example "S" and "C" above explained on the next chart.)

Measurements are not totally accurate and sizes can vary slightly depending upon which portion of the animal is measured; whether or not it is fluffy or it has been squeezed down slightly from storage and packing; and so forth. The size is the longest measurement of the animal, except for a long tail, or the height of the animal, except for protruding ears. The Merrythought catalogs list all sizes in inches only.

Materials

For animals designed *before* 1975, the alphabet letter(s) given with the stock number can designate the type of material from which the animal was made. The prefix letters on the following chart apply ONLY TO ANIMALS MADE BEFORE 1975. WITH THE EXCEPTION OF TEDDY BEARS.

Materials	
Letter	Material/color
AS	art silk plush
AX	mohair; old gold
BB	mohair; burnished bronze
BLT	plush; blue
BT	plush; dark mink
BX	mohair; old gold

Materials	
Letter	Material/color
CDR	woolly plush
CM	mink plush
CT	simulated mink plush
F	curly piled mohair
GM	mohair; super London gold
GT	mohair; London gold
H	medium mohair (kapok filled)
L	mohair; London gold (kapok filled)
LLT	mohair; gold
LM	modacrylic plush; champagne
LT	plush; champagne
M	mohair; old gold
MCE	plush; amber (kapok filled)
MCN	plush; amber (kapok filled)
MM	modacrylic plush; gold
MP	"Movie Toys"
MT	mohair (*Cheeky*)
NM	mohair (kapok filled)
NY	nylon; brown
O	nylon (open mouth *Cheeky*)
PAT	silk plush; various colors (*Cheeky*)
PKT	plush; pink (*Cheeky*)
Q	mohair (long curly pile)
RS	plush (long pile)
S	art silk plush
T	mohair (long pile tipped with dark color)
T	mohair; gold (*Cheeky*)
TAS	rayon silk plush; old gold (*Cheeky*)
TNY	nylon *Cheeky*

Note: Before 1975 these letters also designated materials:

A	white alpaca plush
B	long grey pile mohair
C	woolly plush

After 1975 (see Chart "Stock Numbers") these single letters, A, B, C, denoted the date the animal was designed:

A	1975-1978
B	1978-1981
C	1981-1983

See also Chart "BEAR CHART" in Chapter II, TEDDY BEARS

One more chart is necessary to explain prefex letters that designate dates of Merrythought catalogs:

Prefix letters	Date of Catalog
CE	1947
CN	1948

Presentation of the Merrythought Collection

All of the following charts are taken from the Merrythought catalogs. The catalogs are from 1931 to the present. There are no catalogs for the years of World War II and the years following the war (1940-1947). The Merrythought production is presented in the following order:

CHAPTER II.   Teddy Bears, Polar Bears, Pandas, Koalas.
CHAPTER III.   Dogs, Doggies, Puppies.
CHAPTER IV.   Cats, Kitties, Kittens.
CHAPTER V.   Rabbits, Bunnies, Hares.

CHAPTER VI.	Domestic Animals. These are mostly animals found on farms like pigs, cows and lambs. The camels are listed in this section.
CHAPTER VII.	Wild Animals. These are animals that live in the wild like foxes, kangaroos, mice and tortoises.
CHAPTER VIII.	Jungle Animals. These are the animals that are native to jungles and animals that are native to Africa like monkeys, lions and zebras. Tigers are also included in this section, although they are not found in Africa, having had an origin in Iran and presently found in Asia.
CHAPTER IX.	Fantastic Animals. These are animals that never existed, like dragons.
CHAPTER X.	Birds and insects. These include ducks, geese and parrots; ladybirds (ladybugs) and caterpillars.
CHAPTER XI.	Dolls.
CHAPTER XII.	Walt Disney Designs. These are toys that are based on the creations of Walt Disney from movie cartoons.
CHAPTER XIII.	Famous Artists' Designs. These are all the toys that were designed from the creations and renderings of famous artists other than Merrythought designers and Walt Disney.
CHAPTER XIV.	Movie, Television and Cartoon Characters. These are licensed characters like *Tom* and *Jerry* and *Rin Tin Tin*.
CHAPTER XV.	Toys. This section includes baby toys, push toys, riding toys and animated toys that include stuffed animals in the design.
CHAPTER XVI.	Nightdress cases. These are dolls, animals and other figures that have a zipper compartment or pocket for storing a child's night clothing.
CHAPTER XVII.	Miscellaneous. These are non-toy items like artificial Christmas trees, purses and hassocks.

Within each chapter, or section, most items are listed by the year of production. DOGS are listed alphabetically according to breed, followed by "Dog" for undetermined breeds and are in order according to the year produced. BEARS, CATS and RABBITS are listed according to the year produced, although BEARS are in seven different categories for Teddy Bears, followed by Polar Bears, Pandas and Koalas. All other animals are listed first alphabetically and then according to the production years. DOLLS are listed according to the years of production. WALT DISNEY DESIGNS are listed alphabetically, with the title of the film from which they came cited. FAMOUS ARTISTS' DESIGNS are listed alphabetically by the last name of the artist and then alphabetically by the name of the item. MOVIE, TELEVISION AND CARTOON CHARACTERS are listed alphabetically by the name of the show or film from which they derived. TOYS and NIGHTDRESS CASES are all listed according to the above system. The MISCELLANEOUS section is listed alphabetically by the name of the item, and then by the year of production.

Illustration 1. Mr. John Harrington of Jackfield, Shropshire, posed for a studio photograph with the No. 1477 Merrythought *Sealyham* in December of 1939 at the age of one year, nine months. *Photograph courtesy of John Harrington.*

Illustration 2. In 1779 the world's first iron bridge was built across the Severn River by Abraham Darby, III, who was the first iron worker to smelt with coke at his foundry in Coalbrookdale, Shropshire, England. The bridge is close to the Merrythought factory in Ironbridge.

Illustration 3. The Merrythought factory in Ironbridge, Shropshire. Most of the production for Merrythought Toys is done in the building shown in the right foreground. This shop was built in about 1898 as part of the Coalbrookdale Company foundry, the ironworks that constructed the world's first iron bridge in 1779.

Illustration 3-A. A view inside the Merrythought factory in the 1930s, showing toys being assembled. *Merrythought photograph.*

Illustration 3-B. Another view of the Merrythought factory, which was once an iron foundry, showing some of the staff in the 1930s working on Merrythought toys. *Merrythought photograph.*

Illustration 4. Oliver Holmes, Managing Director of Merrythought Limited, is a hot air balloon enthusiast. Here he prepares to launch the Merrythought balloon.

Illustration 5. The Merrythought balloon over Shropshire.

Illustration 6. Oliver Holmes and his father, Trayton Holmes, the Chairman of the Board of Merrythought Limited, are about to ascend in the Merrythought balloon with the GM40 Merrythought Teddy Bear.

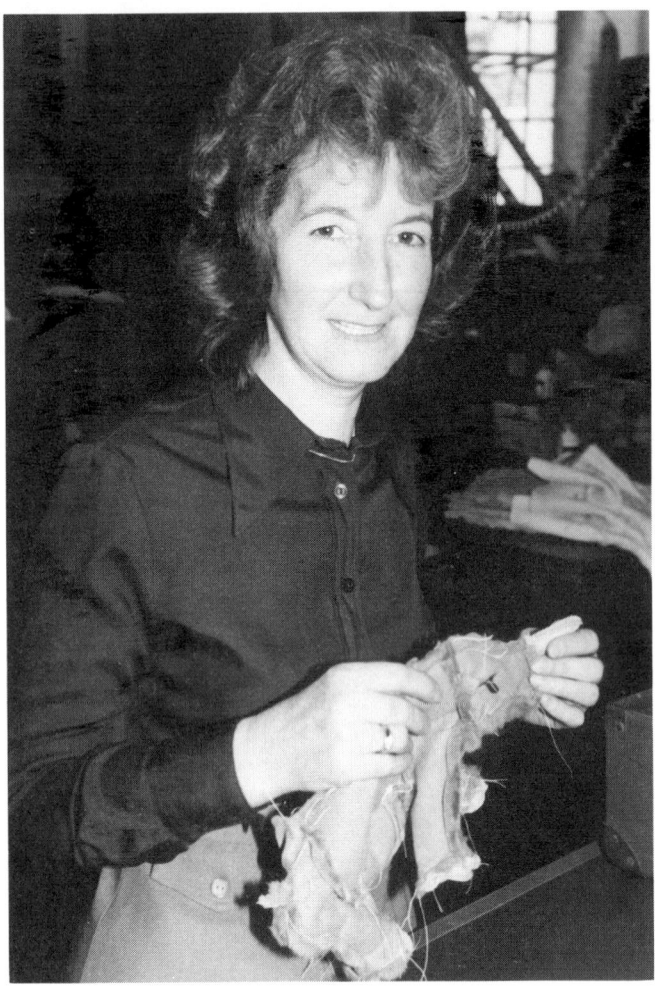

Illustration 7. Esther Walters, Merrythought sewing machine supervisor, in the factory.

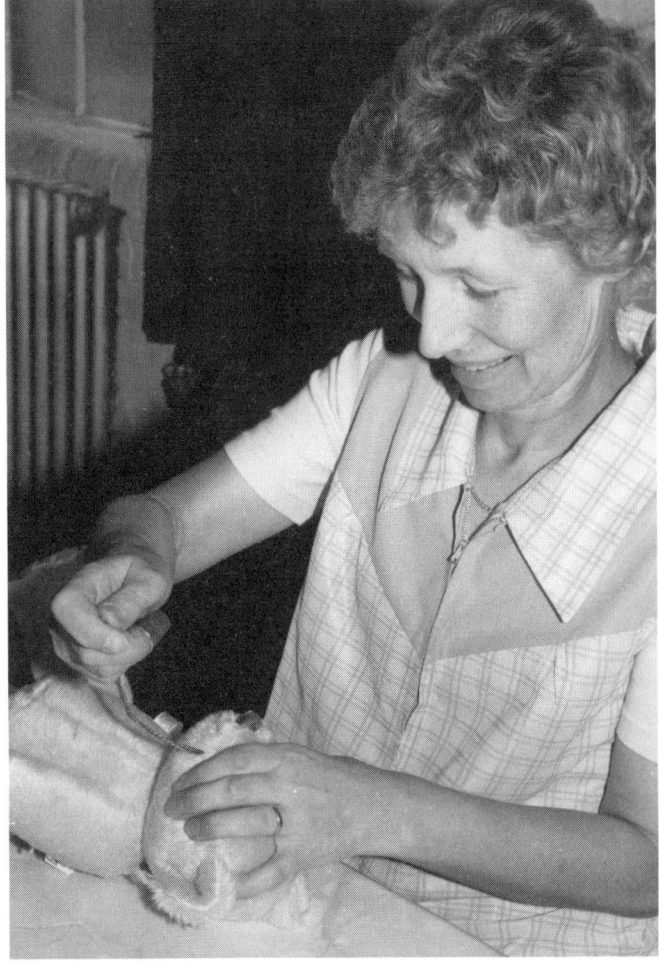

Illustration 8. Marjorie Wilde, Merrythought supervisor, sewing on a Teddy Bear's nose by hand.

Illustration 9. Teddy Bears passing inspection at the Merrythought factory in Ironbridge.

Illustration 10. Harrods Department Store in London with large Merrythought animals included in the display.

Illustration 11. Walt Disney star Annette Funicello and English rock star Cliff Richard with the 187 Merrythought *Giraffe* in about 1960. © Walt Disney Productions Limited.

Illustration 12. Queen Elizabeth II examines a Merrythought No. 1989 *Corgi* at the British Industries Fair, late 1950s, presented by Jimmy Matthews, Merrythought's Sales Director.

Illustration 13. Jimmy Matthews shows *Splasher Duck*, No. 1968, to Princess Margaret Rose and Queen Mother Elizabeth at the British Industries Fair, late 1950s.

BELOW: Illustration 14. Jimmy Matthews with Prince William of Gloucester in the Merrythought booth at the British Industries Fair, 1950s.

Illustration 15. Jimmy Matthews and B.T. Holmes were presented with the Retailers Association of Merit Award, 1970s. In the background are Merrythought animals.

Illustration 16. Prince Charles holds the Merrythought No. 493 *Hippo*, which was given to him for his new son, Prince William, at the Brixton branch of the department store Marks and Spencer by a store employee on July 2, 1982.

II. TEDDY BEARS, POLAR BEARS, PANDAS, KOALAS

Shortly after the turn of the 20th century in the United States Teddy Bears became very popular toys for children. They are still one of the staples of the toy market. In recent times collectors have become more and more interested in preserving them and the history associated with them. A Teddy Bear is actually a caricature of a bear because it is a bear in a humanized form. Teddy Bears are stuffed with a filling material such as kapok, and the "better" ones have jointed heads, arms and legs.

Merrythought began Teddy Bear production in the first year of the company and Teddy Bears are still one of its most important products. The first Teddy Bear was called *The Magnet Bear* and it was advertised as "A really cheap line — Gold or Colours," referring to the selling price, not the quality. In 1931 toy animals made from mohair cloth sold for less than those made from "art silk plush," a synthetic material. In 1931 the wholesale price for a dozen 12½ inch (31.8cm) bears was 42 Pounds; a dozen 13 inch (33cm) art silk bears sold for 60 Pounds. (Note: One current Pound equals 20 old Pounds.)

The early Merrythought Teddy Bears of mohair have survived in excellent condition, except of course, for those who have had their noses and eyes "kissed off" by loving owners or whose fur has worn off from too much attention. The very nature of a Teddy Bear invites a lot of hugging!

Teddy Bears are listed in the order of manufacture, within seven different categories — 1. Traditional Merrythought Teddy Bears, 2. the *Bingie Family*, 3. *Cheeky Bears*, 4. *London Bears*, 5. *Aristocrat Bears*, 6. other Teddy Bears, and 7. Tide-Rider, Inc. Limited Edition Teddy Bears.

The following charts show the 1985 Teddy Bears from Merrythought. These charts can also be used to designate the bears made within the last few years.

First letter = color		second letter = style	
A	gold*	M	Traditional Bear
B	blue	E	Edwardian Bear
C	caramel*	R	Snout bear w/ M body
D	toffee	Y	Merry Bear
E	old gold*	T	T Bear
F	white*	H	T head; M body
G	gold*	O	Snout Bear
H	beige*	U	Special bear for English market
I	grey*	G	(discontinued)
J	brown*	S	Aristocrat Bear
K	mandarin		
L	champagne		
M	melia		
N	surprise*	* pure mohair pile	
O	tilsit		
Q	autumn	these letters after the size indicate:	
R	lamb	MU	Music box
S	grey*	GR	Growler inside
T	gold*		
U	bronze*		
V	grey*		
W	peach*		
X	special*		

SIZE	Style of Bear									SIZE
	M	E	R	Y	T	H	O	U	G	S	
8					X						8
10	X				X						10
11	X	X						X			11
12	X				X					X	12
13	X							X			13
14	X	X		X	X					X	14
15	X							X			15
16	X				X		X			X	16
17	X							X			17
18	X	X		X	X					X	18
20	X										20
21	X									X	21
24		X			X						24
32	X									X	32
40	X									X	40

Examples:
EO16GR = Old gold mohair/Snout Bear/16 inches
(40.6cm) tall/has growler
SM40 = grey mohair/Traditional Bear/40 inches
(101.6cm) tall

TEDDY BEARS

	Stock No.	Name	Size inches centimeters	Year
1. Traditional Merrythought Teddy Bears	M1006/3	The Magnet Bear (mohair-gold or colors; soft stuffed)	12½ (31.8)	1931
	/5		15½ (39.4)	
	/8		19½ (49.6)	
	/11		24 (61.0)	
	B1021/1	The Merrythought Bear (mohair-light gold)	12 (30.5)	1932-1933
	/3		13 (33.0)	1931-1933
	/4		14 (35.6)	
	/5		15 (38.1)	
	/6		16 (40.6)	
	/7		17 (43.2)	
	/8		18 (45.7)	
	/9		19 (48.3)	
	/10		21 (53.3)	
	/11		24 (61.0)	
	/12		26 (66.0)	
	/13		30 (76.2)	1933
	S1021/1	The Merrythought Bear (art silk plush)	12 (30.5)	1932
	/3		13 (33.0)	1931-1932
	/4		14 (35.6)	
	/5		15 (38.1)	
	/6		16 (40.6)	
	/7		17 (43.2)	
	/8		18 (45.7)	
	/9		19 (48.3)	
	/10		21 (53.3)	
	/11		24 (61.0)	1932
	/12		26 (66.0)	
	Q1021/1	The Merrythought Bear (long curly mohair)	12 (30.5)	1932
	/3		13 (33.0)	
	/4		14 (35.6)	
	/5		15 (38.1)	
	/6		16 (40.6)	
	/7		17 (43.2)	
	/8		18 (45.7)	
	/9		19 (48.3)	
	/10		21 (53.3)	
	/11		24 (61.0)	
	/12		26 (66.0)	
	BX1021/1	The Merrythought Bear (mohair — old gold)	12 (30.5)	1932
	/3		13 (33.0)	
	/4		14 (35.6)	

Stock No.	Name	Size inches	centimeters	Year
/5	*The Merrythought Bear* (mohair — old gold), continued	15	(38.1)	
/6		16	(40.6)	
/7		17	(43.2)	
/8		18	(45.7)	
/9		19	(48.3)	
/10		21	(53.3)	
/11		24	(61.0)	
/12		26	(66.0)	
F1021/1	*The Merrythought Bear* (curly piled mohair)	12	(30.5)	1933
/3		13	(33.0)	
/4		14	(35.6)	
/5		15	(38.1)	
/6		16	(40.6)	
/7		17	(43.2)	
/8		18	(45.7)	
/9		19	(48.3)	
/10		21	(53.3)	
/11		24	(61.0)	
/12		26	(66.0)	
/13		30	(76.2)	
M/1	*Merrythought Teddy Bear* (gold long pile mohair; kapok filled)	12	(30.5)	1936
/3		13	(33.0)	
/4		14	(35.6)	
/5		15	(38.1)	
/6		16	(40.6)	
/7		17	(43.2)	
/8		18	(45.7)	
/9		19	(48.3)	
/10		21	(53.3)	
/11		24	(61.0)	
/12		26	(66.0)	
/13		30	(76.2)	
AS/1	*Merrythought Teddy Bear* (art silk plush in seven shades; kapok filled)	12	(30.5)	1936-1938
/3		13	(33.0)	
/4		14	(35.6)	
/5		15	(38.1)	
/6		16	(40.6)	
/7		17	(43.2)	
/8		18	(45.7)	
AX/0	*Merrythought Teddy Bear* (old gold short plush)	10½	(26.7)	1936-1938
/1		12	(30.5)	
/3		13	(33.0)	
/4		14	(35.6)	
/5		15	(38.1)	
/6		16	(40.6)	
/7		17	(43.2)	
/8		18	(45.7)	
/9		19	(48.3)	
/10		21	(53.3)	
/11		24	(61.0)	
/12		26	(66.0)	
T/4	*Merrythought Teddy Bear* (long pile mohair of biscuit brown tipped with darker color)	14	(35.6)	1936-1938
/6		16	(40.6)	
/8		18	(45.7)	
/10		21	(53.3)	
/12		26	(66.0)	
H/12	*Merrythought Teddy Bear* (medium pile mohair; medium soft stuffed)	12	(30.5)	1936-1938
/15½		15½	(39.4)	
/17		17	(43.2)	
/21		21	(53.3)	
M/1	*Merrythought Teddy Bear* (gold long pile mohair)	12	(30.5)	1937-1938
/13		13	(33.0)	
/14		14	(35.6)	
/15		15	(38.1)	
/16		16	(40.6)	
/17		17	(43.2)	
/18		18	(45.7)	
/19		19	(48.3)	
/21		21	(53.3)	
/24		24	(61.0)	
/26		26	(66.0)	
/30		30	(76.2)	
BB/1	*Merrythought Teddy Bear* (burnished bronze mohair)	12	(30.5)	1939
/13		13	(33.0)	
/14		14	(35.6)	

Stock No.	Name	Size inches	Size centimeters	Year
/15	*Merrythought Teddy Bear* (burnished bronze mohair), continued	15	(38.1)	
/16		16	(40.6)	
/17		17	(43.2)	
/18		18	(45.7)	
/19		19	(48.3)	
/21		21	(53.3)	
/24		24	(61.0)	
/26		26	(66.0)	
MCE/13	*Merrythought Teddy Bear* (amber plush; kapok filled)	13	(33.0)	1947
/15		15	(38.1)	
/17		17	(43.2)	
MCN/14	*Merrythought Teddy Bear* (amber plush; kapok filled)	14	(35.6)	1948
/16		16	(40.6)	
/18		18	(45.7)	
/21		21	(53.3)	
HCE/12	*Merrythought Teddy Bear* (gold short plush; kapok filled)	12	(30.5)	1947
/15		15½	(39.4)	
/17		17	(43.2)	
HCN/15	*Merrythought Teddy Bear* (gold short plush; kapok filled)	15	(38.1)	1948
/17		17	(43.2)	
/21		21	(53.3)	
H/11	*Merrythought Teddy Bear* (gold shaggy mohair; kapok filled)	11	(27.9)	1955-1957
/12		12	(30.5)	1954
/13		13	(33.0)	1955-1957
/15		15	(38.1)	1950-1954
/16		16	(40.6)	1955-1957
/17		17	(43.2)	1950-1957
/21		21	(53.3)	1950-1957
M/14	*Merrythought Teddy Bear* (gold medium pile mohair; kapok filled)	14	(35.6)	1950-1962
/16		16	(40.6)	
/18		18	(45.7)	
/21		21	(53.3)	
/30		30	(76.2)	1951-1962
AS/9	*Merrythought Teddy Bear* (art silk plush)	9	(22.9)	1954-1956
L/9	*Merrythought Teddy Bear* (London gold mohair; kapok filled)	9	(22.9)	1955-1956
/11		11	(27.9)	
/13		13	(33.0)	
/15		15	(38.1)	
NM/14	*Traditional Teddy Bear* (mohair; kapok filled)	14	(35.6)	1963-1965
/16		16	(40.6)	
/18		18	(45.7)	
/21		21	(53.3)	
/32		32	(81.3)	
GM/10	*Traditional Teddy Bear* (super London gold pure mohair)	10	(25.4)	1975-1980
/12		12	(30.5)	1981-1985
/14		14	(35.6)	1965-1985
/16		16	(40.6)	
/18		18	(45.7)	
/21		21	(53.3)	
/32		32	(81.3)	
/40		40	(101.6)	
/48		48	(121.9)	1971-1981; 1984
CM/12	*Traditional Teddy Bear* (light champagne mink plush)	12	(30.5)	1981
/14		14	(35.6)	1970-1981
/16		16	(40.6)	
/18		18	(45.7)	
/21		21	(53.3)	
/32		32	(81.3)	
/40		40	(101.6)	1976-1981
/48		48	(121.9)	1971-1981
NY/14	*Traditional Teddy Bear* (brown bears)	14	(35.6)	1974-1975
/16		16	(40.6)	
/18		18	(45.7)	
/21		21	(53.3)	
/32		32	(81.3)	
/48		48	(121.9)	
LM/12	*Traditional Teddy Bear* (Champagne Luxury Bear)	12	(30.5)	1984-1985
/14		14	(35.6)	1982; 1984-1985
/16		16	(40.6)	
/18	plain; growl; or growl with bib	18	(45.7)	
/21		21	(53.3)	
/32		32	(81.3)	
/40		40	(101.6)	

Stock No.	Name	Size inches	centimeters	Year
MM/12	*Traditional Teddy Bear* (Golden Traditional Bear)	12	(30.5)	1984-1985
/14		14	(35.6)	
/16		16	(40.6)	
/18	growl or musical	18	(45.7)	
/21		21	(53.3)	
/32		32	(81.3)	
/40		40	(101.6)	
SM/12	*Traditional Bears* (Ironbridge grey pure mohair)	12	(30.5)	1985
/14		14	(35.6)	
/16		16	(40.6)	
/18		18	(45.7)	
/18GR	w/ growl and bib	18	(45.7)	
/18MU	w/ musical and bib	18	(45.7)	
/21		21	(53.3)	
/32		32	(81.3)	
/40		40	(101.6)	

2. The Bingie Family

Stock No.	Name	inches	centimeters	Year
B1046/1	*Bingie* (sitting cub)	9	(22.9)	1931-1933; 1936-1938
/2		11	(27.9)	1931-1933; 1936-1938
/3		14	(35.6)	1931-1933; 1936-1938
/4		16	(40.6)	1932
/5		19	(48.3)	
/5		18	(45.7)	1936-1938
/7		26	(66.0)	1932
S1046/00	*Baby Bingie*	5¼	(13.4)	1932-1933
/0		7	(17.8)	1932; 1936-1938
MP1165/1	*Cutie Bingie* (a "Movie Toy" which could be placed in many positions.)	7	(17.8)	1932-1933
/2		10	(25.4)	
/3		12½	(31.8)	
		15	(38.1)	
1205/1	*Girl* (dressed)	15	(38.1)	1933
/2		20	(50.8)	
1207/1	*Boy* (dressed)	15	(38.1)	1933
/2		20	(50.8)	
1243/1	*Grenadier Guardsman* (dressed)	20	(50.8)	1933; 1936-1938
/2		27	(68.6)	
1206/1	*Sailor* (dressed)	15	(38.1)	1933; 1936-1938
/2		20	(50.8)	
1242/1	*Ski-Girl* (dressed)	15	(38.1)	1933
/2		20	(50.8)	
1291/1	*Highlander Bingie* (dressed)	16	(40.6)	1934; 1936-1938
/2		20	(50.8)	
1046/0	*Cradle Bingie*	7	(17.8)	1947-1948; 1950-1954
/2		11¼	(28.6)	1948; 1950-1953
/3		14¼	(36.3)	

3. Cheeky Bears (Note: Cheeky not available in Canada.)

Stock No.	Name	inches	centimeters	Year
TAS/1	*Cheeky* (thick silk plush; old gold)	9	(22.9)	1957-1969
/2		11	(27.9)	
/3		13	(33.0)	
/4		15	(38.1)	
/5		25	(63.5)	1958-1969
T/1	*Cheeky* (shaggy gold mohair)	9	(22.9)	1957-1965
/2		11	(27.9)	
/3		13	(33.0)	
/4		15	(38.1)	
/5		25	(63.5)	1958-1965
PAT/1	*Cheeky* (silk plush in assorted colors)	9	(22.9)	1957-1959
/2		11	(27.9)	
/3		13	(33.0)	
/4		15	(38.1)	
/5		25	(63.5)	1958-1959
TNY/1	*Cheeky* (nylon)	9	(22.9)	1960-1961
/2		11	(27.9)	
/3		13	(33.0)	
/4		15	(38.1)	
/5		25	(63.5)	
O/1	*Cheeky with Open Mouth* (honeysuckle nylon plush)	9	(22.9)	1962
/2		11	(27.9)	
/3		13	(33.0)	
/4		15	(38.1)	
/5		25	(63.5)	

Stock No.	Name	Size inches	centimeters	Year
LLT/1	Cheeky (London gold shaggy mohair)	9	(22.9)	1964
/2		11	(27.9)	
/3		13	(33.0)	
/4		15	(38.1)	
/5		25	(63.5)	
GT/1	Cheeky (London gold mohair)	9	(22.9)	1965-1983
/2		11	(27.9)	
/3		13	(33.0)	
/4		15	(38.1)	
/4A		18	(45.7)	1970-1981
/5		25	(63.5)	1965-1983
441/1	Mr. Twisty Cheeky	11	(27.9)	1966-1968
/3		24	(61.0)	
442/1	Mrs. Twisty Cheeky	11	(27.9)	1966-1968
/3		24	(61.0)	
BT/4	Cheeky (super thick dark mink plush)	15	(38.1)	1970
/4A		18	(45.7)	
/5		25	(63.5)	
CT/3	Cheeky (simulated mink)	13	(33.0)	1981
/4		15	(38.1)	1971-1981
/4A		18	(45.7)	
/5		25	(63.5)	
TNY/1	Cheeky (brown drylon)	9	(22.9)	1974-1975
/2		11	(27.9)	
/3		13	(33.0)	
/4		15	(38.1)	
/4A		18	(45.7)	
/5		25	(63.5)	
A46	Bed-Time Bear (Cheeky with removable pyjamas, gown, slippers)	17	(43.2)	1977
BLT/12	Cheeky (blue plush)	12	(30.5)	1982 & 1984
/14		14	(35.6)	1982-1983
/16		16	(40.6)	1982
PKT/12	Cheeky (pink plush)	12	(30.5)	1982 & 1984
/14		14	(35.6)	1982-1983
/16		16	(40.6)	1982
GT/10	Cheeky (London gold mohair)	10	(25.4)	1982-1983
/12		12	(30.5)	
/14		14	(35.6)	
/16		16	(40.6)	
LT.12	Cheeky (champagne plush)	12	(30.5)	1984-1985
MT 10	Cheeky (mohair)	10	(25.4)	1984
12		12	(30.5)	1984-1985
14		14	(35.6)	1984
BT/12	Cheeky (blue)	12	(30.5)	1985
PT/12	Cheeky (pink)	12	(30.5)	1985

4. London Bears

Stock No.	Name	inches	centimeters	Year
716/1	London Guardsman	21	(53.3)	1972-1975
/3		30	(76.2)	
726/1	London Policeman	20	(50.8)	1972-1974
/3		28	(71.1)	
767/1	Beefeater Bear	18	(45.7)	1973-1975
/3		25	(63.5)	
768/1	Highlander Bear	18	(45.7)	1973-1974
/3		25	(63.5)	

5. Aristocrat Bears (long plush)

Stock No.	Name	inches	centimeters	Year
RS/14		14	(35.6)	1983-1985
/16		16	(40.6)	
/18		18	(45.7)	
/18	(also growl and bib)	18	(45.7)	1983
/18	(also musical and bib)	18	(45.7)	
/21		21	(53.3)	
/32		32	(81.3)	
/40		40	(101.6)	

6. Other Teddy Bears

Stock No.	Name	inches	centimeters	Year
M1017/1	Tumpy	12	(30.5)	1931-1932
/2		14½	(36.9)	
/3		17	(43.2)	
S 1064/2	Laughing Baby Bear	12½	(31.8)	1932-1933
/3		15	(38.1)	
/4		18	(45.7)	
1331/17½	Bobby Bruin (w/ "Movie" joints)	17½	(44.5)	1936
/20½		20½	(52.1)	
/26		26	(66.0)	

	Stock No.	Name	Size inches	centimeters	Year
	1422/9	Chubby Bear	9	(22.9)	1936
	/12		12	(30.5)	
	/16		16	(40.6)	
	/20		20	(50.8)	
	1622	Teddy Dofings	22	(55.9)	1937-1938
	1668	Jock (dressed)	15	(38.1)	1938
	1666	Hiker (dressed)	16	(40.6)	1938
	1672/11½	Dutch Bear (dressed)	11½	(29.2)	1938
	/16		16	(40.6)	
	/21		21	(53.3)	
	1673/7	Dutch Teddies (wear pants)	7	(17.8)	1938
	/9		9	(22.9)	
	/11½		11½	(29.2)	
	/14		14	(35.6)	
	/16		16	(40.6)	
	/19		19	(48.3)	
	/21½		21½	(54.6)	
	/26½		26½	(67.3)	
	1725/0	Teddie (fitted voice)	9	(22.9)	1939
	1803/1	Cuddlepup (boy)	10	(25.4)	1939
	/2		13	(33.0)	
	/3		16	(40.6)	
	1804/1	Cuddlepup (girl)	10	(25.4)	1939
	/2		13	(33.0)	
	/3		16	(40.6)	
	1737	Baby Bruin (fitted voice)	10	(25.4)	1939
	4601/12	Print Teddy (fitted squeaker)	12½	(31.8)	1948
	4624/2	Tummykins (squeeze voice)	12½	(31.8)	1948; 1950-1953
	/3		14½	(36.9)	
	/4		16½	(41.9)	
	?	Punkinhead (This was a special made for Eaton's Department Store in Toronto, Canada.)	9	(22.9)	1949-1956
			16	(40.6)	
			24	(61.0)	
	2023/1	Pastel Bear (white and various shades of silk plush)	12	(30.5)	1957
	/2		18	(45.7)	
	252/1	Peter Bear (velveteen face and feet)	13	(33.0)	1962-1963
	371/1	Mr. Twisty Bear	11	(27.9)	1965
	/3		24	(61.0)	
	372/1	Mrs. Twisty Bear	11	(27.9)	1965
	/3		24	(61.0)	
	439/1	Mr. Twisty Bear	11	(27.9)	1966-1971
	/3		24	(61.0)	
	440/1	Mrs. Twisty Bear	11	(27.9)	1966-1971
	/3		24	(61.0)	
	A91	Standing Bear	12	(30.5)	1979-1981
	D38/1	Softie Bear	15	(38.1)	1985
	/2		24	(61.0)	
	D60/1	Beefeater (mohair)	18	(45.7)	1985
	D61/1	Guardsman (mohair)	18	(45.7)	1985
7. Tide-Rider, Inc. Limited Edition Teddy Bears	AC16	Anniversary Bear	16	(40.6)	1982
	AE18	Edwardian Old Gold Bear	18	(45.7)	1983
	CE14	Edwardian Bear (w/ growler)	14	(35.6)	1984*
	EO16	Snout Bear (w/ growler)	16	(40.6)	1984*
		Seasonal Bears:			1984**
	FA14	Teacher's Pet Fall	14	(35.6)	
	SP14	Blossom Spring			
	WI14	Jingle Winter			
	SU14	Sunshine Summer			
	XE18	Edwardian Surprise Bear with Growler	18	(45.7)	1985**
	WE18	Edwardian with Growler	18	(45.7)	1985**
	GE1114	Pair of Bears	11	(27.9)	1985**
			14	(35.6)	
	HU16	Noel	16	(40.6)	1985**

* Limited to 2500 pieces world-wide.

** Limited to 1000 pieces world-wide.

All the Limited Edition Bears from Tide-Rider, Inc. have a tag that is signed by Mr. B.T. Holmes, Merrythought's Chairman.

POLAR BEARS

Stock No.	Name	Size inches	centimeters	Year
S 1155/1	Sammy (Baby Polar Bear)	12	(30.5)	1932-1933
/2		14¾	(37.6)	1932
/3		19	(48.3)	1932
MP1156/2	Polar Bear Cub ("Movie Toy")	18	(45.7)	1932-1933
2032/1	Polar Bear	9	(22.9)	1957
/3		15	(38.1)	
566/3	Polar Bear and Cub	22	(55.9)	1969
845/0	Floppy Polar Bear	16	(40.6)	1979-1981
/1		27	(68.6)	1976-1981
B99/0	Polar Bear	12	(30.5)	1982-1985
/1		18	(45.7)	
/3		36	(91.4)	1982
D18/1	Softie Polar Bear	15	(38.1)	1985
/2		24	(61.0)	

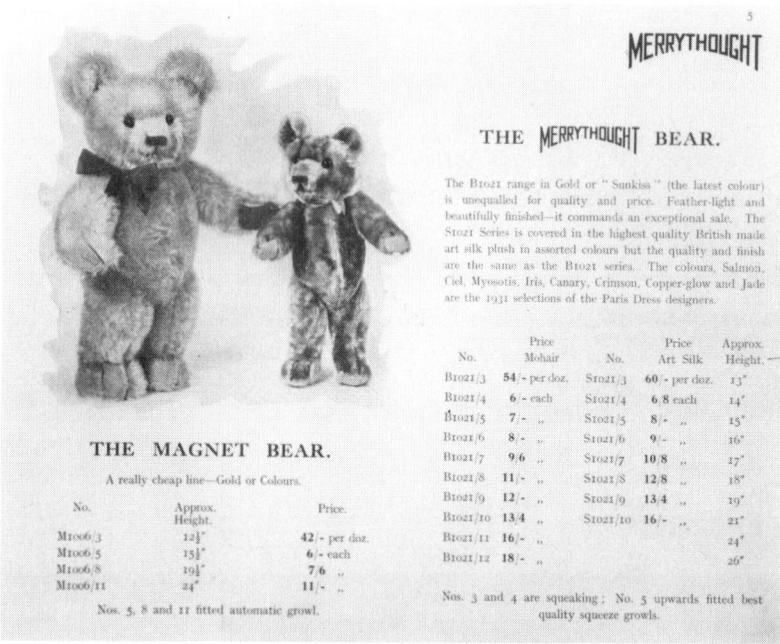

Illustration 17. From the first Merrythought catalog, 1931: At left is the *Magnet Bear* in mohair; at the right is the *Merrythought Bear* in art silk plush.

LEFT: Illustration 18. An "M" Teddy Bear, 1930s. He is gold mohair and stands 15½ inches (39.4cm) tall. *Phyllis Taylor Collection.*

Illustration 19. The woven cloth tag attached to Phyllis Taylor's bear. This is the kind of tag used by Merrythought before World War II. All Merrythought toys have a similar label attached.

Illustration 20. From the 1982 Merrythought catalog: At the bottom left are the six sizes of the *GM Traditional Bear* in mohair; the white bears are the *LM Traditional Bears* in champagne plush; at the top left are *Cheeky* bears in pink and blue; at the bottom right *Cheeky* appears in gold mohair.

Illustration 21. The front cover of the 1984 Merrythought catalog showed the 40 inch (101.6cm) *Champagne Luxury Bear* (No. LM40) and the *Golden Traditional Bear* (No. MM40) in the same size. (The Rocking Horses are the "Rocking Toys" *Rocking Shirehorse* (No. RH02) and *Rocking Dappled Grey Horse* (No. RH05), both available since 1982.)

Illustration 22. Current Merrythought Teddy Bears. From left to right: *Cheeky Bear*, which comes in sizes of 10 inches (25.4cm), 12 inches (30.5cm) and 14 inches (35.6cm); the *Champagne Luxury Bear*, which comes in seven sizes from 12 inches (30.5cm) to 40 inches (99cm); the *Golden Traditional Bear*, which comes in the same sizes as the *Champagne Luxury Bear*; and the *Aristocratic Bear*, which is in sizes of 14 inches (35.6cm), 16 inches (40.6cm) and 18 inches (45.7cm). These bears are made of mohair and plush. *Merrythought photograph.*

Illustration 23. A page from the 1936 Merrythought catalog, featuring the Bears of the "Bingie Family."

Illustration 24. *Cheeky* was first produced in 1957; he is still in production. In the early years he was either mohair or art silk plush; now he is modacrylic plush or mohair. He also came in various pastel colors. This example is mohair and he is 15 inches (38.1cm). *Phyllis Taylor Collection.*

Illustration 26. A large dressed *Cheeky* from the early 1960s. *Merrythought photograph.*

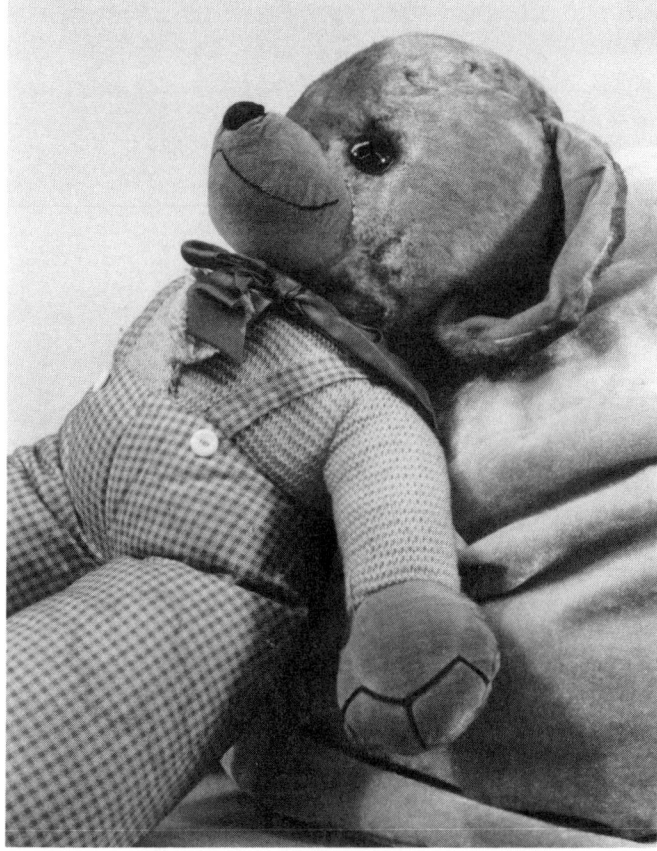

Illustration 25. A dressed *Cheeky* from the late 1950s. *Merrythought sample.*

Illustration 27. The cover of the 1978 Merrythought catalog featured a London gold mohair *Cheeky* (No. GT) and a simulated mink *Cheeky* (No. CT) with *Rocking Pablo Donkey* (No. 185/3).

Illustration 28. Two models of the "London Bears." In the dark uniforms are the *London Policemen* (No. 726) in sizes of 20 inches (50.8cm) and 28 inches (71.1cm); the other two are the *London Guardsmen* (No. 716) who are 21 inches (53.3cm) and 30 inches (76.2cm). 1972 Merrythought catalog illustration.

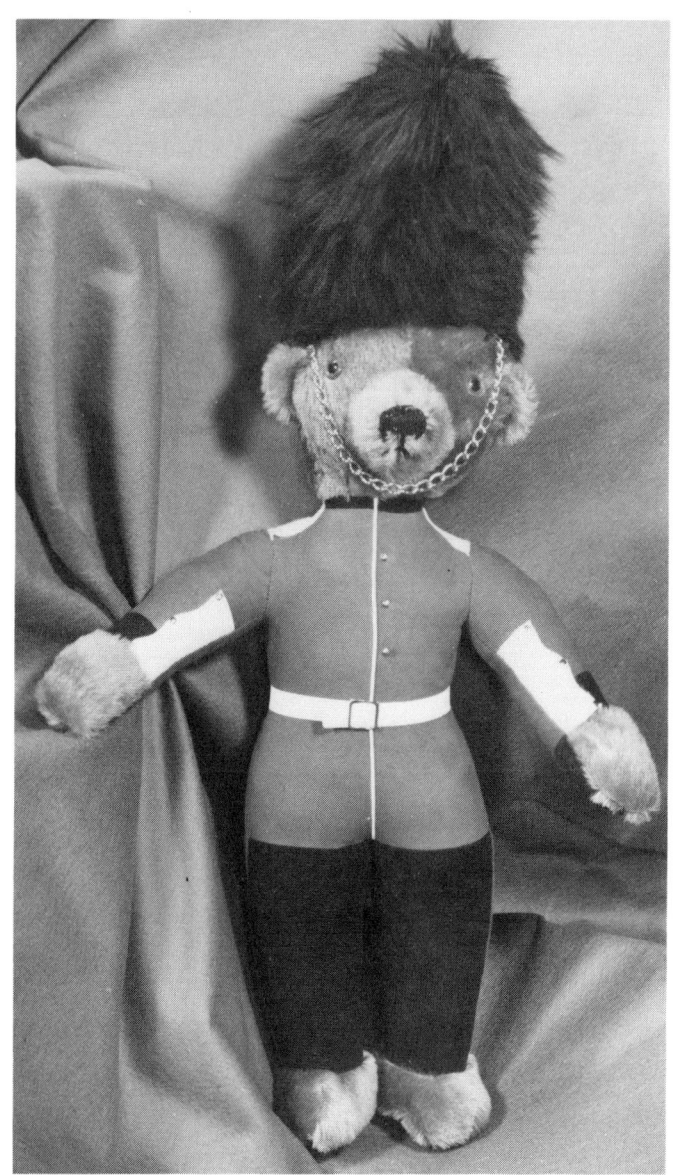

Illustration 29. The *London Guardsman* (No. 726), 1972-1975. *Merrythought photograph.*

Illustration 30. The *London Guardsman* is from 1972 and he is 21 inches (53.3cm) tall, No. 716; *Beefeater Bear* (No. 767) and *Highlander Bear* (No. 768) are from 1973 and they are 18 inches (45.7cm) tall. The "bear" parts are mohair plush; the outfits are formed as part of the bodies. *Phyllis Taylor Collection.*

THE MERRYTHOUGHT BEAR CUBS

"TUMPY"

The baby Bear Cub that appeals, appeals, and appeals! Made in soft woolly plush, dainty colours, white nose and chest, feather-light, soft and most attractive.

No.	Price.	Aprox. Height.
M1017/1	54/- per doz.	12"
M1017/2	72/- " "	14½"
M1017/3	8/- each	17"

"BINGIE"

Sitting Cub in tipped brown and white curly plush. Cuddley and winsome.

No.	Price.	Approx. Height.
B1046/1	66/- per doz.	9"
B1046/2	90/- " "	11"
B1046/3	10/6 each	14"

Illustration 31. *Tumpy* and *Bingie* from the 1931 Merrythought catalog.

MERRYTHOUGHT Teddy Doofings.

(Patented and registered).

His arms move, his fingers move. His eyes shut and open, all of him is movable. How completely a child can play with "Teddy Doofings"! So much playability has never before been incorporated in a single toy.

No. 1622.
Very soft and made in brown, blue, pink and green.
(Brown is the most popular).

He can laugh, he can cry
He can sing, he can sigh
He can sweep, he can sleep
He can box and darn socks
He can play any way.

Send for Show Card.

LEFT: Illustration 32. *Teddy Doofings* from the 1937 Merrythought catalog. The catalog stated, "His arms move, his fingers move. His eyes shut and open, all of him is movable." He was No. 1622 and 22 inches (55.9cm) tall.

Illustration 33. The *Dutch Teddies* from the 1938 Merrythought catalog. All *Dutch Teddies* had pants with pockets.

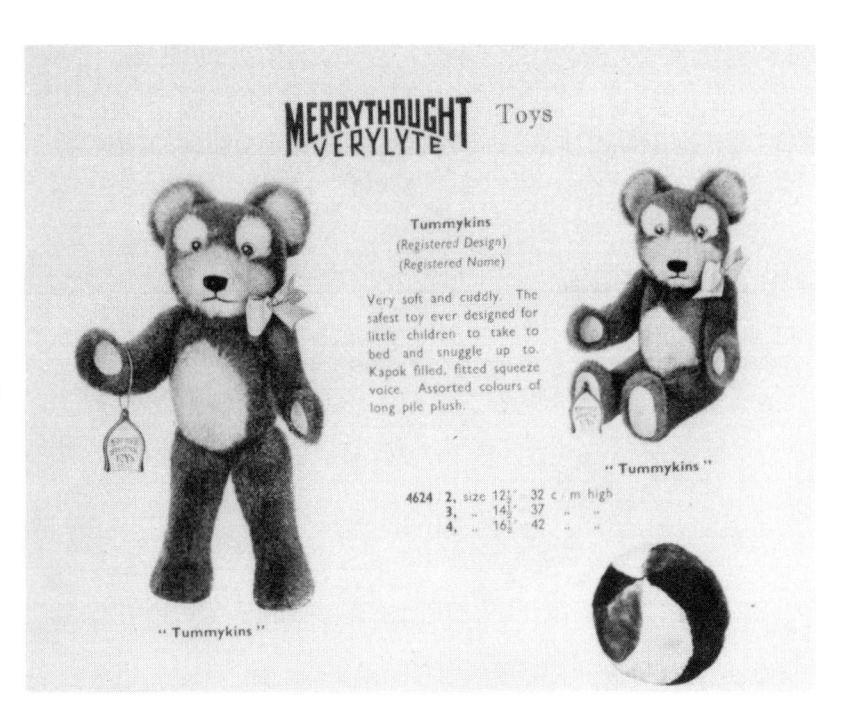

Illustration 34. *Tummykins* from the 1950 Merrythought catalog.

Illustration 35. *Peter Bear* is 13 inches (33cm) and he has a velveteen face and feet and the rest is mohair. He is No. 252/1 and was made in 1962 and 1963. Merrythought sample.

Illustration 36. The *Pastel Bear* is No. 2023 from 1957. He was soft stuffed in pink, blue, red, yellow and dark blue with white trim. He is of "silk plush" and he has bells in his ears. He came in sizes of 12 inches (30.5cm) and 18 inches (45.7cm). Merrythought photograph.

Illustration 37. These *Twisty Bears* and *Cheeky* are from the 1966 Merrythought catalog. They have suede bodies and removable clothing; the heads are mohair plush. An internal frame permits the bears to "twist" and turn into various positions. The stock numbers tell the bear's names: No. 439 is *Mr. Twisty Bear*, No. 440 is *Mrs. Twisty Bear*, No. 441 is *Mr. Twisty Cheeky* and No. 442 is *Mrs. Twisty Cheeky*.

Illustration 38. One of the three 1984 Limited Edition Merrythought offerings from Tide-Rider, Inc. These are the four 14 inch (35.6cm) *Seasonal Bears* and the edition is restricted to 1000 sets, with each set signed by Merrythought's Chairman, B.T. Holmes. The bears are made of pure, short mohair pile. Left to right: These rascals are *Teacher's Pet* for Fall, *Blossom* for Spring, *Jingle* for Winter and *Sunshine* for Summer. *Photograph courtesy of Tide-Rider, Inc.*

Illustration 39. The standing *Polar Bear* is from 1957 and came in sizes of 9 inches (23cm) and 15 inches (38.1cm). He is of white silk plush and has bells inside the ears. *Merrythought photograph.*

PANDAS

Pandas are erroneously called "Panda Bears." They are not part of the bear family, but are related to the American raccoons. They reside in the wild in the hillsides of eastern Tibet and Szechwan province in southwestern China. They are about six feet long and weigh about 300 pounds. Their thick, dense fur is white except for black legs, shoulders, ears and the area around the eyes. Each foot has five clawed toes and the forefeet have a small pad which is used for grasping, like a thumb. The Panda was not known in the western world until 1869 when the French missionary Père David made its existence known. Many Pandas now live in western zoos and they are very difficult to breed.

In 1939 a Panda was born in the London Zoo. At the request of the zoo, Merrythought Limited made a large Panda, measuring 32 inches (81.3cm) long and 21 inches (53.3cm) high that could be used as a stand-in for baby pandas in the zoo during filming, so as not to disturb the real one too much. Pandas became so popular in 1939 in England that Merrythought issued a special catalog of the company's panda toys.

The Pandas are listed in chronological order.

Stock No.	Name	Size inches	centimeters	Year
1641/1	The Panda Bear	17	(43.2)	1937-1939
/2		21	(53.3)	
1643/9	Panda Teddy Bear	9	(22.9)	1939
/10		10	(25.4)	
/B		12	(30.5)	
/D		14	(35.6)	1937-1939
/F		16½	(41.9)	
/H		18	(45.7)	
/J		21	(53.3)	
/K		25	(63.5)	
1643/00	Mascot Panda Teddy	5½	(14.0)	1939
/0		7½	(19.1)	
1840/1	Chummy Panda	9	(22.9)	1939
/2		11	(27.9)	
/3		14	(35.6)	
/4		16	(40.6)	
/5		18	(45.7)	
1843/2	Cuddly Panda Doll	11½	(29.2)	1939
?	Giant Panda	21	(53.3)	1939
CE 1643/10	Panda Teddy	10	(25.4)	1947
/14		14	(35.6)	
1950/1	Panda Bear	10½	(26.7)	1955-1957
/2		14	(35.6)	
462/1	Panda	14	(35.6)	1969-1970
774/1	Standing Panda	16	(40.6)	1973
828	Floppy Panda	24	(61.0)	1975
B18/0	Panda	9½	(24.2)	1982-1985
/1		12	(30.5)	1980-1985
/2		15	(38.1)	
/3		30	(76.2)	
D17/1	Softie Panda	15	(38.1)	1985
/2		24	(61.0)	

39

Illustration 40. The *Merrythought Giant Panda* from a 1939 advertisement. This is the Panda that was used as a stand-in for the London Zoo's live baby panda during film preparations. He is 32 inches long (81.3cm) and 21 inches high (53.3cm).

Illustration 41. Pandas from Merrythought's 1939 catalog.

Illustration 42. *Panda*, No. 462/1, 1969-1970. He is black and white silk plush and is 14 inches (35.6cm) tall. *Dorothy Guest Collection.*

ABOVE LEFT: Merrythought gold Teddy Bear.

ABOVE RIGHT: *Cheeky* was first produced in 1957; he is still in production. In the early years he was either mohair or art silk plush; now he is plush or mohair. He also came in various pastel colors. This example is mohair and he is 15 inches (38.1cm). *Phyllis Taylor Collection.*

RIGHT: On the left: 18 inch (45.7cm) *Beefeater Bear*, plush, 1973-1975; at right: *Beefeater*, No. D60/1, 1985; with mohair bear parts and a jointed head.

41

Limited Edition *Snout Bear* from Tide-Rider, Inc., 1984. 16 inches (40.6cm), fully-jointed of mohair and has a growler. B. T. Holmes signed the tags on each bear in this edition. *Photograph by Harvey Dresner.*

18 inch (45.7cm) *Highlander*, 1986. The head is jointed and is mohair. The clothing is a dress Stewart kilt and plaid with a green velvet hat and jacket, trimmed with white silky Russian braid and silver colored studs. *Merrythought photograph.*

The Elizabethan Bear is a new design for 1986. Fully-jointed of London gold mohair and fitted with a growler. 14 inches (30.5cm) tall. *Merrythought photograph.*

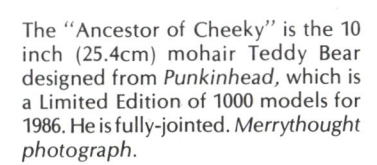

The "Ancestor of Cheeky" is the 10 inch (25.4cm) mohair Teddy Bear designed from *Punkinhead*, which is a Limited Edition of 1000 models for 1986. He is fully-jointed. *Merrythought photograph.*

43

Two Merrythought Teddy Bears with medium length gold mohair pile from the 1930s. Both bears are fitted with growlers. The bear at the left has a pewter button in the ear, which was used by Merrythought in the late 1930s. *Dorothy Guest Collection.* The bear on the right had an eye "kissed off" by a young companion in his youth. This design is the "M" line, which began with Merrythought's first porudction year, 1931. *Phyllis Taylor Collection.* The bears are 15 inches (39.4cm) tall. Note the Merrythought label on the feet.

40 inch (101.6cm) *Traditional Teddy Bear,* No. MM/40, 1984-1985, in all-mohair and fully-jointed.

Cheeky on trolley, a prototype that was not produced.

Tide-Rider, Inc. Limited Edition Teddy Bears from 1983. At the left are two gold mohair *Anniversary Bears*, No. AC16, which are 16 inches (40.6cm) tall and are fully-jointed; at the right is the 18 inch (45.7cm) *Edwardian Old Gold Bear*, No. AE18, also fully-jointed. *Photograph by Harvey Dresner.*

ABOVE: Merrythought Teddy Bear with medium length gold mohair pile from the late 1930s. He is fully-jointed and fitted with a growler. The pewter button in the ear was used in the period prior to World War II. *Dorothy Guest Collection.*

RIGHT: *Cheeky*, from various Merrythought catalogs.

LEFT: Gold mohair Teddy Bear with a pewter button in his ear, late 1930s. He is 10½ inches (26.7cm) tall. *Helen Sieverling Collection.*

ABOVE: *Panda*, No. 462/1, 1969-1970. Black and white silk plush; 14 inches (35.6cm). *Dorothy Guest Collection.*

A 1984 pure mohair bear which was produced in a limited edition of 2500 pieces. *Photograph Courtesy of Tide-Rider, Inc. Photograph by Harvey Dresner.*

A gold mohair Teddy Bear from the 1940s which has been "loved to pieces." *Jane Holmes Rowan Collection.*

Bed-Time Bear is a 17 inch (43.2cm) *Cheeky* dressed for bed, 1977. Merrythought sample.

ABOVE: An assortment of Merrythought factory sample bears.

LEFT: *Punkinhead* was a special for Eaton's Department Store in Toronto, Canada, from 1949 to 1956. He came in sizes of 9, 16 and 24 inches (22.9cm, 40.6cm and 61cm). Merrythought sample.

48

KOALAS

Koalas are called the Australian Teddy Bear but they are not a member of the bear family; they are part of the same family as opossums. They have also been called bangaroos, koolewongs, narnagoons, buidelbeers, native bears, karbors, callawines, colos, koala wombats and New Holland sloths. The koala is like a small bear and is about two feet tall and weighs up to 33 pounds. It has upright tufted ears, small eyes and a bear-like snout. It has cheek pouches for storing food and the breeding pouch of the female opens backwards. All four feet are grasping, an aid to the koala because he is essentially a tree dweller. Koalas eat mostly eucalyptus and gum tree leaves, without which they cannot survive; they do not drink water. Koalas are native to Queensland, in northeastern Australia.

Koalas are listed in chronological order.

Stock No.	Name	Size inches	centimeters	Year
S1111/1	Bush Baby	7	(17.8)	1932-1933
/2		10	(25.4)	
/3		12	(30.5)	
/4		14	(35.6)	
1273/1	Koala (Australian Bear)	11	(27.9)	1934
/2		13½	(34.3)	
/3		16½	(41.9)	
2109/1	Koala Bear	6	(15.2)	1959
/2		8	(20.3)	
/3		9	(22.9)	
/4		11	(27.9)	
109/0	Koala Bear	5	(12.7)	1966-1967
/1		6	(15.2)	1960-1967
/2		8	(20.3)	
/3		9	(22.9)	1960-1966
/3		10	(25.4)	1967
/4		11	(27.9)	1960-1966
/4		12	(30.5)	1967
209/5	Koala Bear	5	(12.7)	1968-1973
/7		7	(17.8)	
/9		9	(22.9)	
/11		11	(27.9)	
A79	Koala with Baby	16	(40.6)	1978-1980
C91/1	Koala Bear	6	(15.2)	1984-1985
/2		8	(20.3)	
/3		13	(33.0)	

Illustration 43. No. 2109 *Koala Bear*, 1959. Merrythought photograph.

Illustration 44. *Koala with Baby,* No. A79, 1978. The mother is 16 inches (40.6cm) tall. Both are made of plush. Merrythought samples.

III. DOGS

Of all the types of animals that were produced by Merrythought over the years, there is a greater variety of dogs than any other kind. During the 1930s there was a very wide range of dogs in various sizes; the number of different types has diminished since World War II. The dogs in production during the various time periods reflects the dogs that have been popular in those eras. In the 1930s the terrier breeds — Skyes, Sealyhams, Aberdeens, Cairns, West Highland Whites and Scottish — dominated; in the 1950s it was Collies and Cocker Spaniels; in the 1960s it was Poodles; in the 1970s and 1980s it has been hounds and large dogs, like the Corgis (which Queen Elizabeth II raises) and the St. Bernards.

The dogs are listed in two sections:
1. Alphabetically by classified breeds of dogs.
2. All other dogs that are not a standard breed, including "Spaniels" and "Terriers."

Within both sections the dogs are listed in chronological order.

Note: In England they are called Alsatians; in the United States the name of the breed is German Shepherd. Alsatians are listed under German Shepherds.

1. DOGS, BY BREEDS

Stock No.	Type of Dog	Name	Size inches	centimeters	Year
MP1038/1	**Aberdeen Terrier**	Robbie (A "Movie Toy" which could be placed in many positions.)	11	(27.9)	1932
/2			12½	(31.8)	
/3			13	(33.0)	
/4			16	(40.6)	
MP1287/1		Aberdeen Terrier (a dressed "Movie Toy")	11	(27.9)	1934-1935
/2			14	(35.6)	
/3			17½	(44.5)	
1038/1		Robbie	11	(27.9)	1936-1938
/2			12½	(31.8)	
/3			13½	(34.3)	
/4			16	(40.6)	
/5			18	(45.7)	
1403		Aberdeen	13	(33.0)	1936-1937
1605/1		Aberdeen	12	(30.5)	1937-1938
/2			14	(35.6)	
/3			17	(43.2)	
1764/1		Jock	6	(15.2)	1939
/2			8	(20.3)	
/3			10	(25.4)	
/3			11½	(29.2)	1948
/4			12	(30.5)	1939
1765/2		Angus	11	(27.9)	1939
/3			14	(35.6)	
/4			16	(40.6)	
1765/3		Angus	12½	(31.8)	1948-1952
1765/3		Angus	11½	(29.2)	1953
1765/1		Angus	9	(22.9)	1954-1959
1764		Jock	11½	(29.2)	1950-1953
2055/0		Standing Aberdeen	8	(20.3)	1958-1959
/1			14	(35.6)	1958
123/1		Angus	9	(22.9)	1960-1962
C77/1	**Afghan Hound**	Afghan Hound	14	(35.6)	1984
/3			30	(76.2)	
1252/1	**Airedale Terrier**	Airedale Terrier	9	(22.9)	1934
/2			10½	(26.7)	
/3			12	(30.5)	
/4			14½	(36.9)	
/5			17½	(44.5)	
C52		Airedale	18	(45.7)	1983-1984
	Alsatian	(See German Shepherd)			
504/1	**Basset Hound**	Bassett Hound [sic]	14	(35.6)	1968-1970
/3			20	(50.8)	1968
A58		Bashful Bassett [sic]	16	(40.6)	1977
1311/16	**Bedlington Terrier**	Bedlington Terrier	16	(40.6)	1934; 1936-1937
706	**Bloodhound**	Bloodhound	13	(33.0)	1972-1974
D40/1		Sitting Bloodhound	15	(38.1)	1985
/3			20	(50.8)	
1967	**Border Collie**	Sheep Dog	16	(40.6)	1955-1958
1967/3			36	(91.4)	1956-1958
C51		Border Collie	16	(40.6)	1983-1985

51

Stock No.	Type of Dog	Name	Size inches	centimeters	Year
1966/1	**Boxer**	Boxer	15	(38.1)	1955-1957
149/1		Boxer Pup	8	(20.3)	1960-1983
/3			24	(61.0)	1962-1969
D13		Boxer	9	(22.9)	1985
1601/1	**Bull Dog**	Bulgie	6½	(16.5)	1937
/2			9½	(24.2)	
4626/2		Dinkie	6	(15.2)	1949
594/1		Bulldog	15	(38.1)	1969-1974
/2			20	(50.8)	1969-1973
D22/1		Standing Bulldog	15	(38.1)	1985
/3			21	(53.3)	
B1041/1	**Cairn Terrier**	Bruce	11	(27.9)	1931-1933; 1936-1938
/2			12½	(31.8)	
/3			14	(35.6)	1931
/3			13	(33.0)	1932-1933
/3			13½	(34.3)	1936-1938
/4			18	(45.7)	1931
/4			16	(40.6)	1932-1933; 1936-1938
/5			18	(45.7)	1932-1938
MP1041/1		Bruce (a "Movie Toy")	11	(27.9)	1932
/2			12½	(31.8)	
/3			13	(33.0)	
/4			16	(40.6)	
BT1098/0		Cairn Lying Puppy	6	(15.2)	1932
/1			8	(20.3)	
/2			10	(25.4)	
/3			13	(33.0)	
MP1288/1		Cairn Terrier (a dressed "Movie Toy")	11	(27.9)	1934-1935
/2			14	(35.6)	
/3			17½	(44.5)	
1404		Cairn	13	(33.0)	1936-1937
1606/1		Cairn	12	(30.5)	1937-1938
/2			14	(35.6)	
/3			17	(43.2)	
721	**Chihuahua**	Chihuahua	11	(27.9)	1972-1976
1692/1	**Chow**	The Royal Chow Puppy (cream color)	12	(30.5)	1938
/2			15¼	(38.8)	
/3			19½	(49.6)	
1693/1		The Royal Chow Puppy (gold color)	12	(30.5)	1938
/2			15¼	(38.8)	
/3			19½	(49.6)	
1694/3		The Royal Chow Puppy (red color)	19½	(49.6)	1938
BT1101/0	**Cocker Spaniel**	Cocker Lying Puppy	6	(15.2)	1932
/1			8	(20.3)	
/2			10	(25.4)	
/3			13	(33.0)	
2035/1		Cocker Spaniel	11	(27.9)	1957-1959
/2			16	(40.6)	1957-1958
/3			30	(76.2)	1958
035/1		Cocker Spaniel	11	(27.9)	1960-1961
1329/12	**Collie**	Dandy	12	(30.5)	1936-1938; 1947
/14			14	(35.6)	
/16			16	(40.6)	1936-1938
/18			18	(45.7)	
1310		Collie Pup	17	(43.2)	1949
1310/15		Collie Pup (with growler)	17	(43.2)	1950-1956
B52/1		Collie	16½	(41.9)	1981-1985
/3			25½	(64.8)	
1989	**Corgi**	Corgi	14	(35.6)	1956-1958
2037		Floppy Corgi	11	(27.9)	1957
A59		Corgi	14	(35.6)	1977-1978
C95		Corgi	15	(38.1)	1984
D55		Charlie the Corgi	18	(45.7)	1985
S1037/0	**Dachshund**	Jerry	7	(17.8)	1931
/1			9	(22.9)	
/2			12	(30.5)	
/3			15	(38.1)	
1982		Dachshund	17	(43.2)	1956-1958
1993		Mitzi	10	(25.4)	1956-1959
181		Mitzi	10	(25.4)	1960-1968
181/1			10	(25.4)	1969-1977
181/3			24	(61.0)	1968

Stock No.	Type of Dog	Name	Size inches	centimeters	Year
517/1		Bedtime Daxi	11	(27.9)	1968-1969
/3			22	(55.9)	
508/1		Tartan Mitzi	10	(25.4)	1968-1977
122		Psycho Hound	14	(35.6)	1970-1972
1729/1	Dalmatian	Dalmatian Puppy	11½	(29.2)	1938
/2			16	(40.6)	
/3			24	(61.0)	
2075		Spotty Dalmatian	8	(20.3)	1958
2082		Standing Spotty	8	(20.3)	1958
205/1		Sitting Dalmatian	16	(40.6)	1961-1962
C31/1		Sitting Dalmatian	9	(22.9)	1983-1984
/2			12	(30.5)	
C55/1		Lying Dalmatian	18	(45.7)	1983-1984
/2			24	(61.0)	1984
D58/1		Sitting Dalmatian	9	(22.9)	1985
/2			12	(30.5)	
D59/1		Lying Dalmatian	18	(45.7)	1985
/2			23	(58.4)	
	Fox Terrier	(See Wirehaired Fox Terrier)			
2074	German Shepherd	Rinty Alsatian	8	(20.3)	1958
2078		Floppy Alsatian	11	(27.9)	1958
2095		Standing Alsatian	8	(20.3)	1958-1959
849		Alsatian Pup	10	(25.4)	1976-1981
D14		Standing Alsatian Puppy	11	(27.9)	1985
D42/1		Lying Alsatian	16	(40.6)	1985
1665A/1	Great Dane	Great Dane (grey)	11½	(29.2)	1938
/2			16	(40.6)	
/3			24	(61.0)	
1665B/1		Great Dane (brindle)	11½	(29.2)	1938
/2			16	(40.6)	
/3			24	(61.0)	
S1025/0	Irish Terrier	Garry (standing)	5	(12.7)	1931
/1			7	(17.8)	
/2			8½	(21.6)	
/3			10	(25.4)	
/4			12	(30.5)	
S1026/0		Garry (sitting)	5	(12.7)	1931
/1			7	(17.8)	
/2			8½	(21.6)	
/3			10	(25.4)	
/4			12	(30.5)	
1286/2	Maltese	Maltese Pup	13½	(34.3)	1934; 1936-1937
B1232/3	Old English Sheep Dog	Lassie (standing)	15½	(39.4)	1933
B1152/3		Lassie (sitting)	18	(45.7)	1933
1304/3		Bob-Tail Sheep Dog (sitting)	10½	(26.7)	1934
/4			13	(33.0)	
/5			15	(38.1)	
/6			17	(43.2)	
/7			19	(48.3)	
1310/15		Bob-Tail Sheep Dog (standing)	15	(38.1)	1934; 1936-1938
/18			18	(45.7)	
/21			21	(53.3)	
/23			23	(58.4)	1934
/26			26	(66.0)	
840		Old English Sheep Dog	14	(35.6)	1976-1979
C58		Old English Sheep Dog	24	(61.0)	1983-1985
D54		Standing Old English Sheep Dog	13	(33.0)	1985
S1069/2	Pekingese	Winsum	9½	(24.2)	1932-1933
BT1095/0		Peke Lying Puppy	6	(15.2)	1932-1933
/1			8	(20.3)	
/2			10	(25.4)	
/3			13	(33.0)	
4628		Peke Pup	9	(22.9)	1949-1958
2013		Floppy Peke	11	(27.9)	1957-1958
304		Peke Pup	8	(20.3)	1963-1965
433/1		White Peke	12	(30.5)	1966-1970
A93		Pekingese	11	(27.9)	1979-1981
C.83		Pekingese	10	(25.4)	1984-1985
1312/17	Poodle	Poodle	17	(43.2)	1934
1914/1		Poodle	9	(22.9)	1954-1958
/2			14	(35.6)	
/3			18	(45.7)	1955-1958
1977		Jointed Poodle	10	(25.4)	1956
2015		Floppy Poodle	11	(27.9)	1957-1959
2089		Fifi Poodle	8	(20.3)	1958

Stock No.	Type of Dog	Name	Size inches	centimeters	Year
2094		Standing Fifi Poodle	8	(20.3)	1958-1959
094		Standing Fifi Poodle	8	(20.3)	1960-1961
2107/1		Begging Poodle	12	(30.5)	1958-1959
/3			?		1958
2119/1		Curly Poodle	10½	(26.7)	1959
/2			15½	(39.4)	
/3			24	(61.0)	
119/1		Curly Poodle	10½	(26.7)	1960-1966
/2			15½	(39.4)	
/3			24	(61.0)	
2142/1		Miss Poodle	26	(66.0)	1959
142/1		Miss Poodle	26	(66.0)	1960
2144/1		Master Poodle	26	(66.0)	1959
144/1		Master Poodle	26	(66.0)	1960
C119/1		Curly Poodle with Hat & Coat	10½	(26.7)	1961-1963
/2			15½	(39.4)	
/3			24	(61.0)	
S119/1		Cairn Poodle	10½	(26.7)	1962-1965
/2			15½	(39.4)	
/3			24	(61.0)	
287/1		Super Poodle	12	(30.5)	1963-1964
/2			17	(43.2)	
/3			24	(61.0)	
A119/1		Pastel Poodle	10½	(26.7)	1966
/2			15½	(39.4)	
/3			24	(61.0)	
495		Lying Poodle	14	(35.6)	1967
585/1		Poodle	11	(27.9)	1969-1971
/2			15	(38.1)	1969-1970
/3			19	(48.3)	
A94		Poodle	16	(40.6)	1980-1981
D36		Standing Black Poodle	15	(38.1)	1985
D37		Standing White Poodle	15	(38.1)	1985
M1013/3	**Setter**	Red Setter	14½	(36.9)	1932
/5			19	(48.3)	
M1196/1		Sitting Red Setter	7½	(19.1)	1933
/2			8½	(21.6)	
/3			10	(25.4)	
/4			12½	(31.8)	
/5			14	(35.6)	
MP1170/2	**St. Bernard**	St. Bernard Pup (a "Movie Toy")	16	(40.6)	1933; 1935
/3			20	(50.8)	
/4			25	(63.5)	
CN1329/12		Dandy	12	(30.5)	1948
/14			14	(35.6)	
1329/12		Dandy	12	(30.5)	1950-1953
/14			14	(35.6)	1950-1952
821/0		Floppy St. Bernard	19	(48.3)	1981
/1			24	(61.0)	1975-1981
825/1		St. Bernard Pup	9	(22.9)	1975-1977
/2			12	(30.5)	
B16/0		Sitting St. Bernard	15	(38.1)	1980-1981
C16		Sitting St. Bernard	15	(38.1)	1982-1984
B97/1		Lying St. Bernard	17	(43.2)	1982-1985
/2			24	(61.0)	
C34	**Schnauzer**	Schnauzer	16	(40.6)	1983-1984
B1038/1	**Scottish Terrier**	Robbie (standing)	11	(27.9)	1931-1932
/2			12½	(31.8)	
/3			14	(35.6)	
/4			18	(45.7)	
/5			18	(45.7)	1932
B1039/1		Robbie (begging)	9	(22.9)	1931
/2			11	(27.9)	
/3			14	(35.6)	
188/1		Standing Scottie	11	(27.9)	1961-1962
328/2		Scottie	14	(35.6)	1964-1965
C98		Scottie	16	(40.6)	1984-1985
BT1099/0	**Sealyham Terrier**	Sealyham Lying Pup	6	(15.2)	1932
/1			8	(20.3)	
/2			10	(25.4)	
/3			13	(33.0)	
S1045/1		Patch (white art silk)	9	(22.9)	1931
/2			12	(30.5)	
/3			14	(35.6)	
/4			16	(40.6)	

Stock No.	Type of Dog	Name	Size inches	centimeters	Year
/5		*Patch,* continued	18	(45.7)	
A1045/3		*Patch* (natural white alpaca)	14	(35.6)	1931
/4			16	(40.6)	
/5			18	(45.7)	
C1204/2		*Sitting Sealyham*	9	(22.9)	1933
/3			11	(27.9)	
/4			13½	(34.3)	
C1224/2		*Standing Sealyham*	13½	(34.3)	1933
/3			17	(43.2)	
/4			20	(50.8)	
1477/1		*Sealyham*	12½	(31.8)	1936-1938
/2			15	(38.1)	
/3			18	(45.7)	
/4			23	(58.4)	1936
2056/0		*Standing Sealyham*	8	(20.3)	1958-1959
/1			14	(35.6)	1958
190/1		*Standing Sealyham*	11	(27.9)	1961-1962
B1043/1	**Skye Terrier**	*Greyfrairs Bobby (sitting)*	7½	(19.1)	1931-1933
/2			8½	(21.6)	
B1044/1		*Greyfriars Bobby (standing)*	10	(25.4)	1931-1933
/2			12	(30.5)	
/4			18	(45.7)	1932-1933
314/2		*Skye Terrier*	14	(35.6)	1964-1965
BT1106/0	**West Highland White Terrier**	*West Highland Terrier Lying Puppy*	6	(15.2)	1932
/1			8	(20.3)	
/2			10	(25.4)	
/3			13	(33.0)	
MP1067/1		*Mac* (a "Movie Toy" that assumes many positions.)	11	(27.9)	1932
/2			12½	(31.8)	
/3			13	(33.0)	
/4			16	(40.6)	
B1067/1		*Mac*	11	(27.9)	1932-1933; 1936-1938
/2			12½	(31.8)	
/3			13	(33.0)	1932-1933
/3			13½	(34.3)	1936-1938
/4			16	(40.6)	1932-1933; 1936-1938
/5			18	(45.7)	
MP1289/1		*West Highland Terrier* (a "Movie Toy")	11	(27.9)	1934-1935
/2			14	(35.6)	
/3			17½	(44.5)	
1771/1		*Andrew*	6	(15.2)	1939
/2			8	(20.3)	
/3			10	(25.4)	
/4			12	(30.5)	
CE1771/2		*Andrew*	8	(20.3)	1947
1776/2		*Don*	11	(27.9)	1939
/3			14	(35.6)	
/4			16	(40.6)	
CE1776/1		*Don*	8½	(21.6)	1947
/2			11	(27.9)	
/3			14	(35.6)	
B19		*Westie*	12	(30.5)	1980-1983
C97·		*Westie*	16	(40.6)	1984-1985
MP1167/1	**Wirehaired Fox Terrier**	*Boy* (a "Movie Toy" that assumes many positions.)	11	(27.9)	1932-1933
/2			13½	(34.3)	
/3			16	(40.6)	
/4			19½	(49.6)	
1335/10½		*Towzer*	10½	(26.7)	1936-1938
/12			12	(30.5)	
/14			14	(35.6)	
CE1335/1		*Towzer (with voice)*	10½	(26.7)	1947
/2			12	(30.5)	
CN1335/1		*Towzer*	10½	(26.7)	1948
/2			12	(30.5)	
/3			14	(35.6)	
1335/0		*Towzer*	5	(12.7)	1953
/1			10½	(26.7)	1950-1959
/2			12	(30.5)	1950-1956
/3			14	(35.6)	1950-1953
124/1		*Towzer*	10½	(26.7)	1960-1961
225/1		*Fox Terrier*	12	(30.5)	1961-1963
B17		*Fox Terrier*	11	(27.9)	1980-1981

Stock No.	Type of Dog	Name	Size inches	centimeters	Year
770/1	**Yorkshire Terrier**	Yorkshire Terrier	11	(27.9)	1973-1981
/3			19	(48.3)	1973-1979; 1981
C96		Yorkshire Terrier	11	(27.9)	1984-1985

Illustration 45. 1931 Merrythought catalog: *Foo-Foo* is a Chlöe Preston design, No. C1055/2, offered in 1931-1933 and 1936-1937. *Greyfriars Bobby* is a Skye Terrier who was produced from 1931-1933. In the sitting style he was 7½ inches (19.1cm) and 8½ inches (21.6cm); in the standing style he was 10 (25.4cm), 12 (30.5cm), and 18 (45.7cm) inches tall.

RIGHT: Illustration 46. 1935 Merrythought catalog: At the top are *Aberdeen, Cairn* and *West Highland Terriers* dressed in black velvet jackets and tartan trousers. They were "Movie Toys," Nos. MP1287, 1288 and 1289 from 1934-1935. Below is the *St. Bernard Pup*, No. MP1170, a "Movie Toy" from 1933 and 1935.

FAR RIGHT: Illustration 47. 1936 Merrythought catalog: The *Aberdeen* and *Cairn*, Nos. 1403 and 1404, were 13 inches long (33cm) and were made in 1936 and 1937; the *Bobtail Sheepdog*, No. 1310, was made in five sizes from 1934 to 1938; the *Maltese Pups*, No. 1286, were made in 1934 and 1936-1937 in a 13½ inch (34.3cm) size.

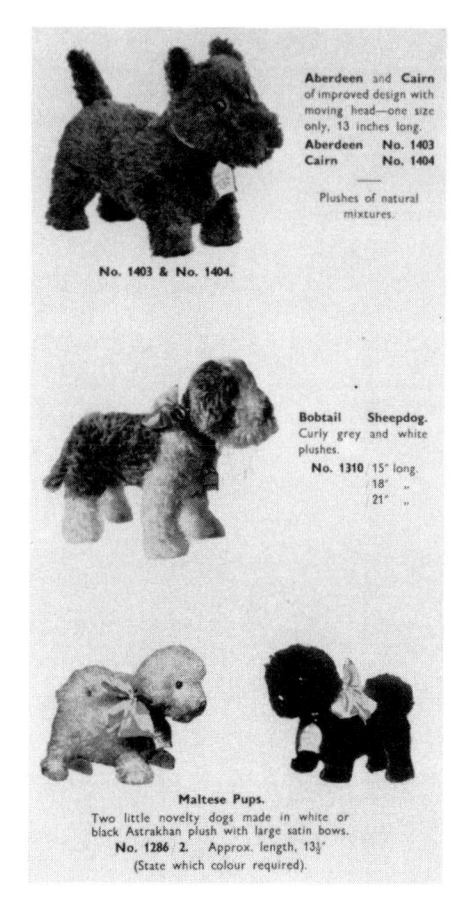

56

ABOVE LEFT: Illustration 48. 1937 Merrythought catalog: The *Black Spaniel*, No. 1475, is from 1936-1937; the *Sealyham*, No. 1477, is from 1936-1938; *Robbie, Aberdeen Terrier*, No. 1038, is from 1936-1938; *Mac, White Highland*, No. 1067, is from 1932-1938; the *Bedlington*, No. 1311, was offered in 1934 and 1936-1937; *Dandy*, a *Collie Pup*, No. 1329, is from 1936-1938 and 1947. All of these dogs were made of mohair.

ABOVE RIGHT: Illustration 49. 1938 Merrythought catalog: The *Dalmatian Puppy*, No. 1729; the *Royal Chow Puppy*, Nos. 1692, 1693, 1694, and the *Great Dane Puppy*, Nos. 1665A and 1665B are all from 1938.

RIGHT: Illustration 50. 1956 Merrythought catalog: *Angus*, the *Aberdeen*, No. 1765/1, is from 1954-1959; the *Boxer*, No. 1966, is from 1955-1957; the *Dachshund*, No. 1982, is from 1956-1958; *Towzer*, the "ever popular *Wire-Haired Terrier*," No. 1335, is from 1950-1959; and the *Sheep Dog* (classified under *Border Collie*), No. 1967, is from 1955-1958.

Illustration 51. 1956 Merrythought catalog: The *Corgi*, No. 1989, is from 1956-1958; the *Poodle*, No. 1914, is from 1954-1958; the *Collie Pup*, No. 1310, is from 1949-1956; and the *Peke Pup*, No. 4628, is from 1949-1958. All of these dogs are made of plush.

Illustration 52. 1965 Merrythought catalog: From the top, going clockwise: No. 119, *Curly Poodle*, 1960-1966; No. 314, *Skye Terrier*, 1964-1965; No. S119, *Cairn Poodle* in mohair, 1962-1965; No. 149, *Boxer Pup*, 1960-1983 (mohair in the earlier years); No. 304, *Peke Pup*, 1963-1965; No. 328, *Scottie*, 1964-1965; No. 309, *Doleful Spaniel*, 1964-1981. In the center: No. 317, *Floppy Doleful*, 1964-1965.

LEFT: Illustration 53. 1978 Merrythought catalog: From the top, going clockwise: No. 840, *Old English Sheepdog*, 1976-1979; No. 770, *Yorkshire Terrier*, 1973-1981; No. A42, *Spaniel Pup*, 1977-1981; No. 849, *Alsatian Pup* (German Shepherd), 1976-1981; No. 309, *Doleful Spaniel*, 1964-1981. All these dogs are made of plush.

ABOVE: Illustration 54. 1981 Merrythought catalog: Clockwise, from top right: No. 821, *Floppy St. Bernard*, 1975-1981; No. B17, *Fox Terrier*, 1980-1981; No. B50, *Standing Spaniel*, 1981; No. B40, *Sitting Spaniel*, 1981-1982; and No. B19, *Westie* (West Highland White Terrier), 1980-1983.

Illustration 55. 1984 Merrythought catalog: Top row: No. C55, *Lying Dalmatian*, 1983-1984; No. C31, *Sitting Dalmatian*, 1983-1984. Center row, left to right: No. C51, *Border Collie*, 1983-1985; No. C97, *Westie* (West Highland White Terrier), 1984-1985; No. C98, *Scottie* (Scottish Terrier), 1984-1985; No. C95, *Corgi*, 1984; No. C56, *Lying Spaniel*, 1983-1984, No. C54, *Sitting Spaniel*, 1983-1984. Bottom center: No. C99, *Lying Rabbit*, 1984-1985.

59

Illustration 56. *Cocker Spaniel,* No. 2035, 1957-1959. He is made of "black and white super silk plush and long shaggy ears." This model is 11 inches (27.9cm) long. Merrythought sample.

Illustration 57. Border Collie, called *Sheep Dog,* No. 1967, 1955-1958. 16 inches (40.6cm) long. Made of black and white plush. Merrythought sample.

2. "DOGS"

Stock No.	Name	Size inches	centimeters	Year
A1048/0	Spot (sitting Terrier)	5	(12.7)	1931
/1		7	(17.8)	
/2		9	(22.9)	
/3		11	(27.9)	
A1049/0	Spot (standing Terrier)	5	(12.7)	1931
/1		7	(17.8)	
/2		9	(22.9)	
/3		11	(27.9)	
M1012/0	Twink (Cubby dog)	6½	(16.5)	1931
/1		8	(20.3)	
/2		9½	(24.2)	
/3		12	(30.5)	
/4		15	(38.1)	
M1004/1	Rex (standing dog)	8	(20.3)	1931
/2		9	(22.9)	
/3		10	(25.4)	
M1007/1	Billy (woolly plush pup)	9	(22.9)	1931
/2		10	(25.4)	
/3		11½	(29.2)	1931-1932
/4		13	(33.0)	
/5		15	(38.1)	
S1007/1	Billy (silk plush pup)	9	(22.9)	1931
/2		10	(25.4)	
/3		11½	(29.2)	
/4		13	(33.0)	
S1028/0	Bogey (Spaniel pup)	5	(12.7)	1931
/1		6	(15.2)	
/2		7	(17.8)	
/3		8	(20.3)	
COT/1	Basket Cradle (with bedding and puppy)	9½	(24.2)	1932
/2		11	(27.9)	
/3		14	(35.6)	
M1001/1	Bobbie	8	(20.3)	1932
/2		11	(27.9)	
M1019/2	Doggie (woolly plush)	10½	(26.7)	1932
S1019/2	Doggie (art silk)	10½	(26.7)	1932
CDR/2½	Doggie (woolly plush)	10½	(26.7)	1933
S1027/2	Standing Bogey (Spaniel)	9	(22.9)	1932
/3		12	(30.5)	
/5		15	(38.1)	
S1028/1	Sitting Bogey (Spaniel)	6	(15.2)	1932
/2		7	(17.8)	
/3		8	(20.3)	
BT1095/0	Black and White Spaniel Lying Puppies	6	(15.2)	1932
/1		8	(20.3)	
/2		10	(25.4)	
/3		13	(33.0)	
MP1163/1	Spandy (a "Movie Toy")	10	(25.4)	1932-1933
/2		12½	(31.8)	
/3		15	(38.1)	
MP1166/1	Cutie Patch (a "Movie Toy")	10	(25.4)	1932-1933
/2		12½	(31.8)	
/3		15	(38.1)	
MP1168/1	Toby (a "Movie Toy")	9¾	(24.9)	1932-1933
/2		12	(30.5)	
/3		14	(35.6)	
/4		16	(40.6)	
M1193/1	Sitting Terrier	7½	(19.1)	1933
/2		8½	(21.6)	
/3		10	(25.4)	
/4		12½	(31.8)	
/5		14	(35.6)	
M1223/2	Towzer (standing Terrier)	11	(27.9)	1933
/3		12½	(31.8)	
/4		15	(38.1)	
1278/3	Slumber Spaniel	16½	(41.9)	1934
/4		19	(48.3)	
/5		21½	(54.6)	
CDR/1½	Dog	9	(22.9)	1935
/2½		10½	(26.7)	1935-1937
1330/12	Happy the Laughing Pup	12	(30.5)	1936
/14		14	(35.6)	
/17		17	(43.2)	

Stock No.	Name	Size inches	centimeters	Year
1394/7½	Jack	7½	(19.1)	1936-1938; 1947
/9		9	(22.9)	
/11		11	(27.9)	1936-1938
/12		12	(30.5)	
1407/7	'Andsome	7	(17.8)	1936
/9½		9½	(24.2)	
/11		11	(27.9)	
1475/1	Black Spaniel (mohair)	12½	(31.8)	1936-1937
/2		15	(38.1)	
/3		18	(45.7)	
/4		23	(58.4)	
1482/1	Booboo-de-bo [sic]	7	(17.8)	1937-1938
/2		10	(25.4)	1936-1938
/3		12½	(31.8)	1937-1938
CE1482/1	Booboo	7	(17.8)	1947
/2		10	(25.4)	
1667A/1	Booboo-de-bo	9	(22.9)	1938
/2		11	(27.9)	
/3		13	(33.0)	
1732	Slumber Puppy	13	(33.0)	1939
1778/1	Dido	5½	(14.0)	1939
/2		7¼	(18.5)	
CE1778/1	Dido	5½	(14.0)	1947
/2		7¼	(18.5)	
1826/1	Mick	8	(20.3)	1939
/2		11	(27.9)	
/3		13	(33.0)	
CE1826/1	Mick	8	(20.3)	1947
/2		11	(27.9)	
CN1482/1	Booboo	7	(17.8)	1948
/2		10	(25.4)	
/3		13	(33.0)	
1482/0	Booboo	5	(12.7)	1953
/1		7	(17.8)	1950-1955
/2		10	(25.4)	
/3		13	(33.0)	1950-1954
4804/1	Fido (puppy)	6¼	(15.9)	1949-1950
4914/1	Smiler Terrier	11	(27.9)	1951-1953
1945	Merrycot Dog	5	(12.7)	1955-1956
2067/1	Laughing Dog	8	(20.3)	1958-1959
/2		11	(27.9)	
/3		13	(33.0)	
/4		17	(43.2)	
2071	Beauty Spaniel	8	(20.3)	1958
2081	Spotted Dog	12	(30.5)	1958-1959
2122/1	Autograph Hound w/ pen	14	(35.6)	1959
/3		25	(63.5)	
122/1	Autograph Hound w/ pen	14	(35.6)	1960-1961
/2		25	(63.5)	
2138/1	Whiskers	9	(22.9)	1959
/2		12	(30.5)	
/3		26	(66.0)	
138/1	Whiskers	9	(22.9)	1960
/2		12	(30.5)	
/3		26	(66.0)	
309/0	Doleful Spaniel	12	(30.5)	1964-1981
/1		14	(35.6)	
/3		20	(50.8)	
317	Floppy Doleful	9	(22.9)	1964-1965
358/1	Patsy Pup	7	(17.8)	1965
365/1	Wagger Dog	12	(30.5)	1965-1968
/3		22	(55.9)	
383/1	Mr. Twisty Doggie	11	(27.9)	1965-1966
/3		24	(61.0)	
384/1	Mrs. Twisty Doggie	11	(27.9)	1965-1966
/3		24	(61.0)	
458/1	Shaggy Dog	14	(35.6)	1967-1969
/3		22	(55.9)	
571	Lanky Doleful	21	(53.3)	1969
572	Lanky Spaniel	21	(53.3)	1969
804/1	Scampi (matches Chips) Puppy	8	(20.3)	1974-1975
/2		13	(33.0)	1975
807/1	Chips (matches Scampi) Puppy	8	(20.3)	1974-1975
/2		13	(33.0)	1975
A32	Floppy Spaniel	24	(61.0)	1977-1980

Stock No.	Name	Size inches	centimeters	Year
A42	Spaniel Pup	9	(22.9)	1977-1981
A48	Floppy Doleful	24	(61.0)	1977-1978
B40	Spaniel	14	(35.6)	1980
B40/0	Sitting Spaniel	9½	(24.2)	1981-1982
/1		13½	(34.3)	
B50/0	Standing Spaniel	9	(22.9)	1981
/1		12½	(31.8)	
B64	Cuddly Puppy	14½	(36.9)	1981
C56/1	Lying Spaniel	16	(40.6)	1983-1984
/2		24	(61.0)	1983
C54/1	Sitting Spaniel	9	(22.9)	1983-1984
/2		12	(30.5)	
D48/1	Sitting Black and White Spaniel	9	(22.9)	1985
/2		12	(30.5)	
D49/1	Lying Black and White Spaniel	18	(45.7)	1985
/2		23	(58.4)	

Illustration 58. *Angus*, the Aberdeen Terrier, No. 1765/1, 1954-1959; 9 inches (22.9cm) long by 7 inches (17.8cm) high. Merrythought sample.

Illustration 59. *Sitting Dalmatian*, No. 205/1, 1961-1962. Made of "spotted silk plush." 16 inches (40.6cm). *Merrythought photograph.*

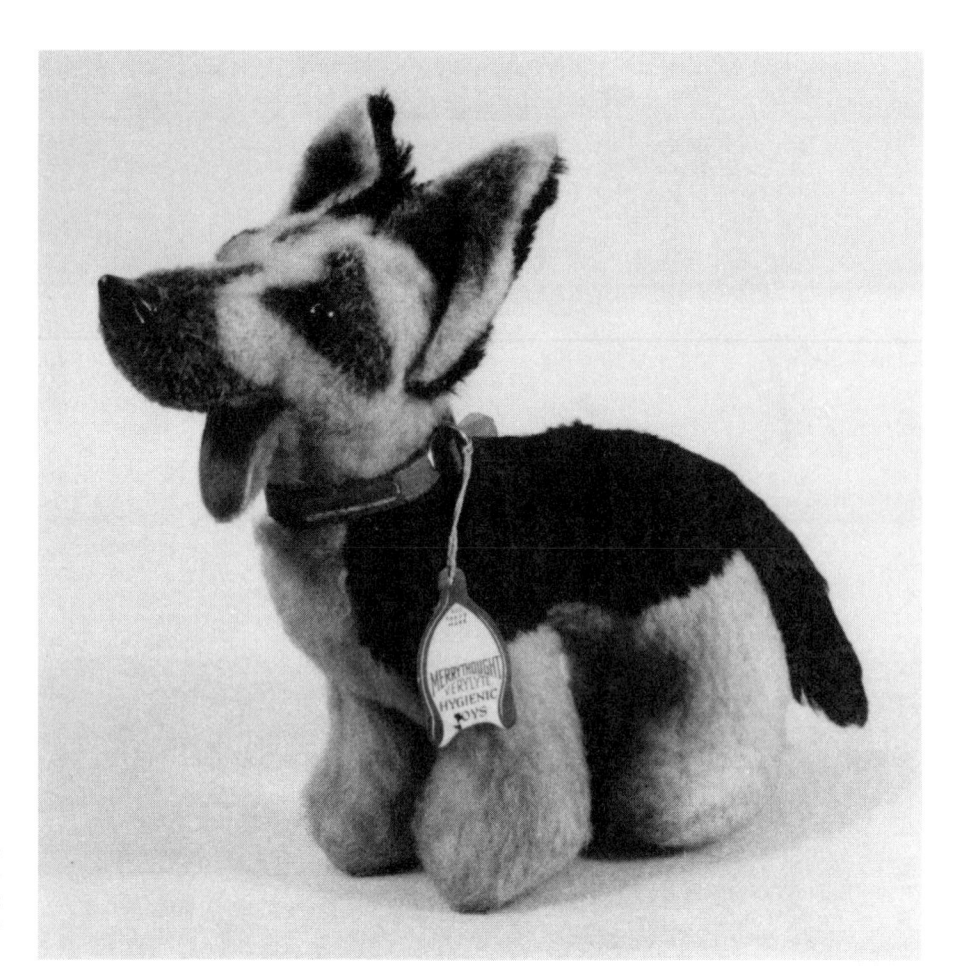

Illustration 60. *Standing Alsatian* (German Shepherd), No. 2095, 1958-1959. Fawn and black plush; soft foam stuffed. 8 inches (20.3cm) tall. Merrythought sample.

Illustration 61. *Old English Sheep Dog,* No. 840, 1976-1979. Made of deep pile white and gray plush. 14 inches (35.6cm) tall. Merrythought sample.

Illustration 62. *Peke Pup*, No. 4628, 1949-1958. He is made of amber and bronze mohair. 9 inches (22.9cm) tall.

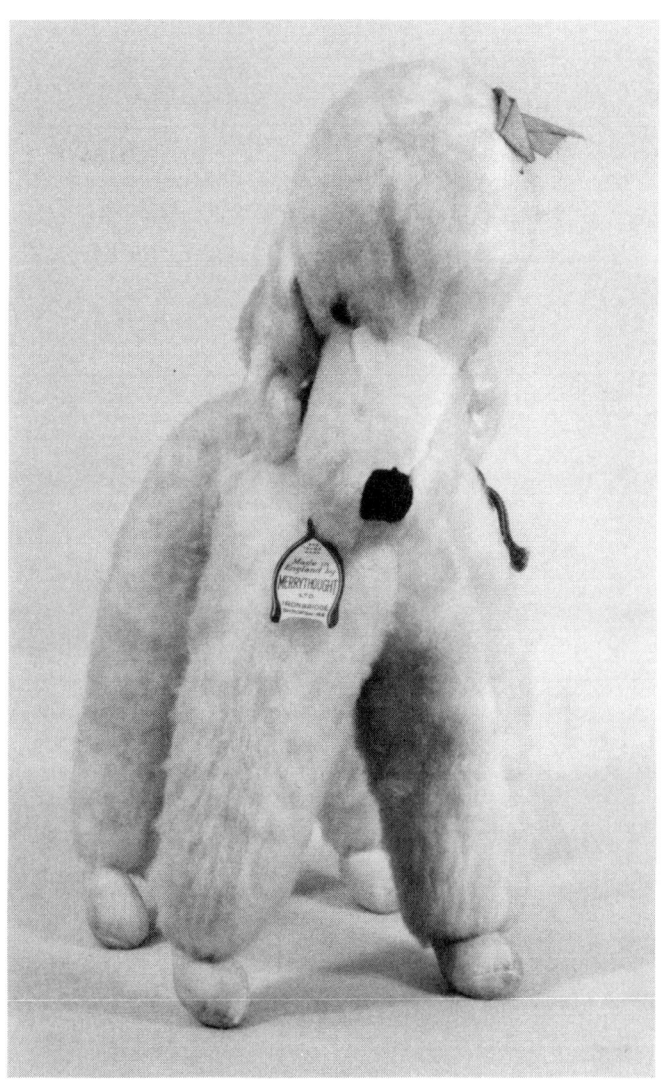

Illustration 63. *Poodle*, No. 1914, 1954-1958. He is made of white plush and white velvet. 16 inches (40.6cm) tall. *Phyllis Taylor Collection.*

Illustration 64. *Begging Poodle*, No. 2107/1, 1958-1959. The "fur" is white wool plush; the body portions are white velvet. 12 inches (30.5cm) tall. Merrythought sample.

Illustration 65. *Curly Poodle*, No. 119, 1960-1966. Made of a special curly plush. This model came in three different sizes, with and without a beret and collar. Merrythought sample.

ABOVE: Illustration 66. *Miss Poodle* and *Master Poodle*, 1959-1960. Each dressed dog is 26 inches (66cm) long. *Merrythought samples.*

RIGHT: Illustration 67. *Towzer*, probably 1950s (No. 1335 series). All-mohair. *Merrythought photograph.*

ABOVE LEFT: Illustration 68. *Towzer,* probably early 1960s. (No. 124/1). All-mohair. 10½ inches (26.7cm). Merrythought sample.

ABOVE RIGHT: Illustration 69. *Booboo-de-boo,* 1936-1938. The two versions at the top are made of cream alpaca plush; the two at the bottom are "spotted white art silk plush." 1938 Merrythought catalog. (These dogs were also called *Booboo.*)

LEFT: Illustration 70. No. 309, *Doleful Spaniel,* 1964-1981. Merrythought sample.

Illustration 71. *Mr. Twisty Doggie* and *Mrs. Twisty Doggie* were made in 1965 and 1966. *Mr. Twisty Doggie* is at the far left; at the bottom left he is next to *Mrs. Twisty Doggie*. The large size is 24 inches (61cm); the small size is 11 inches (27.9cm). At the right are *Mr.* and *Mrs. Twisty Bear*. All "twisties" are fitted with a flexible frame enabling them to be manipulated into any position. They are all dressed with bright colored felt clothes. *Merrythought photograph.*

IV. CATS

The "marvelous Merrythought cats" were made from 1931 through 1981. They are listed chronologically. The measurement is the height of the cat, not including the tail.

Stock No.	Name	Size inches	centimeters	Year
S1051/1	Mopsie	7	(17.8)	1931
/2		10	(25.4)	
/3		13	(33.0)	
M1019/2	Pussy (woolly plush)	10½	(26.7)	1932
S1019/2	Pussy (art silk plush)	10½	(26.7)	1932
CDR/2½	Pussy (woolly plush)	10½	(26.7)	1933
S1110/1	Black Cat (voice)	5	(12.7)	1932-1933
/2		6	(15.2)	
/3		7½	(19.1)	
/4		9	(22.9)	
/5		10½	(26.7)	
B1234/1	Kittums	9	(22.9)	1933
/2		10½	(26.7)	
/3		12	(30.5)	
1255/3	Woosie	16½	(41.9)	1934
/4		19	(48.3)	
/5		21½	(54.6)	
/6		26	(66.0)	
CDR/1½	Cat	9	(22.9)	1935
/2½		10½	(26.7)	1935-1937
* 1680/1	Persian Cat (sitting)	7	(17.8)	1938
/2		8	(20.3)	
/3		10½	(26.7)	
/4		12½	(31.8)	
/5		14½	(36.9)	
/6		16	(40.6)	
* 1681/1	Persian Cat (squatting)	8	(20.3)	1938
/2		10½	(26.7)	
/3		14	(35.6)	
/4		17	(43.2)	
/5		19	(48.3)	
/6		22	(55.9)	
* 1682/1	Persian Cat (standing)	12	(30.5)	1938
/2		14½	(36.9)	
/3		17	(43.2)	
/4		18½	(47.0)	
/5		21	(53.3)	
/6		24	(61.0)	
* 1683/1	Persian Cat (arch back)	7	(17.8)	1938
/2		8	(20.3)	
/3		10½	(26.7)	
/4		12½	(31.8)	
/5		14½	(36.9)	
/6		16	(40.6)	
1685/1	Slumber Cat (dressed)	9½	(24.2)	1938
/2		11	(27.9)	1938; 1951-1955
/3		13½	(34.3)	1938; 1951-1954
/4		16	(40.6)	
/5		18	(45.7)	1938
/6		21	(53.3)	
1786/2	Richard	10½	(26.7)	1939
/3		12	(30.5)	
/4		15	(38.1)	

* Each *Persian Cat* has the following prefix letters to designate color:
- W   White Persian
- G   Ginger
- C   Cream
- P   Persian Blue
- B   Black

Stock No.	Name	Size inches	centimeters	Year
CE1680/1**	*Persian Cat* (sitting)	7	(17.8)	1947
/3**		10½	(26.7)	
CE1681/1**	*Persian Cat* (squatting)	8	(20.3)	1947
/2**		10½	(26.7)	
CE1682/1**	*Persian Cat* (standing)	12	(30.5)	1947
/2**		14½	(36.9)	
CN1680/3***	*Persian Cat* (sitting)	10½	(26.7)	1948
/5***		14½	(36.9)	
CN1681/2***	*Persian Cat* (squatting)	10½	(26.7)	1948
/3***		14	(35.6)	
CN1682/2***	*Persian Cat* (standing)	14½	(36.9)	1948
/3***		17	(43.2)	
1680/3***	*Marvellous Cat* (sitting, squeaker)	10½	(26.7)	1950-1955
/5***		14½	(36.9)	
/6***		16	(40.6)	1950-1953
1681/2***	*Marvellous Cat* (squatting, squeaker)	10½	(26.7)	1950-1955
/3***		14	(35.6)	
/5***		19	(48.3)	1950-1953
1682/2***	*Marvellous Cat* (standing, squeaker)	14½	(36.9)	1950-1955
/3***		17	(43.2)	1950-1954
/4***		18½	(47.0)	
/5***		21	(53.3)	1950-1953
1906	*Cutie Cat* (companion to *Dinkie Dog*)	6	(15.2)	1953-1959
1934/1	*Lucky Cat*	11½	(29.2)	1954-1955
1957	*Merrycot Puss*	6	(15.2)	1955-1956
1958	*Floppy Cat*	14	(35.6)	1955-1956
1680/3	*Sitting Cat* (squeaker)	10½	(26.7)	1956
1992	*Cheshire Cat* (squeaker)	10	(25.4)	1956
1996	*Cuddly Cat* (squeaker)	12	(30.5)	1956-1959
1992/1	*Sitting Cheshire Cat* (bells in ears)	7	(17.8)	1957-1959
/2		8½	(21.6)	
/3	(#3 can have music box)	10	(25.4)	
/4		14	(35.6)	1957-1958
155/1	*Sitting Cheshire Cat*	7	(17.8)	1960-1969
/2		8½	(21.6)	
/3		10	(25.4)	1960-1968
/4		14	(35.6)	1960-1963
2010/1	*Standing Cheshire Cat* (bells in ears)	7	(17.8)	1957-1959
/2		9	(22.9)	
/3	(#3 can have music box)	11	(27.9)	
/4		13	(33.0)	
010/1	*Standing Cheshire Cat*	7	(17.8)	1960-1969
/2		9	(22.9)	
/3		11	(27.9)	1960-1963
/4		13	(33.0)	1960-1962
2012	*Floppy Puss* (bells in ears)	11	(27.9)	1957-1959
012	*Floppy Puss*	11	(27.9)	1960-1963
2076	*Siamese Kitten*	8	(20.3)	1958
151	*Cuddly Cat*	12	(30.5)	1960-1968
211	*Lucy Cat*	18	(45.7)	1961
244/1	*Standing Cat*	10	(25.4)	1962
262/1	*Sarah Cat* (w/ baby in pocket)	16	(40.6)	1963-1964
/3		30	(76.2)	
276/1	*Simon Cat*	16	(40.6)	1963-1964
/3		30	(76.2)	
293/2	*Sitting Cat*	8	(20.3)	1963-1965
/3		11	(27.9)	1963-1964
373/1	*Mr. Twisty Puss*	11	(27.9)	1965-1967
/3		24	(61.0)	
374/1	*Mrs. Twisty Puss*	11	(27.9)	1965-1967
/3		24	(61.0)	
382/1	*Lucky Cat*	11	(27.9)	1965-1966
A151	*Pastel Cat* (same as *Cuddly Cat*)	12	(30.5)	1966-1968
010/1	*Standing Cheshire Cat*	7	(17.8)	1970-1977
/2		9	(22.9)	1970-1973

** Each *Persian Cat* from 1947 had the following letter added to show color:
P   Persian blue
B   Black

*** These letters added to show color:
P   Persian blue
B   Black
C   Cream

Stock No.	Name	Size inches	centimeters	Year
674/1	Mother Cat	15	(38.1)	1971-1972
769/1	Lucky Cat	9	(22.9)	1974
/2		14	(35.6)	1973-1976
784	Siamese Cat	10	(25.4)	1974-1975
788	Sitting Cat	13	(33.0)	1974-1979
A16	Siamese Cat	17	(43.2)	1976-1980
B20/1	Standing Kitten	11	(27.9)	1980-1981
/2		14	(35.6)	1980
B21/1	Sitting Kitten	10	(25.4)	1980-1981
/2		14	(35.6)	1980
B45/1	Standing Tabby	11	(27.9)	1981
B46/1	Sitting Tabby	10	(25.4)	1981
B63	Cuddly Cat	15	(38.1)	1981

Illustration 72. Advertisement for *Merrythought Marvelous Cats*, 1938. This basic cat was No. 1682 and it came in Persian blue, white Persian, ginger, and cream in six different sizes. The catalogs stated, "There are no toy cats so life-like as the Merrythought Cats, being made by a special and secret process."

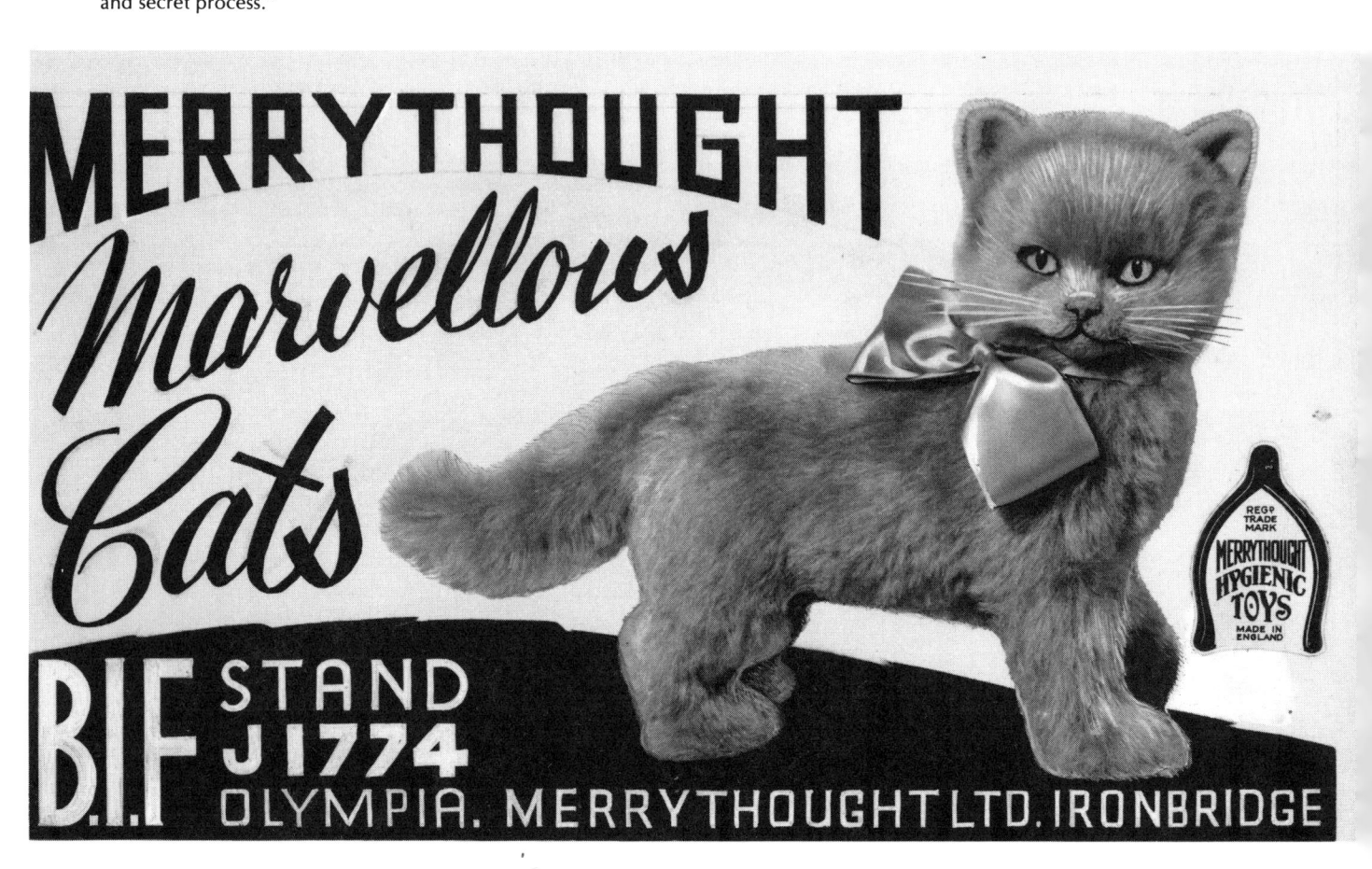

Illustration 73. The No. 1682, *Marvelous Cat*, made from 1938 to 1956. *Merrythought photograph.*

Illustration 74. The sitting *Persian Cat*, No. 1680, 1938-1956. She came in six different sizes in these colors: Cream, blue, white, ginger and black. *Merrythought photograph.*

Illustration 75. *Marvellous Cat*, Standing Series, 1938-1956. (No. 1682). *Dorothy Guest Collection.*

Illustration 77. *Slumber Cat*, No. 1685, 1938; 1951-1955. This cat is made of art silk plush. The head, hands and feet are a cat color; the body portion, simulating pajamas, came in several different pastel colors. *Merrythought photograph.*

Illustration 76. *Cutie Cat*, No. 1906, 1953-1959. 6 inches (15.2cm). This cat was made in black and white velvet and she was a companion to *Dinky Dog*. *Merrythought photograph.*

Illustration 78. *Cheshire Cat*, No. 1992, 1956. 10 inches (25.4cm). Made of silk plush. *Dorothy Guest Collection.*

Illustration 79. *Lucky Cat*, No. 769, 1973-1976. Made of black plush "in the traditional lucky stance." 14 inches (35.6cm). *Dorothy Guest Collection.*

Illustration 80. From the 1981 Merrythought catalog: In front, from left to right: *Standing Kitten*, No. B20, and *Sitting Kitten*, No. B21, both 1980-1981; *Standing Tabby*, No. B45, and *Sitting Tabby*, No. B46, 1981. The standing cats are 11 inches long (27.9cm); the sitting cats are 10 inches (25.4cm) tall. The dogs are *Collie*, No. B52, at the left, and *Sitting St. Bernard*, No. B16, at the right.

75

v. RABBITS

The following are the Merrythought Rabbits, Hares and Bunnies. They are listed chronologically. Note that during the 1930s there was a far greater line of these animals than since that time. Both natural looking and dressed rabbits must have been very popular in the 1930s as toys.

Stock No.	Name	Size inches	centimeters	Year
C1030/0	Begging Rabbit (wool plush)	9	(22.9)	1931
/1		10½	(26.7)	
/2		14	(35.6)	
S1030/0	Begging Rabbit (art silk plush)	9	(22.9)	1931
/1		10½	(26.7)	
/2		14	(35.6)	
/3		17	(43.2)	
C1031/0	Sitting Rabbit (wool plush)	6½	(16.5)	1931
/1		9	(22.9)	
/2		10½	(26.7)	
/3		13	(33.0)	
S1031/0	Sitting Rabbit (art silk plush)	6½	(16.5)	1931
/1		9	(22.9)	
/2		10½	(26.7)	
/3		13	(33.0)	
S1032/1	Running Rabbit	9½	(24.2)	1931
/2		11	(27.9)	
/3		14	(35.6)	
S1033/1	Cutie Rabbit	13½	(34.3)	1931
/2		17	(43.2)	
/3		21	(53.3)	
S1047/1	Honey-Bunch	9½	(24.2)	1931-1932
/2		12	(30.5)	
/3		13½	(34.3)	
/4		16	(40.6)	
/5		19	(48.3)	1932
/6		21½	(54.6)	
/7		30	(76.2)	
M1019/2	Bunny (wool plush)	10½	(26.7)	1932
S1019/2	Bunny (art silk plush)	10½	(26.7)	1932
M1020/1	New Sitting Rabbit	8	(20.3)	1932
/3		11¼	(28.6)	
/4		13	(33.0)	
/5		15	(38.1)	
C1033/1	Cutie Rabbit	13½	(34.3)	1932-1933; 1935
/2		17	(43.2)	
/3		21	(53.3)	
S1113/1	Brer Rabbit (companion to Brer Fox)	11	(27.9)	1932
/2		14	(35.6)	
/3		19	(48.3)	
/4		24	(61.0)	
/5		28	(71.1)	
/6		33½	(85.1)	
S1153/0	Sitting Rabbit (art silk plush)	7	(17.8)	1932
S1153/1	Silkie	8½	(21.6)	1932
/2		9½	(24.2)	
/3		14½	(36.9)	
/4		16	(40.6)	
M1183/3	'Orace	22	(55.9)	1932
MP1162/1	Cutie Bunny (a "Movie Toy")	10	(25.4)	1932-1933
/2		12½	(31.8)	
/3		15	(38.1)	
CDR/1½	Bunny (wool plush)	9	(22.9)	1935
/2½		10½	(26.7)	1933; 1935
A1031/1	White Angora Rabbit	10	(25.4)	1933; 1935-1938
/2		11½	(29.2)	
/3		14	(35.6)	

76

Stock No.	Name	Size inches	centimeters	Year
M1222/1	Begging Rabbit	12	(30.5)	1933; 1935
/2		14	(35.6)	
/3		16	(40.6)	
/4		20	(50.8)	
M1197/2	Wilfred	15	(38.1)	1933
/3		17½	(44.5)	
/4		20	(50.8)	
M1198/2	Dressed Rabbit	12	(30.5)	1933
/3		14	(35.6)	
/4		16	(40.6)	
/5		18	(45.7)	
1241/2	Ronnie the Rabbit	20	(50.8)	1933
1277/3	Slumber Rabbit	16½	(41.9)	1934
/4		19	(48.3)	
/5		21½	(54.6)	
1284/1	Washable Rabbit	8½	(21.6)	1934
/2		11	(27.9)	
/3		14	(35.6)	
1292/3	Sofa Bunny Doll	33	(83.8)	1934
1314/2	Dutch Bunny	19	(48.3)	1934; 1936-1938
/3		21	(53.3)	1934
/4		23	(58.4)	
/5		28½	(72.4)	
/6		32	(81.3)	
/7		35	(88.9)	
1327/11½	Running Hare (wool)	11½	(29.2)	1935-1938
/14		14	(35.6)	
/17		17	(43.2)	
/22		22	(55.9)	1935-1937
S1327/9½	Running Hare (silk)	9½	(24.2)	1935
/11½		11½	(29.2)	
1334/12	White Angora Rabbit	12	(30.5)	1935
1047/2	Honey-Bunch	12	(30.5)	1935-1937
/4		16	(40.6)	
S1031/1	Sitting Rabbit	10	(25.4)	1936-1938
/2		11½	(29.2)	
S1222/2	Begging Rabbit (silk plush; tinkle chime)	14	(35.6)	1936-1938
/3		16	(40.6)	
T1222/1	Begging Rabbit (mohair; tinkle chime)	12	(30.5)	1936-1938
/2		14	(35.6)	
/3		16	(40.6)	
/4		20	(50.8)	
1277/3	Slumber Honey Bunch (squeaker)	16½	(41.9)	1936-1938;
/4		19	(48.3)	1951-1953
/5		21½	(54.6)	1936-1938
T1402/1	Sitting Rabbit (tinkle)	10	(25.4)	1936-1938
/2		11½	(29.2)	
/3		14	(35.6)	
1499/2	Belgian Hare	11½	(29.2)	1936
/3		14	(35.6)	
CDR/2½	Rabbit	10½	(26.7)	1936-1937
1612	Rabbit Family (Mother and 3 Babies)	see 1612M see 1623 A, R, S		1937-1938
	Rabbit Family (Mother and 3 Babies in Basket)	see 1612M see 1623 A, R, S		1937-1938
1612M	Mother	?		1937-1938
1623A	Baby (begging)	?		1937-1938
1623R	Baby (running)	?		1937-1938
1623S	Baby (sitting)	?		1937-1938
1563/1	Bunny Bunting	15½	(39.4)	1937-1938
/2		17	(43.2)	
/3		18½	(47.0)	
/4		20	(50.8)	
/5		22	(55.9)	
1600/1	Bunny (sitting)	12	(30.5)	1937-1938
/2		14	(35.6)	
/3		17	(43.2)	
1669	Little Nell	13½	(34.3)	1938
1722/11	Rabbit (squeaker)	11	(27.9)	1938
/14		14	(35.6)	
/16		16	(40.6)	

Stock No.	Name	Size inches	centimeters	Year
1758/1	Sitting Rabbit	6¾	(17.2)	1939
/2		8¾	(22.3)	
/3		10½	(26.7)	
/4		12	(30.5)	
/5		15	(38.1)	
1733	Slumber Bunny (fitted voice)	17	(43.2)	1939
1805/1	Bunnihug (boy)	15	(38.1)	1939
/2		18	(45.7)	
/3		21	(53.3)	
1806/1	Bunnihug (girl)	15	(38.1)	1939
/2		18	(45.7)	
/3		21	(53.3)	
CE1222/1	Begging Rabbit (squeaker)	12	(30.5)	1947
/2		14	(35.6)	
/3		16	(40.6)	
CE1563/1	Bunny Bunting (squeaker)	15½	(39.4)	1947
/2		17	(43.2)	
CE1758/1	Squatting Rabbit (squeaker)	6¾	(17.2)	1947
/2		8¾	(22.3)	
/3		10½	(26.7)	
CE1805/1	Bunnihug (boy)	15	(38.1)	1947
CE1806/1	Bunnihug (girl)	15	(38.1)	1947
CN1805/1	Bunnihug (boy)	14	(35.6)	1948
CN1806/1	Bunnihug (girl)	14	(35.6)	1948
CN1722/14	Rabbit	17	(43.2)	1948
CN1031/1	Sitting Rabbit (squeaker)	9	(22.9)	1948
/2		11	(27.9)	
/3		14	(35.6)	
CN1222/1	Begging Rabbit (mohair; squeaker)	11	(27.9)	1948
/2		13	(33.0)	
CN4602/17	Dressed Rabbit (squeaker)	16½	(41.9)	1948
4803/1	Begging Rabbit	13	(33.0)	1949-1950
1805/1	Bunnyhug (boy)	14	(35.6)	1950-1954
1806/1	Bunnyhug (girl)	14	(35.6)	1950-1954
1722/14	Rabbit	17	(43.2)	1948; 1950-1955
4602/17	Dressed Rabbit	16½	(41.9)	1950-1959
1031/0	Sitting Rabbit (squeaker)	5	(12.7)	1953
/1		9	(22.9)	1950-1956
/2		11	(27.9)	
/3		14	(35.6)	1950-1954
S1222/1	Begging Rabbit (squeaker)	11	(27.9)	1950-1954
/2		13	(33.0)	
1941/1	Begging Rabbit (squeaker)	9½	(24.2)	1955-1957
/2		12	(30.5)	1955-1956
1943	Merrycot Bun	5	(12.7)	1955-1956
1944	Merrycot Rabbit	8	(20.3)	1955-1956
1962/1	Flexibun (boy; squeaker)	18	(45.7)	1955-1956
/2		24	(61.0)	
1973/1	Flexidoe (girl; squeaker)	18	(45.7)	1955-1956
/2		24	(61.0)	
1990/1	Mr. Rabbit (squeaker)	11	(27.9)	1956-1959
1991/1	Mrs. Rabbit (squeaker)	11	(27.9)	1956-1959
2016/1	Binnie Bunny (girl; bells in ears)	18	(45.7)	1957-1958
/2		27	(68.6)	1957
/3		34	(86.4)	
2031/1	Binnie Boy (bells in ears)	18	(45.7)	1957-1958
/2		27	(68.6)	1957
/3		34	(86.4)	
132/1	Mr. Rabbit	11	(27.9)	1960-1961
131/1	Mrs. Rabbit	11	(27.9)	1960-1961
133	Dressed Rabbit	16½	(41.9)	1960-1966
157/1	Fur Rabbit	10	(25.4)	1960
141/1	Cheeky Rabbit	14	(35.6)	1961-1983
/1		15	(38.1)	1984
/2		19	(48.3)	
/3		26	(66.0)	1965-1968
/3		22	(55.9)	1982-1983
191/1	Bunnikin Rabbit (chime)	10	(25.4)	1961-1976
369/1	Mr. Twisty Bun	11	(27.9)	1965-1974
/3		24	(61.0)	
370/1	Mrs. Twisty Bun	11	(27.9)	1965-1974
/3		24	(61.0)	

Stock No.	Name	Size inches	centimeters	Year
725	Sleepy Rabbit	14	(35.6)	1972-1974
795	Hare	18	(45.7)	1974-1979
841	Standing Hare	15	(38.1)	1976-1978
848	White Rabbit	15	(38.1)	1976-1980
A73	Grey Rabbit	12	(30.5)	1978-1981
B49	Cuddly Bunny	17	(43.2)	1981
B49C	Cuddly Rabbit	16	(40.6)	1982-1983
C15/1	Angora Rabbit	11½	(29.2)	1982-1983
C15/2	Mother Rabbit	16	(40.6)	1983
C.99	Lying Rabbit	14	(35.6)	1984-1985
D.32/1	Mr. Bumpkin Rabbit	9	(22.9)	1985
D.33/1	Mrs. Bumpkin Rabbit	9	(22.9)	1985
D.52	Hoppity Rabbit	16	(40.6)	1985
D.53	Skippity Rabbit	16	(40.6)	1985

Illustration 81. From the 1931 Merrythought catalog: *Honey Bunch* was made in art silk plush in a two-color effect; *Sitting Rabbit* was available in either wool plush or art silk plush — art silk was more expensive then; and the *Begging Rabbit* was also available in either material.

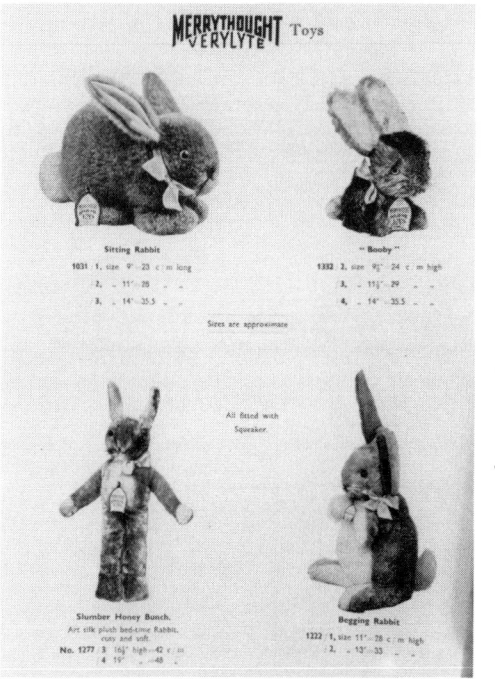

Illustration 82. From the 1952 Merrythought catalog: *Sitting Rabbit* (No. 1031) was a design that was the same from 1931 to 1956; *Booby* was a "Cot Toy" for babies (See Chapter XV.) that was available from 1947 to 1954; *Slumber Honey Bunch* (No. 1277) is a design that was available in 1934 as *Slumber Rabbit* and in 1936 to 1938 and 1951 to 1953 with this name; *Begging Rabbit*, No. 1222, is a design that was available in different materials from 1931 to 1954.

Illustration 83. *Sitting Rabbit*, No. 1031, available from 1931 to 1956. This Merrythought sample is from the later years.

Illustration 84. *Flexidoe*, a dressed rabbit from 1955 to 1956. This Merrythought sample is 18 inches (45.7cm) tall.

Illustration 85. Page from the 1956 Merrythought catalog. On either side is *Mrs. Rabbit* and *Mr. Rabbit*, 1956-1959. In the center is *Dressed Rabbit*, No. 4602, from 1950 to 1959.

Illustration 87. *Binnie Bunny*, No. 2016, is from 1957-1958. She came in three different sizes and wore a red or blue lace-trimmed gingham dress. *Merrythought photograph.*

Illustration 86. *Dressed Rabbit*, No. 4602/17, 1950-1959. He is 16½ inches (41.9cm) high and is of plush. He wears a bright felt coat and print trousers and has a squeaker inside. *Merrythought photograph.*

Illustration 88. *Binnie Boy*, a companion to *Binnie Bunny*, is also from 1957-1958 and he also came in three different sizes. His body is white wool; the clothing is felt. *Merrythought photograph.*

81

Illustration 89. *Mr. Twisty Puss, Mrs. Twisty Puss, Mr. Twisty Bun* and *Mrs. Twisty Bun* from the 1965 Merrythought catalog. The dressed cats were listed from 1965 to 1967; the dressed rabbits from 1965 to 1974. The smaller design is 11 inches (27.9cm); the larger one is 24 inches (61cm). All are dressed in bright felt clothing and have a flexible wire frame inside so that they can be manipulated in many positions.

Illustration 90. The 11 inch (27.9cm) size *Mr. Twisty Bun*, 1965 to 1974. *Merrythought photograph.*

Illustration 91. The *Begging Rabbit* of more recent Merrythought manufacture. This example may be a prototype design that was not put into production.

VI. DOMESTIC ANIMALS

The DOMESTIC ANIMALS are farm animals with the exception of the Camel. The majority of them, with the exception of lambs, are from more recent times. The DOMESTIC ANIMALS are listed alphabetically by the type of animal and then chronologically by dates.

Stock No.	Type of Animal	Name	Size inches	centimeters	Year
463/0	**Bull**	Taurus (Hereford Bull)	12	(30.5)	1969-1985
/1			15	(38.1)	1967-1982
/3			44	(111.7)	1967-1975
S1133/1	**Camel**	Ishmi the Camel	8	(20.3)	1932-1933
/2			10½	(26.7)	
4805/1		Camel	9	(22.9)	1949-1950
771/0		Camel	11	(27.9)	1976-1983
/1			15	(38.1)	1973-1981
/3			30	(76.2)	1974-1977; 1982-1983
C.86/1		Camel	9	(22.9)	1984-1985
/2			11	(27.9)	
/3			18	(45.7)	
S1134/1	**Cow**	Bluebell the Cow	6	(15.2)	1932-1933
/2			8	(20.3)	
/3			10	(25.4)	
/4			12	(30.5)	
529/1		Angus	15	(38.1)	1968-1969
556/0		Moo Cow	11	(27.9)	1968-1969
/1			18	(45.7)	
629/1		Cow (Jersey)	13	(33.0)	1970-1974
/3			30	(76.2)	1971
C23		Daisy	11½	(29.2)	1982
C63		Calf	14	(35.6)	1984
S1149/1	**Donkey**	Nunc the Donkey	6	(15.2)	1932-1933
/2			8	(20.3)	
/3			10	(25.4)	
/4			12	(30.5)	
1269/1		Neddy	6	(15.2)	1937
/2			8	(20.3)	
/3			10	(25.4)	
/4			12	(30.5)	
1762/1		Neddy	9	(22.9)	1939
/2			10	(25.4)	
/3			12	(30.5)	
/4			13	(33.0)	
CE1762/1		Neddy	9	(22.9)	1947
/2			10	(25.4)	
CN1762/2		Neddy	11	(27.9)	1948
/3			13½	(34.3)	
1762/1		Neddy	9	(22.9)	1953-1956
/2			11	(27.9)	1950-1952
/3			13½	(34.3)	1950-1954
1609/1		Donkey Colt	16½	(41.9)	1937; 1950-1958
/2			19	(48.3)	1937
/3			24	(61.0)	
CN1609/1		Donkey Colt	16½	(41.9)	1948
1955/1		Antonio Donkey	12	(30.5)	1955-1959
/3			27	(68.6)	
180/1		Antonio Donkey	12	(30.5)	1960-1976
/3			27	(68.6)	1960-1974
2121/1		Pablo Donkey	18	(45.7)	1959
121/1		Pablo Donkey	18	(45.7)	1960-1980
/3			31	(78.7)	1960-1974

84

Stock No.	Type of Animal	Name	Size inches	centimeters	Year
445/1		Connemara Donkey	14	(35.6)	1966-1976
/2			17	(43.2)	
779/1		Standing Antonio	14	(35.6)	1974-1976
/2			19	(48.3)	1974-1975
817		Floppy Donkey	24	(61.0)	1975-1977
819/1		Donkey	15	(38.1)	1976-1977
B67		Donkey	19	(48.3)	1981-1982
C35/1		Lying Pedro	18	(45.7)	1983
/2			24	(61.0)	
/3			32	(81.3)	
C60/1		Swivel Pedro	12	(30.5)	1983
/2			18	(45.7)	
S1180/1	Goat	Standing Kid	7	(17.8)	1932
/2			8	(20.3)	
/3			9½	(24.2)	
/4			11	(27.9)	
S1181/0		Sitting Kid	6½	(16.5)	1932
775		Goat	14	(35.6)	1974-1976
B65/1		Goat	16	(40.6)	1981-1985
/3			22	(55.9)	
/6			39	(99.0)	1982
D.19	Guinea Pig	Guinea Pig	8	(20.3)	1985
S1148/1	Horse	Nobber the Horse	6	(15.2)	1932-1933
/2			8	(20.3)	
/3			10	(25.4)	
/4			12	(30.5)	
1333/9½		Old Faithful	9½	(24.2)	1935-1937
/11			11	(27.9)	
/12½			12½	(31.8)	
/14			14	(35.6)	
1610/1		Pony Colt	12½	(31.8)	1937
/2			16½	(41.9)	
/3			21	(53.3)	
1761/1		Old Faithful Dobbin	9½	(24.2)	1939
/2			11	(27.9)	
/3			12½	(31.8)	
CE1761/1		Old Faithful	9½	(24.2)	1947
/2			11	(27.9)	
CN1333/9½		Old Faithful	10½	(26.7)	1948
/12			13½	(34.3)	
1333/9½		Old Faithful	10½	(26.7)	1950-1955
/12			13½	(34.3)	
1956/1		Dappled Pony	12	(30.5)	1955-1959
/3			24	(61.0)	1957-1959
179/1		Dappled Pony	12	(30.5)	1960
/3			24	(61.0)	
1974/1		Pony	11	(27.9)	1956-1957
/2			14	(35.6)	1956
2136/1		Henry Horse	?		1959
/2			?		
/3			?		
136/1		Henry Horse	13	(33.0)	1960
176/1		Palamino Pony	11	(27.9)	1960-1961
224/1		Horse	15	(38.1)	1961-1962
/2			19	(48.3)	
/3			24	(61.0)	
/4			36	(91.4)	
662/1		Horse	16	(40.6)	1972
A49		Floppy Horse (Shetland)	24	(61.0)	1977
A89		Shirehorse	18	(45.7)	1979-1981
B61		Standing Shirehorse	18	(45.7)	1982
C53/1		Swivel Shirehorse	12	(30.5)	1983-1984
/2			18	(45.7)	1983-1985
B54		Standing Skewbald	17	(43.2)	1981-1982
B56		Standing Dappled Grey	17	(43.2)	1981-1982
M1002/1	Lamb	Baba	7	(17.8)	1931
/2			8	(20.3)	
/3			9½	(24.2)	
/4			11	(27.9)	
S1029/0		Mary	5	(12.7)	1931
/1			6	(15.2)	
/2			7½	(19.1)	
/3			9	(22.9)	
M1000/3		Lamb	9	(22.9)	1932-1933
/4			11	(27.9)	

Stock No.	Type of Animal	Name	Size inches	centimeters	Year
/5		Lamb, continued	13	(33.0)	
/6			16	(40.6)	
S1029/1		Mary the Lamb	6	(15.2)	1932-1933
/2			7½	(19.1)	
/3			9	(22.9)	
A1000/3		Willie the Lamb	9	(22.9)	1933
/4			11½	(29.2)	
/5			14	(35.6)	
/6			16	(40.6)	
S1326/5½		Baby Lamb	5½	(14.0)	1935
/6½			6½	(16.5)	1935-1938
/7½			7½	(19.1)	
/8½			8½	(21.6)	
/9½			9½	(24.2)	
/11			11	(27.9)	
1728/1		Sitting Lamb	10	(25.4)	1939
/2			13	(33.0)	
/3			16	(40.6)	
4801/1		Lamb	8	(20.3)	1949-1950
1858/0		Curly Lamb (squeaker)	11	(27.9)	1951-1954
/1			13	(33.0)	1951-1953
1937/1		Honey Lamb	10	(25.4)	1954-1959
/3			18	(45.7)	1955-1959
150/1		Honey Lamb	10	(25.4)	1960-1969
/3			18	(45.7)	1960-1968
1942		Merrycot Lamb	5	(12.7)	1955-1956
2104/1		Sugar Lamb	12	(30.5)	1958-1959
/2			19	(48.3)	
/3			26	(66.0)	
148/1		Little Lambkin (black or white)	7½	(19.1)	1960-1961
/2			12	(30.5)	
/3			15	(38.1)	
198/2		Little Lambkin (black only)	12	(30.5)	1961
243/1		Lamb	8½	(21.6)	1962-1965
/2			12	(30.5)	
/3			15½	(39.4)	
568		Baa Baa Lamb	12	(30.5)	1969-1971
150/1		Honey Lamb	10	(25.4)	1970-1981
A83		Floppy Lamb	27	(68.6)	1978-1980
A90		Lamb	13	(33.0)	1979-1981
D.43		Curly the Lamb	13	(33.0)	1985
S1150/1	**Pig**	Posy the Pig	7½	(19.1)	1932-1933
/2			8½	(21.6)	
/3			12	(30.5)	
/4			14	(35.6)	
/5			17	(43.2)	
559/1		Pig	8	(20.3)	1969
744		Pink Pig	12	(30.5)	1973
A88		Pig	12	(30.5)	1979-1981
C.25/1		Piglet	9	(22.9)	1983-1985
/2			12	(30.5)	
/3			18	(45.7)	
/4			24	(61.0)	
/5			30	(76.2)	1985
630/1	**Ram**	Ram	16	(40.6)	1970-1974
/3			32	(81.3)	1971-1972
B87/1		Standing Ram	20	(50.8)	1982-1984

ABOVE: Illustration 92. *Taurus, the Hereford Bull,* 1969-1985. These examples are 12 inches (30.5cm) and 44 inches (111.7cm) long and are made of brown and white plush. *Merrythought photograph.*

RIGHT: Illustration 93. No. 1609 *Donkey Colt* from the 1950s. Merrythought sample.

Illustration 94. 11 inch (27.9cm) *Palamino Pony*, 1960-1961. He is made of mohair plush with a real fur mane and tail. *Merrythought photograph.*

Illustration 95. *Horse* from the 1950s. Merrythought sample.

TOP LEFT: Illustration 96. *Curly Lamb,* No. 1858, 1951-1954. He is of a very curly plush and is fitted with a squeaker. *Merrythought photograph.*

TOP RIGHT: Illustration 97. *Sugar Lamb,* No. 2104, 1958-1959. This lamb is curly white plush with blue hooves and ear linings. *Merrythought sample.*

RIGHT: Illustration 98. *Little Lambkin,* No. 148, 1960-1961. This model is white curly plush. *Merrythought photograph.*

Illustration 99. Domestic Animals from the 1971 Merrythought catalog. Going clockwise, from top right: *Pablo Donkey*, No. 121, 1960-1980; *Cow*, No. 629, 1970-1974; *Taurus the Herefordshire Bull*, No. 463, 1969-1985; *Ram*, No. 630, 1970-1974; *Honey Lamb*, No. 150/1, 1970-1981 in 10 inch (25.4cm) size only; and *Connemara Donkey*, No. 445, 1966-1976.

Illustration 100. From the 1976 Merrythought catalog. Clockwise, from top right: *Connemara Donkey*, No. 445, 1966-1976; *Goat*, No. 775, 1974-1976; *Standing Antonio* (donkey), No. 779, 1974-1976; and *Pablo Donkey*, No. 121, 1960-1980. In the center is *Taurus*, the bull.

VII. WILD ANIMALS

This section includes all the animals who are not tame and who live in the wild, mostly in forests. All animals from jungles and tropical regions are classified under JUNGLE ANIMALS. The WILD ANIMALS are classified alphabetically and are then listed by the dates of manufacture by Merrythought.

Stock No.	Type of Animal	Name	Size inches	centimeters	Year
505/1	**Armadillo**	Armadillo	16	(40.6)	1968
444/1	**Badger**	Badger	9	(22.9)	1966-1967
773/1		Badger	12	(30.5)	1973-1976
/3			30	(76.2)	1973-1974
B58		Badger	17	(43.2)	1981-1983
C81		Badger	18	(45.7)	1984
D.28/1		Mr. Bumpkin Badger (dressed)	9	(22.9)	1985
D.29/1		Mrs. Bumpkin Badger (dressed)	9	(22.9)	1985
B43/1	**Buffalo**	Buffalo	16	(40.6)	1981
/3			30	(76.2)	
A78/1	**Chipmunk**	Chipmunk	11	(27.9)	1978-1985
/3			15	(38.1)	1980-1985
815	**Cougar**	Floppy Puma	24	(61.0)	1975
A77/1		Mountain Lion	24	(61.0)	1978-1980
/3			36	(91.4)	1978
A81/1		Floppy Mountain Lion	27	(68.6)	1978-1979
/3			48	(121.9)	
B41	**Deer**	Floppy Fawn	27	(68.6)	1980
D.21/0	**Dinosaur**	Standing Dinosaur	12	(30.5)	1985
/1			18	(45.7)	
S1071/1	**Fox**	Brer Fox	11	(27.9)	1932
/2			14	(35.6)	
/3			19	(48.3)	
/4			24	(61.0)	
/5			27½	(69.9)	
/6			36	(91.4)	
S1131/1		Reynard	6	(15.2)	1932
/2			8	(20.3)	
/3			11½	(29.2)	
/4			14	(35.6)	
BT1105/0		Lying Fox Cub	6	(15.2)	1932
/1			8	(20.3)	
/2			10	(25.4)	
/3			13	(33.0)	
MP1132/1		Reynard (a "Movie Toy")	8½	(21.6)	1932
/2			11½	(29.2)	
/3			15	(38.1)	
/4			18½	(47.0)	
MP1164/1		Cutie Reynard (a "Movie Toy")	10	(25.4)	1932
/2			12½	(31.8)	
/3			15	(38.1)	
1988/0		Reynard	12	(30.5)	1959
/1			19	(48.3)	1956-1959
/3			42	(106.6)	
A18		Sitting Fox	14½	(36.9)	1977-1982
A26		Floppy Fox	24	(61.0)	1977-1980
C43		Lying Fox	18	(45.7)	1983
D11		Sitting Fox	13	(33.0)	1984
555/1	**Frog**	Freddie Frog	7	(17.8)	1968-1979
/2			9	(22.9)	
/3			12	(30.5)	
B27/1		Handy Frog	13	(33.0)	1980-1981
/2			20	(50.8)	
C.28/1		Frog	8	(20.3)	1983-1985
/2			10	(25.4)	
/3			12	(30.5)	1984-1985
350/1	**Gopher**	Vincent Van Gopher	9½	(24.2)	1964
424/1	**Hedgehog**	Little Hog	8	(20.3)	1966-1981
PA424/1		Road Hog	8	(20.3)	1966-1967

91

Stock No.	Type of Item	Name	Size inches	centimeters	Year
404/1		Mr. Twisty Hedgehog	11	(27.9)	1966-1967
/3			24	(61.0)	
409/1		Mrs. Twisty Hedgehog	11	(27.9)	1966-1967
/3			24	(61.0)	
C14		Squeaker Hog	7	(17.8)	1982-1983
C.14/1		Hedgehog	7	(17.8)	1985
/3			14	(35.6)	
D.34/1		Mr. Bumpkin Hedgehog (dressed)	9	(22.9)	1985
D.35/1		Mrs. Bumpkin Hedgehog (dressed)	9	(22.9)	1985
S1154/1	Kangaroo	Boomer the Kangaroo (with baby in pouch)	10½	(26.7)	1932
/2			13	(33.0)	
/3			16	(40.6)	
223/1		Kangaroo (with baby in pocket)	15	(38.1)	1961-1966
/3			30	(76.2)	1962-1966
345/1		Kanga Two (with twins in pouch)	18	(45.7)	1964-1965
/3			39	(99.0)	1964
A44		Kangaroo (baby in pouch)	21	(53.3)	1977-1981
C17		Kangaroo (baby in pouch)	16	(40.6)	1982
C92/1		Kangaroo (baby in pouch)	15	(38.1)	1984-1985
D.24/1	Mole	Mr. Bumpkin Mole (dressed)	9	(22.9)	1985
D.25/1		Mrs. Bumpkin Mole (dressed)	9	(22.9)	1985
228/1	Mouse	Miss Mouse	13	(33.0)	1961-1964
/3			24	(61.0)	
229/1		Master Mouse	13	(33.0)	1961-1964
/3			24	(61.0)	
462/0		Mouse	4	(10.2)	1967
/1			7	(17.8)	
491/1		Mr. Twisty Mouse	11	(27.9)	1967-1968
/3			24	(61.0)	1968
492/1		Mrs. Twisty Mouse	11	(27.9)	1967-1968
/3			24	(61.0)	1968
B71/0		Mouse	9½	(24.2)	1981-1984
C.75		Squeaker Mouse	6	(15.2)	1984-1985
D.26/1		Mr. Bumpkin Mouse (dressed)	9	(22.9)	1985
D.27/1		Mrs. Bumpkin Mouse (dressed)	9	(22.9)	1985
D.47		Little Nibbler w/ Cheese	10	(25.4)	1985
376/1	Octopus	Octopus	18	(45.7)	1965
843	Otter	Otter	22	(55.9)	1976-1982
C57		Otter	14	(35.6)	1983-1985
B38/1	Racoon	Racoon	11	(27.9)	1980-1983
/2			15	(38.1)	1980-1982
1905/1	Reindeer	Reindeer	14	(35.6)	1953-1956
/2			18	(45.7)	1955-1956
/3			27	(68.6)	
169/1	Seal	Sailor Seal	10	(25.4)	1960-1961
/2			14	(35.6)	
/3			16	(40.6)	
B15/1		Seal	12	(30.5)	1980
/2			22	(55.9)	
C30/1		Seal	18	(45.7)	1983-1985
/2			22	(55.9)	
A43	Skunk	Skunk	14	(35.6)	1977-1978
666/1	Snake	Snake	10	(25.4)	1971-1973
635	Snail	Snail	9	(22.9)	1971-1972
D.44		Sammy Snail	12	(30.5)	1985
S1182/0	Squirrel	Squirrel	7¼	(18.5)	1932
1182/0		Cyril the Squirrel	7	(17.8)	1953-1955
299/1		Tufty (The Official Mascot of the RSPA)	12	(30.5)	1963-1964
/3			24	(61.0)	
780		Squirrel	10½	(26.7)	1974-1984
D.30/1		Mr. Bumpkin Squirrel (dressed)	9	(22.9)	1985
D.31/1		Mrs. Bumpkin Squirrel (dressed)	9	(22.9)	1985
467/1	Tortoise	Tortoise	11	(27.9)	1967-1976
614/0		Flower Tortoise	9	(22.9)	1970-1971
/1			11	(27.9)	1970
A55		Tortoise	11	(27.9)	1977-1978
C.74/1		Tortoise	6	(15.2)	1984-1985
/2			9	(22.9)	
/3			13	(33.0)	

Illustration 101. *Reynard*, the dressed fox, 1956-1959. He wears a red coat, red and white checked jodhpurs and green boots and his limbs are wired for posing. *Merrythought photograph.*

Illustration 102. Another version of *Reynard* from the late 1950s. Merrythought sample.

Illustration 103. *Reindeer,* No. 1905, 1953-1956, in fawn and white wool plush. Merrythought sample.

Illustration 104. Page from the 1977 Merrythought catalog. Clockwise, beginning at top right: *Pablo Donkey; Taurus; Skunk,* No. A43, 14 inches (35.6cm) long in black and cream plush, 1977-1978; *Corgi; Kangaroo,* No. A44, in beige plush with a baby in the pouch, 1977 to 1981, 21 inches (53.3cm) tall.

Great Dane in brindle color, 1938, 16 inches (40.6cm); *John Harrington Collection.* Sitting Rabbit, 1931-1956. 15½ inch (39.4cm) Teddy Bear with pewter button in ear. *Dorothy Guest Collection.*

BOTTOM LEFT: Teddy Bear with pewter button *(Dorothy Guest Collection);* Great Dane *(John Harrington Collection);* Bonzo; Baby Monkey; Sitting Rabbit. (Uncredited items are Merrythought samples.)

BOTTOM RIGHT: *Great Dane,* brindle color, 16 inches (40.6cm), 1938, all-mohair. *John Harrington Collection.*

97

Mickey Mouse, Donald Duck, Great Dane (John Harrington Collection), Teddy Bear (Dorothy Guest Collection), and *Jerry Mouse.*

Teddy Bear *(Dorothy Guest Collection),* Mickey Mouse, Donald Duck *and* Jerry Mouse *that are Merrythought samples.*

98

RIGHT: *Greyfriars Bobby* from the first Merrythought catalog — 1931. The standing dog came in two sizes--10 inches (25.4cm) and 12 inches (30.5cm) long. The seated version was either 7½ inches (19cm) high or 8½ inches (21.6cm) high. He was made of "undyed plush of very long pile." In the caption for this catalog picture the spelling was *Bobbie*, an error.

BELOW: *Greyfriars Bobby* of 1986 is 12 inches (30.5cm) tall. He was redesigned by John Axe from the original model which was the first toy in the first Merrythought catalog of 1931. His head is jointed, permitting him to assume different poses and expressions. Limited Edition for 1986. *Merrythought photograph.*

Sheep Dog (Border Collie), 1955-1958. 16 inches (40.6cm) long, black and white plush. Merrythought sample.

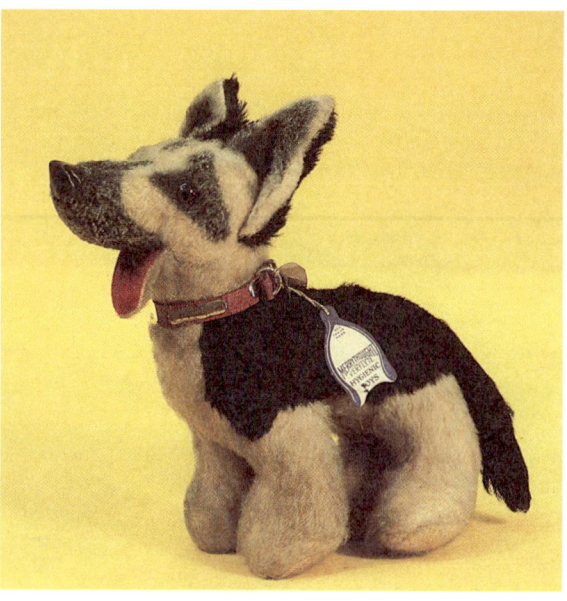

Alsatian (German Shepherd), No. 2095, 1958-1959. Fawn and black plush; soft foam stuffed; 8 inches (20.3cm) tall. Merrythought sample.

Collie Pup, 1310/15, 1950-1956, and *Peke Pup*, 4628, 1949-1958. Merrythought photograph.

Chlöe Preston's *Dinkie* in various colors of velvet. This version is from 1950 to 1959 and is 6 inches (15.2cm) tall and 6 inches (15.2cm) long.

Two "Nightdress Cases:" *Golden Cocker Spaniel* and *Black Cocker Spaniel*, both from 1949 to 1959.

Black and White Spaniel nightdress case, dating from 1948; 1950-1959.

101

Sitting White Persian Cat, 1938.

Sitting Persian Cat, No. 1680, 1938-1956.

White Persian Cat, 1938.

Peke nightdress case, No. ZNC1487/2, made in 1936; 1938; 1948; 1950-1957.

Persian Blue Cat, 1938.

Ginger Persian Cat, 1938.

103

The *Marvelous Cat*, No. 1682, 1938-1956.

Cream Persian Cat, 1938.

VIII. JUNGLE ANIMALS

The JUNGLE ANIMALS are the animals of Africa, except for the Tiger, which is native to India and Asia, and is not found in the wild in Africa. All these animals are listed alphabetically and then in order by the year of manufacture.

Stock No.	Type of Animal	Name	Size inches	centimeters	Year
582/1	**Alligator**	Alligator	26	(66.0)	1969-1972
A68	**Bush Baby**	Bush Baby	12	(30.5)	1978-1980
A86	**Cheetah**	Sitting Cheetah	20	(50.8)	1979-1980
812	**Crocodile**	Crocodile	30	(76.2)	1975
B68		Crocodile	21	(53.3)	1981-1983
S1036/1	**Elephant**	Pimpo	5	(12.7)	1931
/2			6	(15.2)	
/3			7½	(19.1)	
/4			9	(22.9)	
S1120/1		Pimpo	6½	(16.5)	1932-1933
/2			8	(20.3)	1932-1933;
/3			9½	(24.2)	1935-1937
/4			11½	(29.2)	
/5			14	(35.6)	
/6			16	(40.6)	1932-1933; 1935
1763/1		Jumbo	7½	(19.1)	1939
/3			10¼	(26.1)	
CE1763/1		Jumbo	8	(20.3)	1947
/2			9½	(24.2)	
4802/1		Elephant (felt)	6¼	(15.9)	1949-1950
2002/1		Elephant	11	(27.9)	1956-1958
2100/1		Bessie Elephant	11	(27.9)	1958-1959
/2			15	(38.1)	
/3			30	(76.2)	
2120/1		Nellie Elephant	16	(40.6)	1959
100/1		Bessie Elephant	11	(27.9)	1960-1962
/2			15	(38.1)	
/3			30	(76.2)	
120/1		Nellie Elephant	16	(40.6)	1960-1978
/3			21	(53.3)	1959-1977
325/2		Standing Elephant	17	(43.2)	1964
100/1		Pastel Bessie	11	(27.9)	1966-1967
A67/1		Standing Elephant	20	(50.8)	1978
/3			30	(76.2)	
A66		Floppy Elephant	24	(61.0)	1978
B44		Sitting Elephant	12½	(31.8)	1981
B70		Elephant	15	(38.1)	1981
B76		Pink Elephant	26	(66.0)	1982
C68/1		Elephant	9	(22.9)	1984
/2			12	(30.5)	
/3			18	(45.7)	
D56		Sitting Jumbo Elephant	11	(27.9)	1985
187/1	**Giraffe**	Giraffe	23	(58.4)	1961-1963
/1			24	(61.0)	1976-1981
/2			36	(91.4)	1961-1963; 1970-1972; 1976-1981
/5			72	(182.8)	1970-1971
C11/0		Giraffe	18	(45.7)	1985
/1			24	(61.0)	1982-1985
/2			30	(76.2)	1982-1984
B53	**Gorilla**	Gorilla	21	(53.3)	1981
B77/1		Gorilla	14	(35.6)	1982
/2			19	(48.3)	
B77/1		Gorilla	11	(27.9)	1983-1985
/2			14	(35.6)	1983-1984
/3			19	(48.3)	1983-1985
493/1	**Hippopotamus**	Hippo	9	(22.9)	1967-1985

Stock No.	Type of Animal	Name	Size inches	centimeters	Year
/2		Hippo, continued	12	(30.5)	
/3			18	(45.7)	
/4			28	(71.1)	1976-1985
/5			40	(101.6)	1968-1985
589		Lanky Hippo	23	(58.4)	1969
D15/2		Sitting Hippo	10	(25.4)	1985
/3			14	(35.6)	
/4			18	(45.7)	
/5			22	(55.9)	
BT1103/0	Leopard	Lying Leopard	6	(15.2)	1932
/1			8	(20.3)	
/2			10	(25.4)	
/3			13	(33.0)	
MP1169/1		Leopard Cub (a "Movie Toy")	15	(38.1)	1932-1933
/2			18	(45.7)	
/3			21½	(54.6)	
S1056/1		Leopard (sitting; pull growl)	6½	(16.5)	1932-1933
/2			9½	(24.2)	
/3			12½	(31.8)	
/4			15	(38.1)	
/5			18	(45.7)	
/7			30	(76.2)	
S1057/1		Leopard (standing; pull growl)	8½	(21.6)	1932-1933
/2			13	(33.0)	
/3			16½	(41.9)	
/4			20	(50.8)	
/5			24	(61.0)	
/6			27	(68.6)	
A31/0		Floppy Leopard	16	(40.6)	1978-1981
/1			24	(61.0)	1977-1981
/3			48	(121.9)	
C18/1		Lying Leopard	18	(45.7)	1982-1985
/2			24	(61.0)	
/3			33	(83.8)	
C20		Standing Leopard	16	(40.6)	1982-1984
MP1160/1	Lion	Lion Cub (a "Movie Toy")	15	(38.1)	1932-1933
/2			18	(45.7)	
/3			21½	(54.6)	
2039/1		Lion	10	(25.4)	1957-1959
/2			16	(40.6)	
2102/1		Car Mascot Lion	9	(22.9)	1958-1959
/3			?		1958
153/1		Lion	12	(30.5)	1960-1961
/2			18	(45.7)	
/3			24	(61.0)	
239/1		Lion	12	(30.5)	1962-1964
/2			18	(45.7)	1962-1963
/3			24	(61.0)	
675/1		Lion	11	(27.9)	1971-1974
/3			32	(81.3)	1973-1974
808/1		Standing Lion	15	(38.1)	1974-1976
/2			18	(45.7)	
/3			40	(101.6)	1975
809/1		Squatting Lion	16	(40.6)	1974-1976
/2			21	(53.3)	
/3			44	(111.7)	1975
811		Lion Cub	9	(22.9)	1975-1981
847/0		Floppy Lion	16	(40.6)	1978-1981
/1			27	(68.6)	1976-1981
/3			48	(121.9)	
A51		Standing Lion	18	(45.7)	1977-1981
A52		Squatting Lion	21	(53.3)	1977-1981
B66		Cuddly Lion	14	(35.6)	1981
B91/1		Lying Lion	18	(45.7)	1982-1985
/2			24	(61.0)	
/3			33	(83.8)	
C19		Standing Lion	16	(40.6)	1982-1985
1279/3	Monkey	Slumber Monkey	16½	(41.9)	1934
/4			19	(48.3)	
/5			21½	(54.6)	
1648/10½		Chimp	10½	(26.7)	1939
/14			14	(35.6)	
/17			17	(43.2)	

Stock No.	Type of Animal	Name	Size inches	centimeters	Year
4806/1		Jacko (felt)	12	(30.5)	1949-1950
313		Baby Monkey	10	(25.4)	1964-1965
420/1		Mr. Twisty Monkey	11	(27.9)	1966
421/1		Mrs. Twisty Monkey	11	(27.9)	1966
553		Monkey	18	(45.7)	1969
822		Floppy Monkey	24	(61.0)	1975
B36/1		Handy Monkey	13	(33.0)	1980
/2			20	(50.8)	
C12/1		Monkey	13	(33.0)	1982-1983
/2			17	(43.2)	
C76/1		Merry Monkey	13	(33.0)	1985
/2			18	(45.7)	
596/1	**Rhinoceros**	Rhino	16	(40.6)	1970-1971
B69		Rhino	16	(40.6)	1981
C94/1		Rhino	12	(30.5)	1984-1985
/2			14	(35.6)	
/3			18	(45.7)	
/4			36	(91.4)	1985
BT1102/0	**Tiger**	Lying Tiger	6	(15.2)	1932
/1			8	(20.3)	
/2			10	(25.4)	
/3			13	(33.0)	
MP1161/1		Tiger Cub (a "Movie Toy")	15	(38.1)	1932-1933
/2			18	(45.7)	
/3			21½	(54.6)	
S1059/1		Tiger (sitting; pull growl)	6½	(16.5)	1932-1933
/2			9½	(24.2)	
/3			12½	(31.8)	
/4			15	(38.1)	
/5			18	(45.7)	
/7			30	(76.2)	
S1960/1		Tiger (standing; pull growl)	8½	(21.6)	1932-1933
/2			13	(33.0)	
/3			16½	(41.9)	
/4			20	(50.8)	
/5			24	(61.0)	
/6			27	(68.6)	
245/1		Tiger	21	(53.3)	1962
717/1		Tiger	14	(35.6)	1972-1973
/2			19	(48.3)	
/3			36	(91.4)	1973
797/1		Squatting Tiger	16	(40.6)	1974-1976
/2			21	(53.3)	
/3			44	(111.7)	1975
798/1		Standing Tiger	15	(38.1)	1974-1976
/2			19	(48.3)	
/3			40	(101.6)	1975
824		Tiger Cub	9	(22.9)	1975-1981
846/0		Floppy Tiger	16	(40.6)	1979-1981
/1			27	(68.6)	1976-1981
/3			48	(121.9)	
A53		Standing Tiger	18	(45.7)	1977-1981
A54		Squatting Tiger	21	(53.3)	1977-1981
B62		Cuddly Tiger	14	(35.6)	1981
B95/1		Lying Tiger	18	(45.7)	1982-1985
/2			24	(61.0)	
/3			33	(83.8)	
C21		Standing Tiger	16	(40.6)	1982-1985
C46/1	**Zebra**	Lying Zebra Foal	18	(45.7)	1983
/2			24	(61.0)	
/3			32	(81.3)	
C59/1		Swivel Zebra	12	(30.5)	1983
/2			18	(45.7)	

Illustration 105. *Pimpo,* a well-modeled elephant of mohair, 1931-1937. 1935 Merrythought catalog illustration.

Illustration 106. *Elephant,* No. 2002/1, 1956-1958. Grey-brown plush with pink velvet ears and white tusks. 11 inches (27.9cm) long. *Merrythought photograph.*

Illustration 107. The three lions at the top are: *Squatting Lion*, No. 809, 1974-1976; *Lion Cub*, No. 811, 1975-1981, and *Standing Lion*. No. 808, 1974-1976. The three tigers are: *Standing Tiger*, No. 798, 1974-1976, *Tiger Cub*, No. 824, 1975-1981, and *Squatting Tiger*, No. 797, 1974-1976. Each animal is made of nylon plush. *Merrythought photograph*.

LEFT: Illustration 108. From the 1979 Merrythought catalog. Each "Floppy" Jungle Animal is shown in two sizes. From the top row down: *Floppy Lion*, No. 847; *Floppy Tiger*, No. 846; *Floppy Polar Bear*, No. 845; and *Floppy Leopard*, No. A31. Each animal was made from 1976 to 1981, except for the Leopards, which were from 1977 to 1981. All are made of synthetic plush.

ABOVE: Illustration 109. *Baby Monkey*, No. 313, 1964-1965. He is 10 inches (25.4cm) tall and is of brown mohair. Merrythought sample.

BELOW: Illustration 110. *Tiger*, No. 245/1, 1962. He has black painted stripes on brown mohair and he is 21 inches (53.3cm) long, excluding the tail. Merrythought sample.

IX. FANTASTIC ANIMALS

FANTASTIC ANIMALS are animals that never existed, such as the Unicorn. The only FANTASTIC ANIMAL that was made by Merrythought is the Dragon. The company considered producing a Yeti, the fabled "Abominable Snowman" of the Himalayas, but the piece was never produced.

Stock No.	Type of Item	Name	Size inches	centimeters	Year
610/1	**Dragon**	Dragon	16	(40.6)	1971
/3			24	(61.0)	
B74		Dragon	11	(27.9)	1982-1983
B74		Red Dragon	11	(27.9)	1984-1985

Illustration 111. This 6 inch (15.2cm) *Yeti, the Abominable Snowman of the Himalayas,* is a prototype toy that Merrythought did not produce after it was designed.

x. BIRDS and INSECTS

All of the Merrythought BIRDS are listed in alphabetical order by the type of bird and then chronologically by year of manufacture. The BIRDS are followed by the INSECTS, of which there are only the Caterpillar, the Ladybug and the Bumble Bee.

Stock No.	Type of Item	Name	Size inches	centimeter	Year
D46	**Bird of Paradise**	Bird of Paradise	21	(53.3)	1985
C1054/1	**Chicken**	Chirpie (chick)	6½	(16.5)	1932
S1219/2		Cocky the Cockerel	18	(45.7)	1933
S1219/2		Cocky the Cockerel	16½	(41.9)	1935
S1253/2		Hen	14½	(36.9)	1935
1254/2		Chick	4½	(11.5)	1935-1936; 1953
4911/1		Chick	9	(22.9)	1951-1953
/2			10	(25.4)	
/3			11½	(29.2)	
1219/2		Cockerel	17	(43.2)	1954-1955
1253/2		Hen	15	(38.1)	1954-1955
473		Hen	11	(27.9)	1967
475		Cockerel	11	(27.9)	1967-1968
C22		Chic Chick	5½	(14.0)	1982
C61		Hen	10	(25.4)	1983
291/2	**Cockatoo**	Cockatoo (on aluminum triangle)	22	(55.9)	1963-1965
B12		Cockatoo	21	(53.3)	1979-1984
D23		Cockatoo	20	(50.8)	1985
1244/1	**Crow**	Crow	10½	(26.7)	1933
/2			13	(33.0)	
S1050/1	**Duck**	Daddles (natural duck voice)	6	(15.2)	1931-1933; 1935-1937
/2			8	(20.3)	
/3			10½	(26.7)	
/4			12½	(31.8)	
M1003/0		Duck	4	(10.2)	1931
/1			6	(15.2)	1932-1935
/2			7½	(19.1)	
/3			10	(25.4)	
/4			12	(30.5)	
SD1050/3		Drake	10½	(26.7)	1932
S1236/1		Fanny the Fantail	10½	(26.7)	1933
/2			13	(33.0)	
1050/2		Daddles Duck	8	(20.3)	1953-1954
1968/1		Splasher Duck	4½	(11.5)	1955-1958
/2			6½	(16.5)	1955-1957
1972		Merrycot Duck	5	(12.7)	1955-1956
2118/1		Sailor Duck	11	(27.9)	1959
118/1		Sailor Duck	11	(27.9)	1960
337/1		Standing Duck	10	(25.4)	1964
381/1		Duck	13	(33.0)	1965
494/1		Duck	8	(20.3)	1967-1981
/2			13	(33.0)	1967-1969
/3			24	(61.0)	1968-1971
528		Dutch Duck	12	(30.5)	1968-1969
718		Mrs. Duck	12	(30.5)	1972-1974
722		Mr. Duck	12	(30.5)	1972-1974
A45		Mallard	12	(30.5)	1977-1985
A47		Baby Mallard	6	(15.2)	1977-1982
B35/1		Handy Duck	13	(33.0)	1980-1981
/2			20	(50.8)	
B39/1		Standing Duckling	10	(25.4)	1981-1982
/2			14	(35.6)	1980-1982
/3			18	(45.7)	1981
D12		Sailor Duck	10	(25.4)	1984
S1208/1	**Goose**	Gandi the Goose	13	(33.0)	1933
/2			16	(40.6)	
/4			19	(48.3)	
/5			22½	(57.2)	

Stock No.	Type of Item	Name	Size inches	centimeters	Year
720		Goose	11	(27.9)	1972-1974
A12/1	**Kingfisher**	Kingfisher	15	(38.1)	1976-1978
/2			22	(55.9)	1977
S1238/1	**Love Birds**	Love Birds	10	(25.4)	1933
S1240/1	**Magpie**	Maggie the Magpie	18	(45.7)	1933
/2			22	(55.9)	
557/1	**Owl**	Tawny Owl	8	(20.3)	1968-1974
/2			15	(38.1)	1968-1973
781		Owl	12	(30.5)	1973
A80/1		Tawny Owl	9	(22.9)	1978-1981
/2			12	(30.5)	
C10/1		Owl	9	(22.9)	1982-1985
/2			11	(27.9)	
/3			14	(35.6)	
1730/15	**Parakeet**	Budgies (in wicker cage)	15	(38.1)	1938
S1239/2	**Parrot**	Flying Parrot	19	(48.3)	1933
S1189/2		Polly the Parrot	19	(48.3)	1933; 1936-1938; 1953-1959
/3			30	(76.2)	1957-1959
1511		Parrot on Stand	21	(53.3)	1937-1938
2073/1		Twin Parrots	12	(30.5)	1958-1959
189/1		Parrot	13	(33.0)	1981-1985
/2			19	(48.3)	1960-1979; 1985
/2			18	(45.7)	1980-1985
/3			30	(76.2)	1960-1984
073/1		Twin Parrots	12	(30.5)	1960-1965
443/1		Musical Parrot	10	(25.4)	1966-1968
446/0		Flying Parrot	12	(30.5)	1966-1969
S1237/2	**Pelican**	Pelly the Pelican	14	(35.6)	1933
/4			17½	(44.5)	
2134/1	**Penguin**	Penguin	8	(20.3)	1959
/2			12	(30.5)	
/3			18	(45.7)	
/4*			?		
134/1		Penguin	8	(20.3)	1960
/2			12	(30.5)	
/3			18	(45.7)	
485		Chime Penguin	9	(22.9)	1967
481/0		Penguin	10	(25.4)	1967-1971; 1974
/1			13	(33.0)	1968-1971; 1974
724/1		Baby Penguin	9	(22.9)	1972-1973
/2			12	(30.5)	
B42/0		King Penguin	9	(22.9)	1983-1985
/1			12	(30.5)	1981-1985
/2			18	(45.7)	
/3			24	(61.0)	
C44	**Puffin**	Puffin	13	(33.0)	1983-1985
B57	**Swan**	Swan	15	(38.1)	1981-1983
B73		Cygnet	8	(20.3)	1982-1985
B75	**Toucan**	Toucan	16	(40.6)	1982-1985
1249/1	**Woodpecker**	Woodpecker	10½	(26.7)	1933
C67		Woodpecker	12	(30.5)	1984-1985
D51	**Bumble Bee**	Stripey the Bumble Bee	14	(35.6)	1985
561/1	**Caterpillar**	Caterpillar	12	(30.5)	1969
/3			25	(63.5)	
468/1	**Ladybug**	Ladybird	7	(17.8)	1967-1985
D50		Spotty the Ladybird	14	(35.6)	1985

*Special Order

Illustration 112. *Cockatoo,* No. B12, 1979-1984. He is 21 inches high (53.3cm) and is made of plush and felt. He sits on an aluminum perch. Merrythought sample.

Illustration 113. *Budgies* in wicker cage, No. 1730, 1938. 15 inches (38.1cm) high. Merrythought catalog illustration. (Budgies are also known as parakeets.)

Illustration 114. From the 1981 Merrythought catalog. The three *Parrots* are No. 189, from 1981 to 1985. At the bottom is the *Cockatoo*, No. B12, 1979-1984.

115

XI. DOLLS

Merrythought has produced some wonderful DOLLS over the years. Of the older ones, the most collectible are the jointed dolls with pressed felt faces from the late 1930s. The first doll made, the *Golliwog*, the "teddy bear's best friend," is still in the Merrythought line. Since World War II the Merrythought DOLLS have been more in the nature of toys for young children. The DOLLS are all listed in the order of manufacture from the catalogs. Note that there were more doll designs produced from 1936 to 1939 than any other time period, but this is not indicative of the quantity of dolls made by the company, as the number of designs never reflected the quantity of items produced for any item in the catalogs. See also WALT DISNEY DESIGNS and FAMOUS ARTISTS' DESIGNS for more dolls made by Merrythought.

Stock No.	Name	Size inches	centimeters	Year
S1147/3	Golliwog (black)	16	(40.6)	1932
/4		18½	(47.0)	
/5		22½	(57.2)	
S1183/1	Gnome	12¼	(31.2)	1932-1933
1202/1	Tinkabell (Mama voice)	9	(22.9)	1933
/2	(chimes)	11	(27.9)	1933; 1935
/3	(Mama voice)	13	(33.0)	1933
M1201/1	Bunting Doll	13	(33.0)	1933; 1936-1937
/2		15	(38.1)	
/3		16	(40.6)	
/4		17½	(44.5)	
/5		19½	(49.6)	
/6		25	(63.5)	1933
M1221/1	Eska Doll	14½	(36.9)	1933
/2		15½	(39.4)	
/3		16½	(41.9)	
/4		18	(45.7)	
/5		21½	(54.6)	
/6		25	(63.5)	
/7		31	(78.7)	
S1023/1	Humpty Dumpty	8	(20.3)	1933
/2		10½	(26.7)	
/3		13	(33.0)	
/4		15	(38.1)	
/5		18	(45.7)	
S1112/1	Cuddly Coo (art silk)	10	(25.4)	1932-1933
/2		12	(30.5)	
C1112/1	Cuddly Coo (woolly plush)	10	(25.4)	1932-1933
/2		12	(30.5)	
S1147/2	Golliwog (black)	10½	(26.7)	1933
/3		15½	(39.4)	
/4		17½	(44.5)	
/5		21	(53.3)	
Showpiece		42	(106.6)	
S1235/1	Pixie (Mama voice)	17½	(44.5)	1933
/2		20	(50.8)	
/3		26	(66.0)	
1261/00	Dixie Bébé (jolly "Piccaninny")	10	(25.4)	1934; 1936-1938
/0	(Mama voice)	12	(30.5)	
/1		17	(43.2)	
/2	(Mama voice)	20	(50.8)	
/3		24	(61.0)	1934
1262/00	Patsie	10	(25.4)	1934
/0		12½	(31.8)	

Stock No.	Name	Size inches	centimeters	Year
/1	*Patsie*, continued	17	(43.2)	
/2		20	(50.8)	
/3		24	(61.0)	
1265/1	*Babette*	8	(20.3)	1934; 1936-1938
/2		11	(27.9)	
/3		13	(33.0)	
1275/1	*Mitzie* (doll in bunny outfit)	16	(40.6)	1934
/2		18	(45.7)	
/3		21	(53.3)	
/4		24	(61.0)	
/5		26½	(67.3)	
/6		31	(78.7)	
1276/1	*Slumber Golliwog* (black)	13	(33.0)	1934
/2		15½	(39.4)	
/3		16½	(41.9)	
/4		19	(48.3)	
/5		21½	(54.6)	
/6		26	(66.0)	
1280/3	*Slumber Dolly*	16½	(41.9)	1934
/4		19	(48.3)	
/5		21½	(54.6)	
1306/2½	*Dutch Doll* (velveteen)	17	(43.2)	1934; 1936-1938
/3		20	(50.8)	
/24		24	(61.0)	1936-1938
/30.n		30	(76.2)	1934
1307/1	*Dutch Doll* (art silk)	12	(30.5)	1934
/2		16	(40.6)	
/3		20	(50.8)	
1315/2	*Red Riding Hood*	16	(40.6)	1934; 1936
/3		18	(45.7)	
/4		20	(50.8)	
/5		24	(61.0)	
1203/1	*Humpty-Dumpty*	8	(20.3)	1935
/2		10½	(26.7)	
/3		13	(33.0)	
T1203/1	*Humpty-Dumpty* (musical tinkle)	8	(20.3)	1936-1938
/2		10½	(26.7)	
/3		13	(33.0)	
1235/00	*Pixie*	11	(27.9)	1936-1938
/0		13½	(34.3)	
/0½		15	(38.1)	
/1		17½	(44.5)	
/2		20	(50.8)	
/3		26	(66.0)	
1280/3	*Slumber Silk Plush Dollie*	16½	(41.9)	1936-1938
/4		19	(48.3)	
/5		20½	(52.1)	
1281/1	*Coloured Art Silk Bunting Doll*	13	(33.0)	1936-1938
/2		15	(38.1)	
/3		16	(40.6)	
/4		17½	(44.5)	
/5		19½	(49.6)	
1320/18	*Cupie*	18	(45.7)	1936-1938
1345/1	*Golliwog* (black)	14	(35.6)	1936-1938
/2		15	(38.1)	
/3		16	(40.6)	
/4		19	(48.3)	
/5		21	(53.3)	
/5½		25	(63.5)	
1373/13	*Elfie*	13	(33.0)	1936
/15		15	(38.1)	
/17		17	(43.2)	
/20½		20½	(52.1)	
1409/15	*Harlequin*	15	(38.1)	1936-1938
/20		20	(50.8)	
/24		24	(61.0)	
1410/2½	*Checka Doll*	17	(43.2)	1936
/3		20	(50.8)	
/24		24	(61.0)	
1411/13	*Baby Betty*	13	(33.0)	1936
/15		15	(38.1)	
/17		17	(43.2)	
/21		21	(53.3)	

Stock No.	Name	Size inches	centimeters	Year
/24	Baby Betty, continued	24	(61.0)	
1413/1	Buddy, the Cowboy	12	(30.5)	1936-1938
/2		15½	(39.4)	
/3		23	(58.4)	
1414/1	Nobby, the Sailor	11	(27.9)	1936-1938
/2		14	(35.6)	
/3		21	(53.3)	
1421/12	Clown	12	(30.5)	1936-1938
/16		16	(40.6)	
/23		23	(58.4)	
1560/1	Dolly Drummer	12	(30.5)	1937-1938
/2		13¼	(33.7)	
/3		15	(38.1)	
/4		17½	(44.5)	
/5		24	(61.0)	
1571/1	Art Silk Plush Muff Doll	10	(25.4)	1937-1938
/2		12	(30.5)	
/3		14	(35.6)	
/4		16	(40.6)	
/4		17½	(44.5)	1951-1955
/5		19	(48.3)	1936-1938
/6		21	(53.3)	
1572/1	Turkish Delight	10½	(26.7)	1937-1938
/2		14	(35.6)	
/3		22	(55.9)	
1564	Little Oliver	8	(20.3)	1937-1938
1565	Gnome	8	(20.3)	1937-1938
1566	Topsy (black)	8	(20.3)	1937-1938
1567	Chef Yah Sah (black)	8	(20.3)	1937-1938
1568	Puck	8	(20.3)	1937-1938
1569	King Cole	8	(20.3)	1937-1938
1631/2	Fairy Elf	20	(50.8)	1937-1938
1717/1	Puck (girl in bunny outfit)	15	(38.1)	1938
/2		17	(43.2)	
1718P	Humpty Dumpty (music box) press bellows	8	(20.3)	1938
1718W	key wind	8	(20.3)	
1719W	clockwork	9	(22.9)	
1718T	Humpty Dumpty	8	(20.3)	
1719T		9	(22.9)	
1674/15	Dutch Girl — Gretel	15	(38.1)	1938
/17		17	(43.2)	
/22½		22½	(57.2)	
1675/15	Dutch Boy — Hans	15	(38.1)	1938
/17		17	(43.2)	
/22½		22½	(57.2)	
1759/2	Hans	11½	(29.2)	1939
/3		13½	(34.3)	
/4		17½	(44.5)	
/5		20	(50.8)	
/6		22	(55.9)	
1760/2	Gretel	14	(35.6)	1939
/3		15	(38.1)	
/4		17	(43.2)	
/5		21	(53.3)	
/6		24	(61.0)	
1767/1	Dimples	10	(25.4)	1939
/2		11	(27.9)	
/3		13	(33.0)	
1787	Sonja	15½	(39.4)	1939
1789/1	Willum	12	(30.5)	1939
/2		18	(45.7)	
/3		21	(53.3)	
1795/14	Red Riding Hood	14	(35.6)	1939
1796/14	Miss Muffett	14	(35.6)	1939
1797/14	Boy Blue	14	(35.6)	1939
1798/14	Prince Charming	14	(35.6)	1939
1799/14	Alice of Wonderland	14	(35.6)	1939
1800/14	David	14	(35.6)	1939
1801/14	Goldilocks	14	(35.6)	1939
1807	Aladdin	18	(45.7)	1939
1808	Jester	17	(43.2)	1939
1809	José (black)	17	(43.2)	1939

Stock No.	Name	Size inches	centimeters	Year
1810	Kentucky Minstrel (black)	17	(43.2)	1939
1811	Sambo (black)	10	(25.4)	1939; 1948; 1950-1955
1812	Bell Boy	10	(25.4)	1939
1813	Garge	10	(25.4)	1939
1825/1	Cosy Cot Babies	14	(35.6)	1939
/2		15	(38.1)	
/3		16½	(41.9)	
/4		19	(48.3)	
1837/2½	Print Dutch Soft Doll	16	(40.6)	1939
/3		19	(48.3)	
CE1261/0	Dixie ("Piccaninny")	12	(30.5)	1947
/1		17	(43.2)	
CE1632/2	Fairy Elf	20	(50.8)	1947
CE1767/1	Dimples (squeaker)	10	(25.4)	1947
/2		13	(33.0)	
CE1795	Red Riding Hood	14¼	(36.3)	1947
CE1797	Boy Blue	14¼	(36.3)	1947
CE1801	Goldilocks	14¼	(36.3)	1947
CE1825/1	Caressa	14	(35.6)	1947
/3		16½	(41.9)	
CN1201/2	Coloured Plush Bunting Doll	15	(38.1)	1948
CN1306/2½	Dutch Doll	16½	(41.9)	1948
/3		18½	(47.0)	
CN1345/1	Golliwog (fitted voice; black)	13	(33.0)	1948
/3		16	(40.6)	
CN1767/1	Dimples (squeaker)	9	(22.9)	1948
/2		11	(27.9)	
CN1825/2	Baby Royal (squeaker)	14	(35.6)	1948
CN4623/10	Black Mammy	10¾	(27.4)	1948
/14		14½	(36.9)	
4807/12	Jollywogs (Black)	12	(30.5)	1949-1955
/17		16	(40.6)	
1201/2	Coloured Plush Bunting Doll	15	(38.1)	1950-1953
1306/2½	Dutch Doll (voice)	16½	(41.9)	1950-1953
/3		18½	(47.0)	1950-1951
1345/1	Golliwog (voice; black)	13	(33.0)	1950-1952
/3		16	(40.6)	
1767/1	Dimples (squeaker)	9	(22.9)	1950-1956
/2		11	(27.9)	1950-1953
1825/2	Baby Royal (squeaker)	14	(35.6)	1950
4623/10	Black Mammy	10¾	(27.4)	1950-1954
/14		14	(35.6)	1950-1953
T1203/1	Humpty-Dumpty	8	(20.3)	1951-1957
/2		10½	(26.7)	1951-1959
1759/2	Hans	12	(30.5)	1953-1954
1825/2	Stockinette Doll	14	(35.6)	1953-1954
5219/1	Golliwog (black)	15	(38.1)	1953
/2		19	(48.3)	
/3		24	(61.0)	
1932/0	Golliwog (black)	12	(30.5)	1954-1959
/1		15	(38.1)	
/2		19	(48.3)	
/36		36	(91.4)	1959
1976/1	Swingalong Kate (rag doll)	19	(48.3)	1956-1959
Z2090	Clown	6	(15.2)	1958
2103/1	Happy Clown	14	(35.6)	1958-1959
/3		20	(50.8)	
127/1	Swingalong Kate	19	(48.3)	1960-1972
/3		30	(76.2)	1962-1972
143/0	Golliwog	12	(30.5)	1960-1964
/1		15	(38.1)	
/2		19	(48.3)	
/3		36	(91.4)	1960-1963
184	Humpty-Dumpty (musical tinkle)	10½	(26.7)	1960-1964
192	Cotton Golliwog (black)	18	(45.7)	1961
344/0	Jointed Golliwog (black)	12	(30.5)	1964-1966
/1		15	(38.1)	
/2		19	(48.3)	
346/1	Minstrel (black)	14	(35.6)	1964-1965
/2		19	(48.3)	1964
354/1	Honey Bebe	10	(25.4)	1964
359/1	Lanky Joe (black)	21	(53.3)	1965-1966

Stock No.	Name	Size inches	centimeters	Year
/3	Lanky Joe (black), continued	35	(88.9)	
395/1	Merry Dumpty Humpty-Dumpty (chime)	7	(17.8)	1965-1967
396/1	Lanky Kate (rag doll)	24	(61.0)	1966
/3		36	(91.4)	
461/1	Clown	22	(55.9)	1967-1968
484/0	Chime Golliwog (musical chime)	12	(30.5)	1967-1979
/1		15	(38.1)	1967-1975
/2		20	(50.8)	1967-1985
/3		38	(96.5)	1968-1975
511	Bella (black)	19	(48.3)	1968
540	Eskie Boy (chime)	7	(17.8)	1968-1969
541	Eskie Girl (chime)	7	(17.8)	1968-1969
578/1	Psycho Kate (rag doll)	19	(48.3)	1969
/3		30	(76.2)	
608/1	Mermaid	18	(45.7)	1970
C88/1	Humpty Dumpty	7	(17.8)	1984-1985
/3		14	(35.6)	
D41	Zurich the Gnome	15	(38.1)	1985
D45	Father Christmas	15	(38.1)	1985

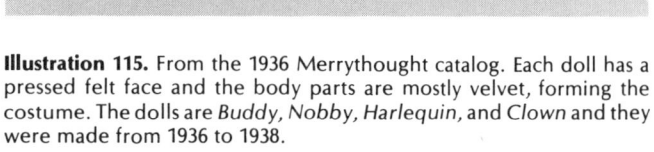

Illustration 115. From the 1936 Merrythought catalog. Each doll has a pressed felt face and the body parts are mostly velvet, forming the costume. The dolls are *Buddy, Nobby, Harlequin,* and *Clown* and they were made from 1936 to 1938.

Illustration 116. A page of 8 inch (20.3cm) "Little People" from the 1937 Merrythought catalog. In the top row are *Puck, Little Oliver* and *King Cole;* in the bottom row are *Gnome, Yah Sah* and *Topsy.* The dolls have felt heads and velvet bodies, which on some of them also form part of the costume. This set was made in 1937 and 1938.

Illustration 117. Merrythought "Cabaret Poupé" from the 1939 catalog. These felt-faced dolls were described as "dressed in silks, velvets, panne velvets, felts, cords and smockettes of brilliant artistic colourings appropriate to the characters." In the top row are *Aladdin, Jester* and *José*. In the bottom row are *Kentucky Minstrel, Sonja* (no doubt a Sonja Henie inspiration) and *Willum*. None of these characters were shown in any other year.

Illustration 118. Merrythought "Fairy Tale Art Dolls" from the 1939 catalog. Each doll is 14 inches (35.6cm) tall and they were "designed by a world famous Child Artist" (unspecified). The design and the quality seems to be very similar to other "art dolls" of felt from the same time period. In the top row: *Goldilocks, David, Prince Charming* and *Boy Blue*. In the bottom row: *Red Riding Hood, Miss Muffett* and *Alice of Wonderland*.

Illustration 119. Merrythought "Verylyte Dolls" from the 1947 catalog. The three dolls in the top row are designs that were also advertised in 1939 at 14 inches (35.6cm) each; now they are listed at 14½ inches (36.9cm). They are *Red Riding Hood, Goldilocks* and *Boy Blue*. In the bottom row are two dolls from 1947 with felt faces and velvet bodies. They are *Fairy Elf* and *Dixie*, who came in either brown or black velvet.

121

Illustration 120. *Dimples* was shown from 1947 to 1956 in the catalogs. She was called "a Baby's soft Doll. Coloured plushes, fitted with squeaker" and came in sizes of 9 and 11 inches (22.9cm and 27.9cm). Her stock number was 1767; the "150" printed on this post card must have been for another purpose. *Merrythought Collection.*

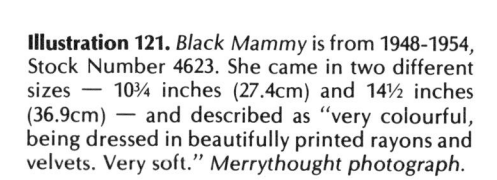

Illustration 121. *Black Mammy* is from 1948-1954, Stock Number 4623. She came in two different sizes — 10¾ inches (27.4cm) and 14½ inches (36.9cm) — and described as "very colourful, being dressed in beautifully printed rayons and velvets. Very soft." *Merrythought photograph.*

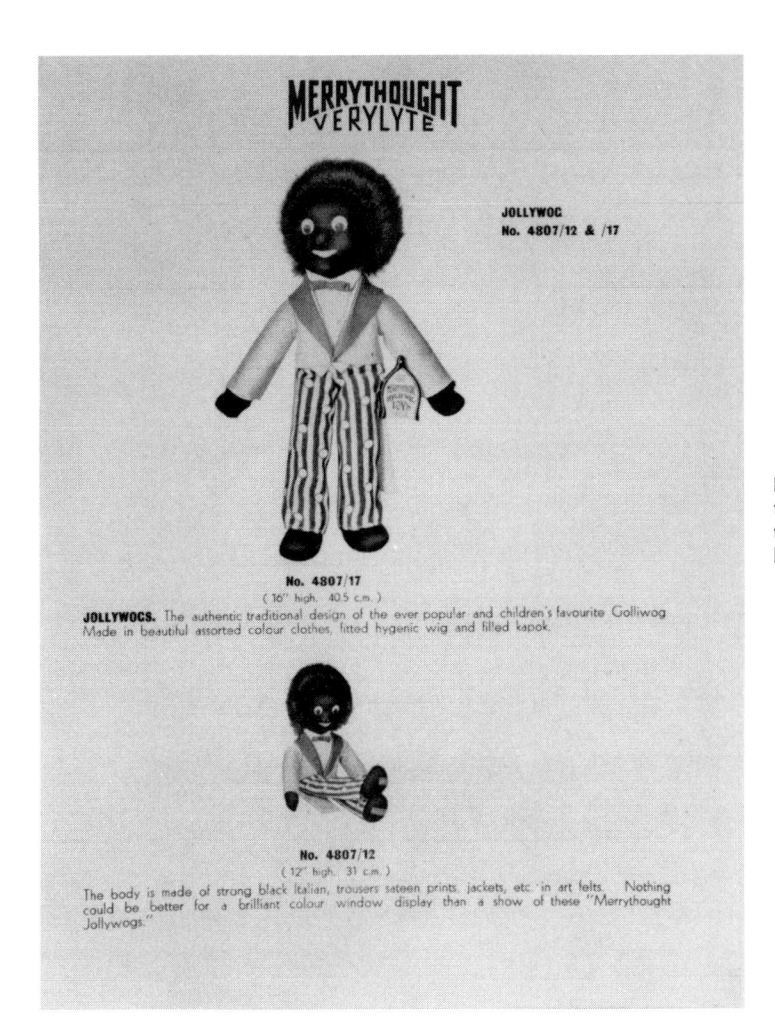

Illustration 122. *Jollywogs*, No. 4807, from the 1949 Merrythought catalog. This is the traditional Golliwog and he is wearing a black wig and is filled with kapok.

Illustration 123. From the 1951 catalog. *Humpty-Dumpty*, T1203, made from 1951 to 1959, is of silk plush and velvet. The *Art Silk Plush Muff Doll* is No. 1571/4 and was made from 1937 to 1955. *Dimples*, No. 1767, was made from 1947 to 1956. The *Bunting Doll* was colored plush except for the face, and is No. 1201, from 1950 to 1953 in a 15 inch (38.1cm) size.

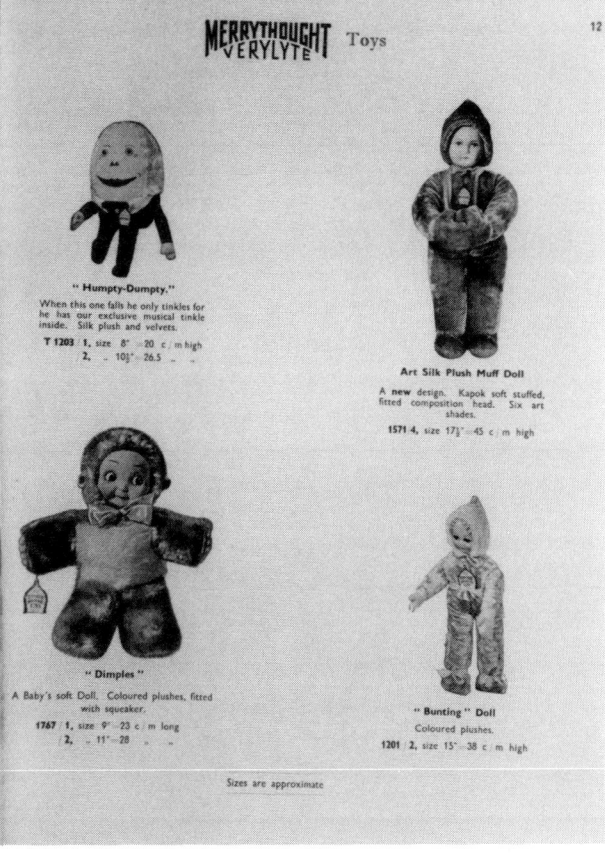

123

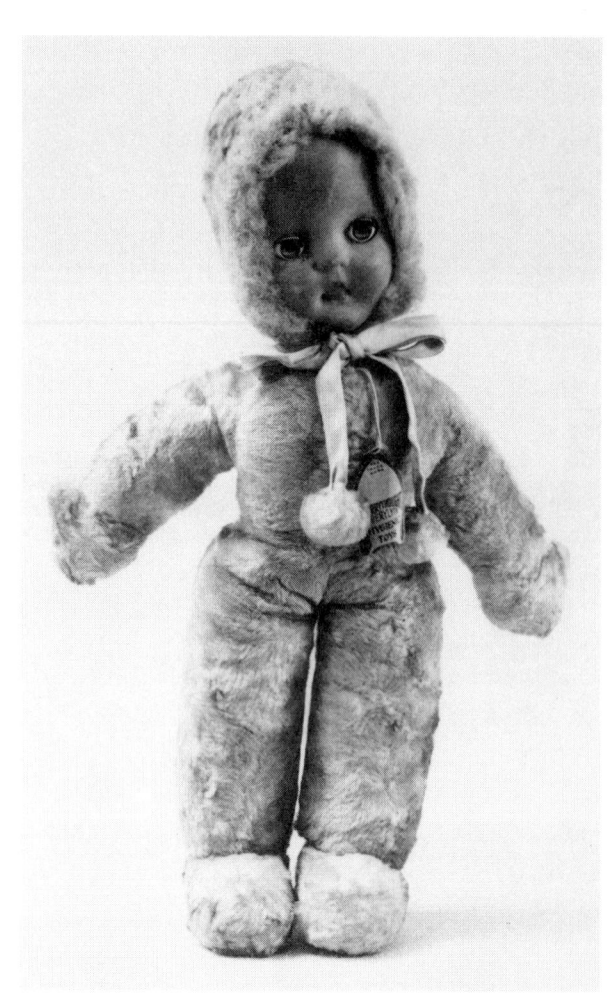

Illustration 124. *Bunting Doll*, No. 1201, from 1950 to 1953 is 15 inches tall (38.1cm) and is all plush except for a felt mask face. Merrythought sample.

Illustration 125. *Golliwog*, No. 5219, 1953. Made in red, blue and yellow felts with movable wired limbs and rolling eyes. Merrythought photograph.

Illustration 126. Clockwise, from top right: *Lanky Joe*, 1965-1966; *Minstrel*, 1964-1965; *Noddy*, 1960-1968 (See Enid Blyton, Chapter XIII.); *Golliwog*, 1964-1966; and *Swingalong Kate*, 1960-1972. *Merrythought photograph.*

LEFT: Illustration 127. 14 inch (35.6cm) *Minstrel*, a Golliwog made from 1964 to 1965. The jacket and the hat are felt. The trousers and the bow tie are cotton. *Dorothy Guest Collection.*

RIGHT: Illustration 128. This 14 inch (35.6cm) Golliwog looks like the *Minstrel* of 1964 to 1965, but the Merrythought catalogs do not show one in this costume. He may be a factory prototype design. *Phyllis Taylor Collection.*

XII. WALT DISNEY DESIGNS

From 1954 to 1980 Merrythought Limited made animals and toys of the characters created by Walt Disney for animated films. These toys are listed in order alphabetically by the name of the item and the film title is cited in the second column. The catalogs stated, "Each character is a perfect model taken from the famous Walt Disney Films made in finest material in realistic colours." The Disney lines were available only in: Great Britain; Near, Middle and Far East; Australia; Sweden; British West Indies; Bahamas; and Bermuda. This was because of licensing requirements.

Stock No.	Disney Film Title	Name	Size inches	centimeters	Year
242/1	**Bambi**	*Bambi*	12	(30.5)	1962-1964
/2			18	(45.7)	
/3			23	(58.4)	
246/1	**101 Dalmatians**	*Lucky Dalmatian*	10½	(26.7)	1962-1963
250		*Floppy Dalmatian*	12	(30.5)	1962-1963
5222/1	various cartoons	*Donald Duck* (squeaker)	12	(30.5)	1953-1959
/25			25	(63.5)	1954-1959
/4			39	(99.0)	1958
163/1		*Donald Duck*	12	(30.5)	1960-1962; 1968-1969
/3			25	(63.5)	1960-1961
162		*Donald Duck*	12	(30.5)	1972-1973
686		*Donald Duck* (muff toy)	14	(35.6)	1972
1912	**Dumbo**	*Dumbo*	6	(15.2)	1954-1956
434/1	**Winnie the Pooh**	*Eeyore* (donkey w/ removable tail)	15	(38.1)	1966-1973; 1976
/3			24	(61.0)	1966-1970; 1976
P31/2		*Eeyore* (push toy)	25	(63.5)	1967
T834		*Eeyore* (toddle toy)	20	(50.8)	1967
286/1	?	*Sitting Fox*	14½	(36.9)	1963
438/1	**Winnie the Pooh**	*Kanga-&-Roo* (Kangaroo; Roo fits in Kanga's pouch)	16	(40.6)	1966-1976
/3			24	(61.0)	
486		*Chime Kanga*	9	(22.9)	1967
1959	**Lady and the Tramp**	*Lady* (Spaniel)	11	(27.9)	1955-1956
1959/1		*Lady*	11	(27.9)	1957-1959
/3			19	(48.3)	
115/1		*Lady*	11	(27.9)	1960-1980
/3			19	(48.3)	
Z2127		*Lady* (nightdress case)	22	(55.9)	1959
870		*Lady* (nightdress case)	22	(55.9)	1960-1978
2008		*Floppy Lady* (bells in ears)	11	(27.9)	1957-1959
008		*Floppy Lady*	11	(27.9)	1960
Z2024		*Floppy Lady* (nightdress case)	14	(35.6)	1957-1959
855		*Lady Sachet* with satin pillow (nightdress case)	12½	(31.8)	1960-1961
2052		*Lady Pup*	8	(20.3)	1958-1959
052		*Lady Pup*	8	(20.3)	1960-1980
5223/1	various cartoons	*Mickey Mouse* (squeaker)	12	(30.5)	1953-1959
/3			36	(91.4)	1958
161/1		*Mickey Mouse* (squeaker)	12	(30.5)	1961-1962; 1968-1969; 1972-1973
685		*Muff Mickey* (muff toy)	14	(35.6)	1972
5224/1	various cartoons	*Minnie Mouse*	12	(30.5)	1954-1959
/3			36	(91.4)	1958
162/1		*Minnie Mouse*	12	(30.5)	1960-1961; 1968-1969
2113	**Old Yeller**	*Old Yeller* (hound)	16	(40.6)	1959
113		*Old Yeller*	16	(40.6)	1960
447/1	**Winnie the Pooh**	*Piglet*	11	(27.9)	1966-1968
/3			24	(61.0)	1967-1968
447/1		*Piglet*	12	(30.5)	1976

Continued

Stock No.	Disney Film Title	Name	Size inches	centimeters	Year
489		*Chime Piglet*	9	(22.9)	1967
966		*Piglet in Bed* (nightdress case)	12½	(31.8)	1967
1910/1	various cartoons	*Pluto* (squeaker)	13½	(34.3)	1954-1959
/29			29	(73.7)	1954
/30			29	(73.7)	1955-1959
105/1		*Pluto* (squeaker)	16½	(41.9)	1960-1961; 1968
/3			29	(73.7)	1960
105		*Pluto* (squeaker)	14	(35.6)	1972
1919		*Pluto Glove Puppet*	9½	(24.2)	1954-1957
ZNC1911		*Pluto* (nightdress case)	22	(55.9)	1954-1957
TT1975/0		*Pluto* (Safety Toddle Toy)	19	(48.3)	1955-1956
460/1	**Winnie the Pooh**	*Rabbit*	13	(33.0)	1967-1968
/3			30	(76.2)	
253/1	?	*Racoon*	11	(27.9)	1962-1963
2051	**Lady and the Tramp**	*Scamp*	8	(20.3)	1958-1959
051		*Scamp*	8	(20.3)	1960-1980
1921/7	**Snow White and the Seven Dwarfs**	*The Seven Dwarfs* (Not known if sold as a set or separately.) *Doc; Dopey; Happy; Sleepy; Sneezy; Grumpy; Bashful*	9½	(24.2)	1954-1955
1929		*The Seven Dwarfs Glove Puppet* (Not known if sold as a set or separately.) *Doc; Dopey; Happy; Sleepy; Sneezy; Grumpy; Bashful*	9½	(24.2)	1954-1955
1920		*Snow White*	14	(35.6)	1954-1955
1987/1	**Bambi**	*Thumper* (rabbit; squeaker)	12	(30.5)	1956-1959
/3			24	(61.0)	
112/0		*Thumper* (squeaker)	10	(25.4)	1960-1980
/1			12	(30.5)	
/3			24	(61.0)	
248/1		*Floppy Thumper*	16	(40.6)	1962
887		*Thumper* (nightdress case)	19	(48.3)	1962-1978
448/1	**Winnie the Pooh**	*Tigger* (tiger)	12	(30.5)	1967-1968
/1			14	(35.6)	1976
/3			27	(68.6)	
1960	**Lady and the Tramp**	*Tramp* (dog)	14½	(36.9)	1955-1956
1960/1		*Tramp*	14½	(36.9)	1957-1959
/3			28	(71.1)	
110/1		*Tramp*	14½	(36.9)	1960-1965; 1974-1980
/3			28	(71.1)	1960-1965
2011		*Floppy Tramp* (bells in ears)	11	(27.9)	1957-1959
011		*Floppy Tramp*	11	(27.9)	1960
Z2025		*Floppy Tramp* (nightdress case)	14	(35.6)	1957-1959
858		*Tramp Sachet* (nightdress case)	12½	(31.8)	1960-1961
435/1	**Winnie the Pooh**	*Winnie the Pooh* (bear)	10	(25.4)	1966-1973; 1976
/3			24	(61.0)	
488		*Chime Pooh*	9	(22.9)	1967
967		*Pooh* (nightdress case)	21	(53.3)	1967-1968
974		*Pooh in Bed* (nightdress case)	14	(35.6)	1967-1973
449/1	**Winnie the Pooh**	*Wol* (owl)	12	(30.5)	1967-1968
/3			24	(61.0)	
490		*Chime Wol*	9	(22.9)	1967
969		*Wol* (nightdress case)	?		1967

ABOVE: Illustration 129. These versions of *Mickey Mouse* and *Donald Duck* were made from 1953 to 1959. Each is 12 inches (30.5cm) tall. They have bodies of art silk plush with felt hands, feet and felt ears for *Mickey* and a felt bill for *Donald*. *Mickey*'s trousers are bright red felt. This is one of the most faithful adaptions ever made of these Disney characters. *Merrythought photograph*.

LEFT: Illustration 130. Prototype model for a *Donald Duck* nightdress case, probably late 1950s.

RIGHT: Illustration 131. Back view of the Merrythought prototype nightdress case using *Donald Duck*.

Illustration 132. Walt Disney designs from the 1972 Merrythought catalog. Beginning with *Mickey Mouse*, and going clockwise: This 12 inch (30.5cm) *Mickey* is No. 161/1, from 1961-1973, and is the same design as No. 5223; *Donald Duck*, No. 162, differs in design from the one shown in *Illustration 129*, and was from 1972 to 1973 also at 12 inches (30.5cm); *Muff Mickey* and *Muff Donald* are both from 1972; *Pluto*, No. 105, is from 1972 and is 14 inches (35.6cm) long and is nylon plush.

BOTTOM LEFT: Illustration 133. *Pluto* is 14 inches long (35.6cm) and made of nylon plush, No. 105 from 1972. *Phyllis Taylor Collection.*

BOTTOM RIGHT: Illustration 134. *Pluto Nightdress Case*, No. ZNC1911, 1954 to 1957. This model of *Pluto* could also be sold in Canada and he is 22 inches (55.9cm) long and is made of fine art silk plush. *Merrythought photograph.*

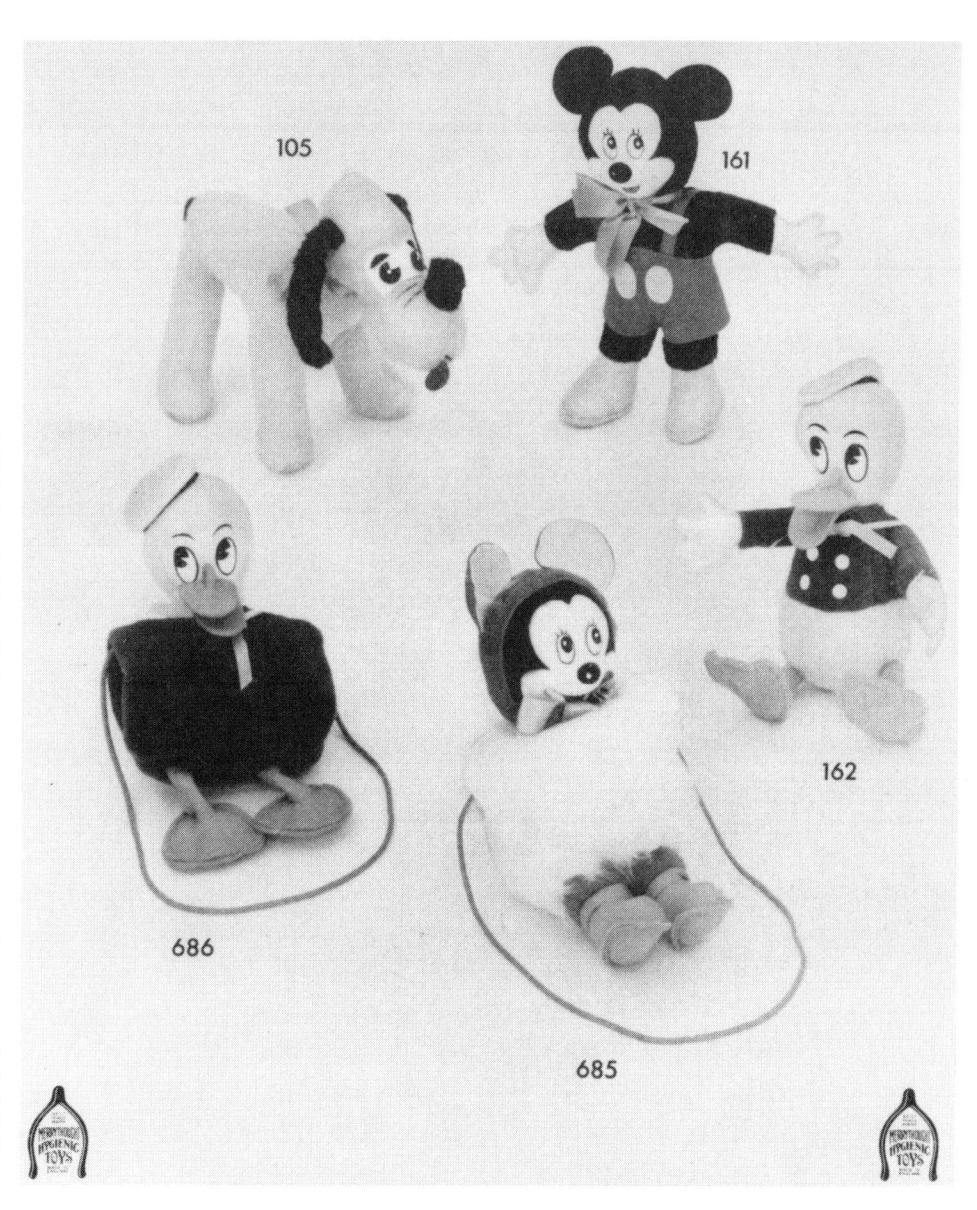

Illustration 135. *Lady and the Tramp* from the Walt Disney film of the same title. *Tramp*, at the left, is No. 110/1 and he is 14½ inches (36.9cm) high; *Lady*, at the right, is No. 115/1 and she is 11 inches (27.9cm) high. Both models were shown from 1960 to 1980 and they are made of plush. *Lady* is from the *Dorothy Guest Collection.*

BOTTOM LEFT: Illustration 136. No. 115/1 *Lady*, 11 inches (27.9cm). *Dorothy Guest Collection.*

BOTTOM RIGHT: Illustration 137. *Scamp*, No. 2051, 1958-1959, is 8 inches (20.3cm) long and is blue-grey and white plush. *Kay Bransky Collection.*

Illustration 138. Walt Disney toys from the 1972 Merrythought catalog. Beginning top right and going clockwise: *Eeyore*, No. 434/1, 1966 to 1976, is 15 inches (38.1cm) long and he has a removable tail and is grey plush. He is from *Winnie the Pooh*, as is *Pooh* himself, No. 435, 1966-1976, fully-jointed in plush with a bright felt jacket. *Lady Pup*, No. 052, is 8 inches (20.3cm) long and is from 1960-1980. *Scamp*, No. 051, is the same size and from the same years. *Lady*, No. 115, is the model from 1960 to 1980. *Thumper*, No. 112, came in three sizes from 1960 to 1980. In the center is *Kanga-&-Roo* from *Winnie the Pooh*, No. 438, from 1966 to 1976.

Illustration 139. This is the prettiest of all the versions of *Lady*. She is No. 1959, from 1955 and 1956 and is the actual coloring of a Golden Spaniel. 11 inches (27.9cm) high. *Merrythought photograph.*

131

Illustration 140. Lady Pup, No. 052, 1960 to 1980. Merrythought photograph.

Illustration 141. From the 1962 Merrythought catalog. More versions of Lady and the Tramp with other Disney characters. At the top right is Bambi, No. 242, 1962 to 1964. Bambi is brown and white mohair plush. At the bottom are No. 246, Lucky Dalmatian, who is 10½ inches (26.7cm) high, and Floppy Dalmatian, No. 250, who is 12 inches (30.5cm) long. These two are from 101 Dalmatians and they are mohair with "lucky" markings and they wear leather collars. They were made from 1962 to 1963.

132

Illustration 142. Still more versions of *Lady and the Tramp* from a 1965 Merrythought photograph. At the top right is *Thumper*, No. 112, from 1960 to 1980, who had a "voice" in his tail. Note: the music box ring on his back was not in the same photograph when it was used in the 1965 Merrythought catalog.

Illustration 143. *Old Yeller* was made in 1959 and 1960 in a 16 inch (40.6cm) size. He is of art silk plush. Merrythought sample.

BELOW: Illustration 144. This set of *Snow White and the Seven Dwarfs* is by Chad Valley Co. Ltd., probably late 1940s to early 1950s. *Snow White* is 17 inches (43.2cm) tall with a pressed felt mask face, a black mohair wig, painted brown eyes and a jointed cloth body. Each dwarf is 9½ inches (24.2cm) tall and they each have a pressed felt mask face with painted blue eyes and attached plush beards. All of the dolls of this set are labeled with a cloth tag. At the back left is *Doc;* to *Snow White's* other side is *Dopey.* In front are *Bashful, Happy, Grumpy, Sleepy* and *Sneezy.*

LEFT: Illustration 145. *Sneezy* from the Chad Valley set of *Snow White and the Seven Dwarfs* from the Walt Disney film of 1937. The face and arms are felt; the body is cotton cloth. The dolls of this set are probably from the late 1940s to early 1950s.

BOTTOM: Illustration 146. Merrythought Limited purchased supplies from Chad Valley and made a set of Walt Disney's *Snow White and the Seven Dwarfs* in 1954 and 1955 that are similar to the Chad Valley set. The painting was done at Merrythought. Note that *Doc* has painted glasses. *Snow White* is 14 inches (35.6cm) and the *Dwarfs* are 9½ inches (24.2cm). These dolls have pressed felt mask faces and cloth bodies like the Chad Valley set. From left to right: *Dopey, Grumpy, Bashful, Snow White, Happy, Doc, Sleepy* and *Sneezy*. Merrythought photograph.

Illustration 147. *Snow White* by Merrythought, 1954-1955. She is 14 inches tall (35.6cm) and has a felt mask face with a black mohair wig and blue painted eyes. The remainder of the fully-jointed doll is cloth. The gown is all of velvet; the top is dark blue and the skirt is yellow. *Phyllis Taylor Collection.*

No. 854 *Rabbit Sachet,* 1960-1961, a nightdress case with a zipper compartment.

Sitting Rabbit, 1931-1956. Merrythought sample.

137

Flexidoe, a dressed rabbit from 1955-1956. This Merrythought sample is 18 inches (45.7cm) tall.

17 inch (43.2cm) *Rabbit*, No. CN1722/14, 1948.

138

Donald Duck, 1953 to 1959, in plush and felt. He is 12 inches (30.5cm) tall. Merrythought sample.

14 inch (35.6cm) *Snow White*, 1954-1955. She has a felt mask face with a black mohair wig and blue painted eyes. The gown is velvet with a dark blue top and yellow skirt. *Phyllis Taylor Collection.*

Mickey Mouse and *Donald Duck*, 1953 to 1959. Each is 12 inches (30.5cm) tall with plush bodies and felt faces, hands and feet.

A Merrythought Artificial Christmas Tree from the early 1950s with *Minnie Mouse*, *Jerry Mouse* and *Bambi*. Doris Morris Collection.

Golliwogs from the 1950 Merrythought catalog, called *Jollywogs*. These are Nos. 4807/12 and 4807/17; they are 12 inches (30.5cm) and 16 inches (40.6cm) tall and date from 1949 to 1955.

The *New Merrythought Golliwog* of 1986 is 19 inches (48.3cm) tall and is made of velvet with velvet clothing. Merrythought photograph.

141

24 inch (61cm) *Gran'pop*, a Lawson Wood design monkey, late 1930s. All-mohair plush. *Helen Sieverling Collection. Photograph by Glenn Sieverling.*

Baby Monkey, No. 313, 1964-1965. He is 10 inches (25.4cm) tall and is of brown mohair. Merrythought sample.

Reynard, the dressed fox, 1956-1959. 19 inches (48.3cm). Merrythought sample.

At the top is *Mr. Jinks* and *Deputy Dawg* is below him. These characters are from the television cartoon show "Deputy Dawg and Friends."

143

Nellie Elephant, No. 120/3, 1959-1977. Mohair with a felt coat. *Kay Bransky Collection.*

Jerry Mouse is 6½ inches tall and is from the MGM cartoon series "Tom and Jerry."

Bonzo, a character designed by G.E. Studdy. He is from 1952 to 1954 and is velvet with painted features and is 9 inches (22.9cm) high.

144

Illustration 148. The pressed felt mask faces that Merrythought used for the *Seven Dwarfs*. These are old factory stock. In the top row are *Doc, Happy, Bashful* and *Grumpy;* in front are *Sleepy, Sneezy* and *Dopey.*

Illustration 149. Merrythought made *Thumper* from Walt Disney's *Bambi* from 1956 to 1980. This Merrythought sample is 12 inches (30.5cm) tall and he has jointed arms.

145

Illustration 150. *Winnie the Pooh* toys from the 1966 Merrythought catalog. At the top is *Winnie*, made of mohair and wearing a jacket, and *Kanga-&-Roo* in plush. At the bottom are *Eeyore* in plush with a removable tail and *Piglet* in pink velveteen and wearing a "smart coat." These characters were made from 1966 to 1976.

Illustration 151. *Winnie the Pooh* from the 1976 Merrythought catalog. This is No. 435/1 and he is 14 inches (35.6cm) tall and is fully-jointed of mohair with an embroidered nose. His bright red felt jacket has his name on the front.

XIII. FAMOUS ARTISTS' DESIGNS

The FAMOUS ARTISTS' DESIGNS by Merrythought are items that originated in the drawings and stories of several famous artists, most of them British. These items are listed under the names of the creators, which appear in alphabetical order with their designs listed in the order in which they were made by Merrythought.

Stock No.	Type of Item	Name	Size inches	centimeters	Year
		CECIL ALDIN:			
C1070/2	Dog	*Woggles* from the *Weekly Sketch*	11½	(29.2)	1932-1933
/3			13½	(34.3)	1932
/4			16	(40.6)	1932-1933
		MABLE LUCIE ATTWELL:			
ZNC1624	Doll	*Slumbering Sam* (nightdress case)	24	(61.0)	1938
ZNC1630	Doll	*Vanity Jane* (nightie case)	24	(61.0)	1938
		ENID BLYTON:			
2070/1	Doll	*Noddy*	12	(30.5)	1958-1959
/3			24	(61.0)	
070/1	Doll	*Noddy*	12	(30.5)	1960-1968
/3			24	(61.0)	1960-1966
168	Muff	*Noddy*	14	(35.6)	1960-1961
881	Doll	*Noddy Sachet* (nightdress case)	12½	(31.8)	1961
2101	Doll	*Big Ears*	13½	(34.3)	1958
/1			13½	(34.3)	1959
/3			22	(55.9)	
101/1	Doll	*Big Ears*	13½	(34.3)	1960-1962
/3			22	(55.9)	
		HARRY CORBETT:			
871	Bear	*Sooty*	18	(45.7)	1960-1962
186	Bear	*Muff Sooty*	14	(35.6)	1961
856	Bear	*Sooty Sachet* (nightdress case)	12½	(31.8)	1960-1961
		PEGGY EARNSHAW:			
S1054/1	Robin	*Tweetie*	6½	(16.5)	1932-1933
/2			8	(20.3)	
/3			10	(25.4)	
		ARTHUR GROOM:			
1985	Duck	*Dimple Duckling* (girl)	10	(25.4)	1956-1957
1986	Duck	*Dilly Duckling* (boy)	10	(25.4)	1956-1957
2043	Duck	*Dilly Duck* (glove toy)	9½	(24.2)	1957
2044	Duck	*Dimple Duck* (glove toy)	9½	(24.2)	1957
		IAN HASSALL:			
1504/2	Cat	*Smuggins*	13	(33.0)	1936
		MARIA PEREGO:			
353/1	Mouse	*Topo Gigio*	11	(27.9)	1965
/3			24	(61.0)	
		CHLOE PRESTON:			
C1055/1	Dog	*Foo-Foo*	8	(20.3)	1932-1933; 1936-1938
/2			10	(25.4)	1931-1933; 1936-1938
/3			13	(33.0)	1932-1933; 1936
/4			16	(40.6)	
/5			20	(50.8)	
C1114/1	Kitten	*Ki-Ki*	9	(22.9)	1932-1933; 1935-1937
/2			10½	(26.7)	
/3			12	(30.5)	1932-1933
1385/1	Dog	*Dinkie*	5	(12.7)	1936-1937
/2			7	(17.8)	
/3			7½	(19.1)	
4626/2	Dog	*Dinkie*	6	(15.2)	1950-1959
		HARRY ROUNDTREE:			
1830	Rabbit	*Robert* (fitted voice)	8¾	(22.3)	1939
1831	Bear	*Bobby* (fitted voice)	8	(20.3)	1939
1834	Fawn	*Flossie*	11	(27.9)	1939

Stock No.	Type of Item	Name	Size inches	centimeters	Year
		LILIAN ROWLES:			
1726	**Doll**	Snow White	14	(35.6)	1938
1727		The Fairy Princess	14	(35.6)	1938
		G. E. STUDDY:			
1505/16	**Pekingese**	Cheekie	16	(40.6)	1936
/18			18	(45.7)	
1466/2	**Horse**	Yop	13	(33.0)	1936
	Little People Dolls:				
1651		Simple Simon	9	(22.9)	1938
1652		Little Turk	9	(22.9)	1938
1653		Farmer's Boy	9	(22.9)	1938
1654		Pixie Man	9	(22.9)	1938
1686		Lucky Sam	9	(22.9)	1938
1687		Eskimo	9	(22.9)	1938
5116/9	**Dog**	Bonzo	9	(22.9)	1952-1954
		BRIAN WHITE:			
1390/13½	**Doll**	Nipper from the *Daily Mail*	13½	(34.3)	1936
1390			13	(33.0)	1937-1938
1644	**Doll**	Nipper's Brother	11	(27.9)	1937-1938
		LAWSON WOOD:			
C1068/1	**Monkey**	Rango	10	(25.4)	1932-1933
/2			12	(30.5)	
/3			14	(35.6)	
ZNC1319/30	**Monkey**	Sleeping Beauty (nightie case)	30	(76.2)	1935-1936; 1938; 1948; 1950-1959
872	**Monkey**	Sleeping Beauty (nightie case)	30	(76.2)	1960-1978
1372/0	**Monkey**	Jubilee Chimp	8½	(21.6)	1936-1938
/2			14	(35.6)	
1465/11½	**Pig**	Twiggie	11½	(29.2)	1936
/14			14	(35.6)	
/17			17	(43.2)	
ZNC1393/17	**Pig**	Twiggie (nightdress case)	17	(43.2)	1936; 1938
1386/17	**Monkey**	Gran'Pop	17	(43.2)	1938
/24			24	(61.0)	
1752/12		Gran'Pop	12	(30.5)	1939
/16			16	(40.6)	
/24			24	(61.0)	
/32			32	(81.3)	
1784/14		Gran'Pop	14	(35.6)	1939
/19			19	(48.3)	
CE1752/1		Gran'Pop (voice)	12	(30.5)	1947
CN1752/1		Gran'Pop (voice)	12	(30.5)	1948
/2			17½	(44.5)	
ZNC1827		Gran'Pop (nightdress case)	25	(63.5)	1939; 1949-1953; 1955-1959
861		Gran'Pop (nightdress case)	25	(63.5)	1960
1752/1		Gran'Pop (voice)	12	(30.5)	1950-1959
/2			17½	(44.5)	1950-1957
/36			36	(91.4)	1954-1957
5218		Gran'Pop (glove toy)	9½	(24.2)	1953-1959
178		Gran'Pop (glove toy)	9½	(24.2)	1960-1962
1965/1		Floppy Gran'Pop	12	(30.5)	1957-1959
/2			15	(38.1)	1955-1959
160/1		Floppy Gran'Pop	12	(30.5)	1960
156/1		Gran'Pop	12	(30.5)	1960-1964
4912/1		Chimpy (boy)	10½	(26.7)	1951-1953
4913/1		Chirpy (girl)	10½	(26.7)	1951-1955
312		Mother Monkey	24	(61.0)	1964-1965

Illustration 152. Enid Blyton's *Noddy*. The 1958-1959 version came in sizes of 12 inches (30.5cm) and 24 inches (61cm). He has wired limbs and a spring-jointed head. He was not available in Canada, Australia, the United States and Ireland. *Merrythought photograph.*

Illustration 153. *Big Ears*, another Enid Blyton design, was made from 1958 to 1962. This version is from 1959 and is 13½ inches (34.3cm) and is constructed like *Noddy*, his companion. *Merrythought photograph.*

Illustration 154. Arthur Groom with his designs, *Dimple Duckling* and *Dilly Duckling*, from 1956 and 1957. The 10 inch (25.4cm) characters are made of plush and felt and are from the children's "Sunny Stories" series of characters. *Merrythought photograph.*

Illustration 155. *Dimple Duckling* and *Dilly Duckling* from Arthur Groom's "Sunny Stories." Merrythought photograph.

Illustration 156. Maria Perego's famous mouse *Topo Gigio* was made of velveteen and suedette in 1965 in sizes of 11 inches (27.9cm) and 24 inches (61cm). This Merrythought factory sample is the smaller version.

"**Dinkie,**" Chloe Preston's famous creation. Beautiful art shades of velvets and very light.

No. 1385/1 5" long.
/2 7" ,,
/3 7½" ,,

Illustration 157. Chlöe Preston's famous character *Dinkie* was made from 1936 to 1959. He came in various shades of velvet. This catalog illustration is from 1936.

36

MERRYTHOUGHT

The Fairy Princess
from Grimm's Fairy Tale.
Snow White
Designed by
LILIAN ROWLES

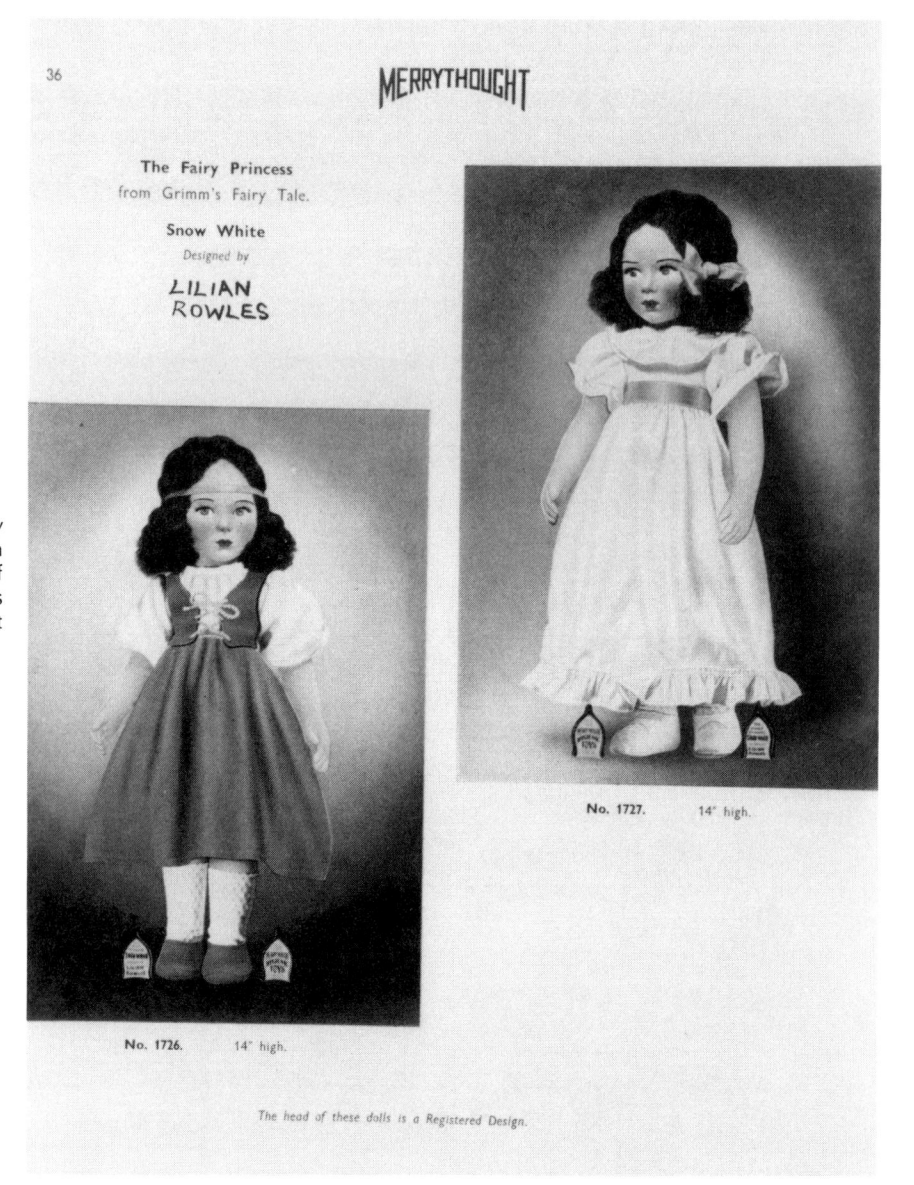

Illustration 158. *Snow White* (left) and *The Fairy Princess* were produced in 1938 from the design of Lilian Rowles and are some of the best of Merrythought's felt "art dolls." Each is 14 inches (35.6cm) tall. From the 1938 Merrythought catalog.

No. 1726. 14" high.

No. 1727. 14" high.

The head of these dolls is a Registered Design.

152

TOP LEFT: Illustration 159. *Bonzo* is a cartoon character that originated in the 1920s. He was designed by G.E. Studdy and produced in velvet with painted features by Merrythought from 1952 to 1954. The body is a pink color and the painted portions are black and red. This 9 inch (22.9cm) dog is one of the cutest items that Merrythought ever manufactured.

TOP RIGHT: Illustration 160. G.E. Studdy's *Bonzo* by Merrythought.

RIGHT: Illustration 161. *Cheekie*, a G.E. Studdy creation, was "Bonzo's Lady Friend, a delightful Pekingese" and was made by Merrythought in 1936. She came in sizes of 16 inches (40.6cm) and 18 inches (45.7cm) and was of white and golden brown plush. 1936 Merrythought catalog illustration.

153

MERRYTHOUGHT

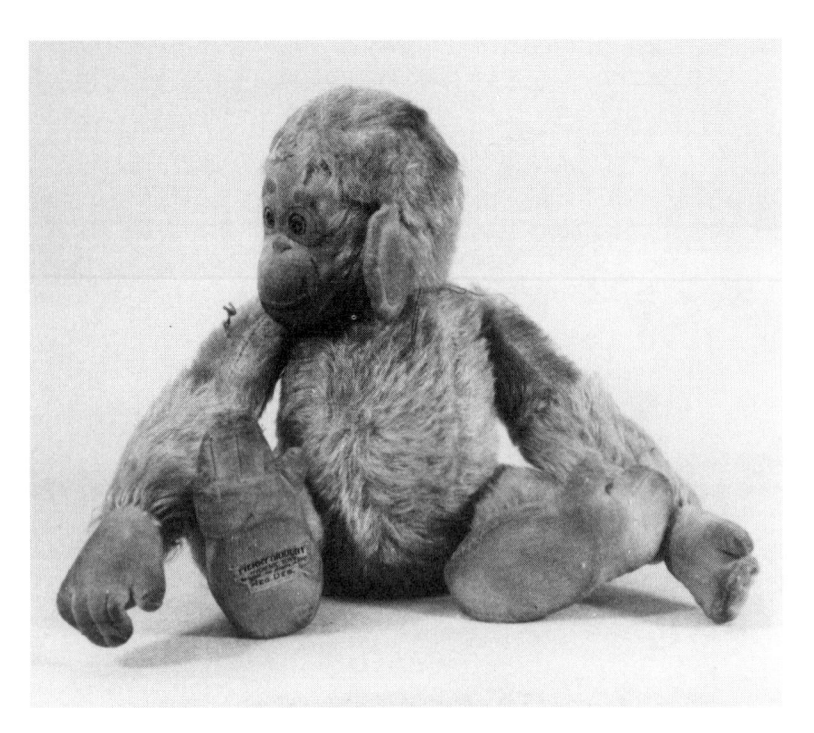

"Gran'pop" designed by
LAWSON WOOD
No. 1386   17 inches high.
/24 "   "

JUBILEE
(or any other baby "Chimp" that monopolizes the children's attention at the Zoos).
Designed by Lawson Wood.
Soft alpaca plush in natural shades.
Soft stuffed.
No. 1372 0   8½" high.
           2 14"   "

Illustration 163. *Gran'pop;* a Merrythought sample, produced from 1950 to 1959. He is of brown plush with a velvet face, hands and feet and is fully-jointed with a "voice" inside. This Merrythought sample is 12 inches (30.5cm).

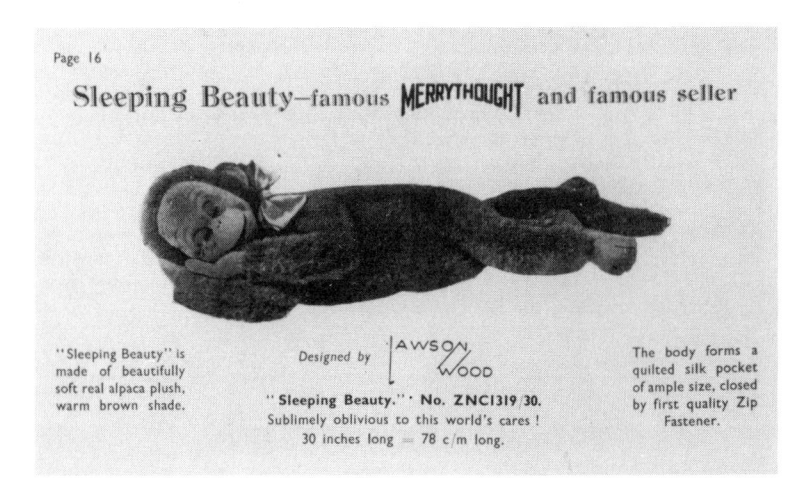

Illustration 162. Lawson Wood's comical monkeys were made by Merrythought from 1932 to 1965. Above is *Gran'pop* from the 1938 catalog. Below is *Jubilee*, the baby Chimp.

Illustration 164. *Sleeping Beauty* nightdress case, a Lawson Wood design of 1935 to 1959. Inside the plush body is a quilted silk pocket for storing a child's sleep wear and it is closed with a zipper. This example is 30 inches (76.2cm) long and is from the 1948 Merrythought catalog.

Page 16
Sleeping Beauty—famous MERRYTHOUGHT and famous seller

"Sleeping Beauty" is made of beautifully soft real alpaca plush, warm brown shade.

Designed by LAWSON WOOD
"Sleeping Beauty." No. ZNC1319/30.
Sublimely oblivious to this world's cares!
30 inches long = 78 c/m long.

The body forms a quilted silk pocket of ample size, closed by first quality Zip Fastener.

Illustration 165. Lawson Wood's *Sleeping Beauty*. Merrythought sample.

Illustration 166. *Gran'pop, Chimpy* and *Chirpy* from the 1951 Merrythought catalog.

Illustration 167. The last Lawson Wood design made by Merrythought was *Mother Monkey* from 1964-1965. She is 24 inches (61cm) tall, fully-jointed and she wears a check pinafore. Her "fur" is synthetic; the face, hands and feet are velveteen. Merrythought sample.

MERRYTHOUGHT VERYLYTE Toys

"Gran'pop"

"Beauty unadorned," designed by LAWSON WOOD

Brown plush and velvet.
1752/1, size 12" = 30.5 c/m high
    /2, „ 17½" = 45 „ „

Two NEW additions to the Merrythought collection specially designed for them by that famous artist LAWSON WOOD

"Chimpy" (Boy)
Size 10½" = 27 c/m high

"Chirpy" (Girl)
Size 10½" = 27 c/m high

XIV. MOVIE, TELEVISION and CARTOON CHARACTERS

This section includes licensed characters from movies and television films that are not WALT DISNEY DESIGNS. They are listed alphabetically by the name of the film or series, with the characters listed chronologically. *Tom* and *Jerry* were made from 1951 to 1979. The other characters were made from 1958 to 1975.

Stock No.	Type of Animal	Name	Size inches	centimeters	Year
		DEPUTY DAWG AND FRIENDS © C.B.S. Films Inc.			
264/1	Cat	Mr. Jinks	12	(30.5)	1963-1964
/3			26	(66.0)	
267	Cat	Mr. Jinks (Trike Toy)	8	(20.3)	1963
349/1	Dog	Deputy Dawg	11	(27.9)	1964-1965
/3			24	(61.0)	
351/1	Mouse	Muskie	8½	(21.6)	1964
		DOUGAL AND THE BLUE CAT © DANOT. Based on the feature film *Dougal and the Blue Cat*.			
723/1	Cat	Blue Cat	15	(38.1)	1972-1974
		HAROLD HARE © Fleetway Publications			
251/1	Rabbit	Harold Hare	16	(40.6)	1962-1963
		THE HERBS from the BBC-TV Series permission Film Fair Parsley			
731	Lion	Mr. Parsley	8	(20.3)	1973-1975
		HUCKLEBERRY HOUND AND FRIENDS © Screen Gems, Inc.			
237/1	Bear	Yogi Bear	11	(27.9)	1961-1964;
/3			27	(68.6)	1971-1973
226/1	Dog	Huckleberry Hound	12	(30.5)	1961-1964;
/3			25	(63.5)	1971-1973
254/1	Mouse	Pixie	8	(20.3)	1963-1975
/3			26	(66.0)	1964-1965
255/1	Mouse	Dixie	8	(20.3)	1963-1975
/3			26	(66.0)	1964-1965
271	Mouse	Pullalong Pixie	8	(20.3)	1963
272	Mouse	Pullalong Dixie	8	(20.3)	1963
265	Bear	Trike Yogi Bear	8	(20.3)	1963
268	Dog	Trike Huckleberry Hound	8	(20.3)	1963
942	Mice	Pixie and Dixie Sachet (nightdress case)	12½	(31.8)	1966-1975
		THE MAGIC ROUNDABOUT BBC-TV Series © Serge Danot, 1972			
732	Dog	Dougal	18	(45.7)	1973-1975
X48	Dog	Dougal (nightdress case)	22	(55.9)	1973-1975
		MARY, MUNGO AND MIDGE permission BBC Television Enterprises			
633/1	Dog	Mungo	12	(30.5)	1971-1972
/3			42	(106.6)	
634/1	Mouse	Midge	10	(25.4)	1971-1973
		MEET THE PENGUINS permission of Bill Hooper and Josephine Smith Wright (television show)			
1916	Penguin	Bo Bo, the Baby Penguin	6½	(16.5)	1954-1955
1918	Penguin	Father Penguin	12	(30.5)	1954-1956

Stock No.	Type of Animal	Name	Size inches	centimeters	Year
		THE PINK PANTHER © Mirisch-Geoffrey D.F., 1964 (television show)			
699/1	Panther	Pink Panther	17	(43.2)	1972
		RIN TIN TIN Official Screen Gems Inc. model			
2065/1	German Shepherd	Rin Tin Tin	14	(35.6)	1958-1959
/2			34	(86.4)	
065/1		Rin Tin Tin (Note: Rin Tin Tin also used for Alsatians, SEE German Shepherds, under DOGS)	14	(35.6)	1960
		ROBIN, from Hulton's National Weekly			
1933	Lion	Richard Lion	11	(27.9)	1955-1956
1951	Cat	Princess Tai-Lu	8	(20.3)	1955-1958
1979	Bear	Woppit	9	(22.9)	1956-1957
		TOM AND JERRY permission of MGM			
4627	Mouse	Jerry the Mouse	6½	(16.5)	1951-1957
4627/1		Jerry the Mouse	6½	(16.5)	1958-1959
/3			24	(61.0)	
182/1		Jerry the Mouse	6½	(16.5)	1960-1979
/2			13	(33.0)	1969-1979
/3			24	(61.0)	1960-1979
1931		Jerry Mouse (glove toy)	9½	(24.2)	1954-1956
275		Pullalong Jerry Mouse	7	(17.8)	1963
522/1	Cat	Tom Cat (squeaker)	12	(30.5)	1954-1956
397/1		Tom Cat	10	(25.4)	1965-1969
/3			24	(61.0)	1965-1968
954		Tom and Jerry Sachet (nightdress case)	12½	(31.8)	1967-1972

Illustration 168. "Deputy Dawg and Friends" cartoon character from television: *Deputy Dawg* is 11 inches (27.9cm) tall in velveteen with a felt cowboy hat. Merrythought sample from 1964-1965.

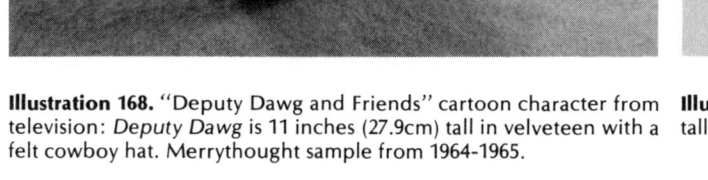

Illustration 169. *Mr. Jinks* from "Deputy Dawg and Friends" is 12 inches tall and is of bright red velveteen, 1963-1964. Merrythought sample.

Illustration 170. From "Meet the Penguins" television show: *Father Penguin* is 12 inches (30.5cm) tall in art silk plush. Merrythought sample from 1954-1956.

Illustration 171. "The Adventures of Rin Tin Tin" was an American television show from 1954 to 1959 and was also shown in Great Britain. From left to right, the stars: Rin Tin Tin, Lee Aaker as Rusty and James Brown as Lt. Rip Masters. Each star has autographed this picture. *Photograph courtesy of Screen Gems, Inc.*

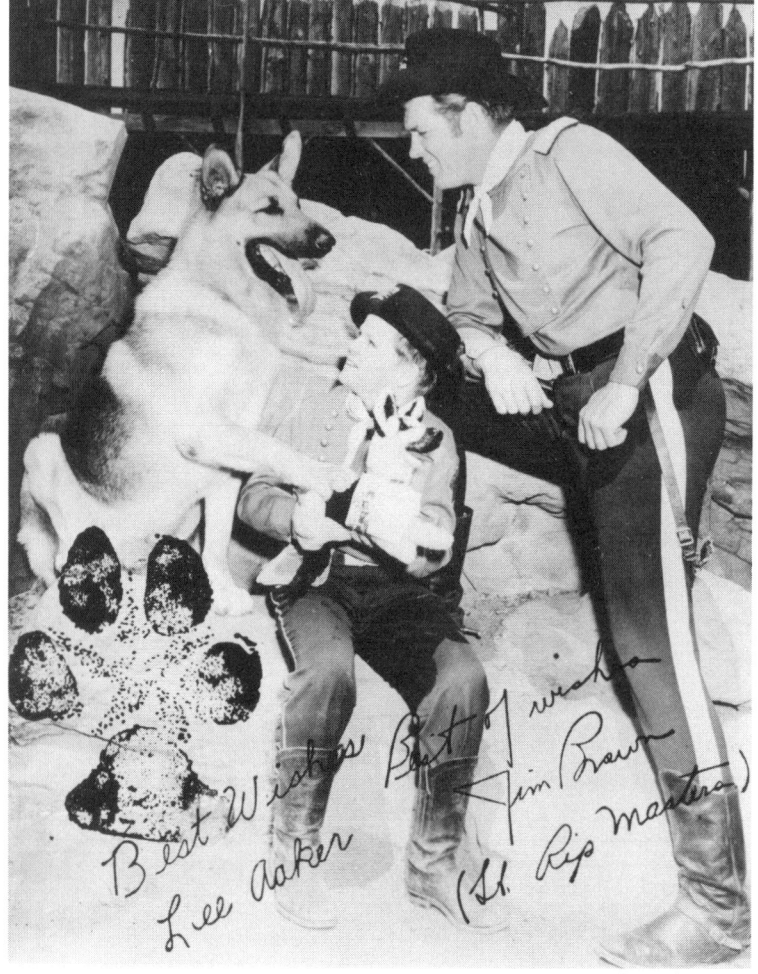

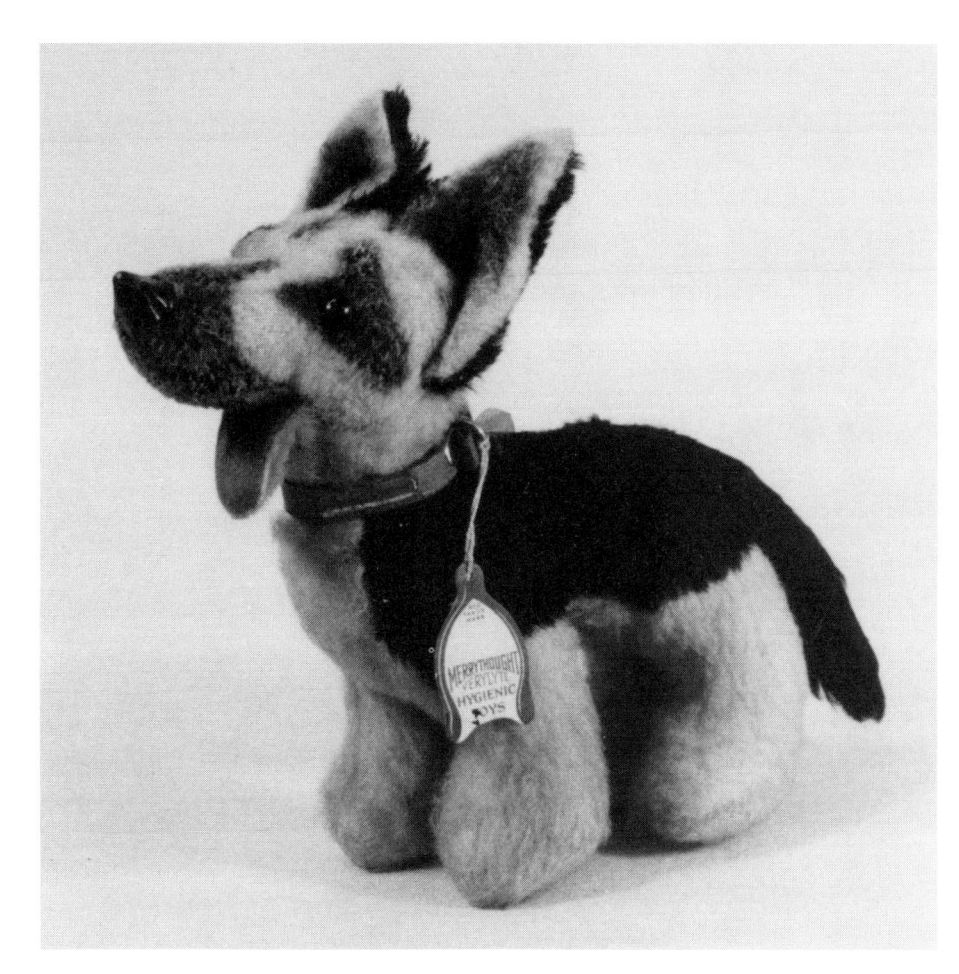

Illustration 172. *Rin Tin Tin*, 1958-1960, was the same dog design that was used for *Alsatian*, No. 2095, 1958-1959. Merrythought sample.

Illustration 173. Character from "Robin," which appeared in Hulton's *National Weekly: Richard Lion*, 1955-1956, golden brown and white plush, moving eyes, fitted with a squeaker, 11 inches (27.9cm). *Dorothy Guest Collection.*

Illustration 174. Also from "Robin," the 9 inch (22.9cm) *Woppit;* brown plush body and wearing a bright red felt coat; 1956-1957. *Merrythought photograph.*

Illustration 175. *Jerry the Mouse* from MGM's "Tom and Jerry" cartoons, 1951-1979. He is 6½ inches (16.5cm) tall and is made of velveteen. This one is from the later production years. The plush ball is probably from the late 1950s. Note the different cardboard tags on each item. The tag on the ball was used in the 1950s and 1960s; *Jerry's* tag began in the late 1960s.

Illustration 176. *Jerry Mouse Glove Toy*, 1954-1956, 9½ inches (24.2cm) high. Velveteen with a stuffed head. The cardboard Merrythought tag is reversed for the "Tom and Jerry" information. *Merrythought sample.*

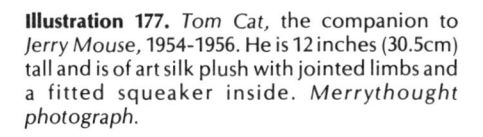

Illustration 177. *Tom Cat*, the companion to *Jerry Mouse*, 1954-1956. He is 12 inches (30.5cm) tall and is of art silk plush with jointed limbs and a fitted squeaker inside. *Merrythought photograph.*

Illustration 178. Page from the 1965 Merrythought catalog. In the top row are *Deputy Dawg*, No. 349, from "Deputy Dawg and Friends" and *Tom Cat*, No. 397, from "Tom and Jerry." In the center row are *Mitzi*, a 10½ inch (26.7cm) long velveteen Dachshund; *Patsy Pup*, a 7 inch tall (17.8cm) velveteen dog; and Maria Perego's famous *Topo Gigio*, the Italian mouse, at 11 inches (27.9cm) in velveteen and suedette. At the bottom are 6½ inch (16.5cm) *Jerry Mouse* and *Pixie* and *Dixie* who are 8 inches (20.3cm) tall each. *Pixie* and *Dixie* are from "Huckleberry Hound and Friends" and they are made of grey velveteen with pink faces and ears. *Dixie* wears a bright red felt coat.

Illustration 179. From the 1969 Merrythought catalog. Across the top are *Standing Panda*, No. 998, who is 18 inches (45.7cm) long, and *Sitting Connemara*, No. 962, who is 18 inches (45.7cm) high in shaggy brown mohair plush. The other three items are "sachets," which have a fitted pocket for storing bed clothing or other things. The dog is *Doleful*, a spaniel, 12½ inches (31.8cm) in diameter with a red velveteen and satin pillow. The *Tom and Jerry* sachet is the same size and their "blanket" is also red velveteen. *Pooh in Bed*, No. 974, includes a brown mohair *Pooh* who has a red velveteen blanket and a satin pillow and the piece is 14 inches long (35.6cm). Each of these last three items has a zipper compartment on the back side.

XV. TOYS

Included in this chapter are various sorts of toys that incorporated Merrythought animals and dolls. These toys are all highly collectible today, as are all mechanical and activated toys that were originally designed for vigorous play use. Animals that were designed with wheels have always had a special fascination for collectors and the rarity of older models makes them all the more desirable. Even such simple items as play balls are quite appealing when displayed with other collectibles, such as a cat with a ball made of felt or plush, and more so when both items were creations of the same company.

The wide range of toys that Merrythought Limited made since they were first introduced in the 1931 catalog are grouped within categories that are listed alphabetically. Within these groups the toys are listed in chronological order. The TOYS are the following:

BALLS. These are soft and were made of art silk and plush.

COT TOYS. Soft, simple toys, designed for babies.

JUMPEE COT TOYS. Baby toys attached to an elastic cord so that they will bounce when mounted over a baby crib.

COT TOY WITH MUSICAL CHIME. Baby toys with bells and chimes built inside.

CUSHIONS. Made only in 1958.

FLEXI TOYS. A flexible wire frame is built inside so that the animal can be placed in different positions, which it will hold.

GLOVE TOYS. These are hand puppets.

ARM LENGTH GLOVE TOYS. Longer hand puppets that fit over the child's arm.

HOBBY TOYS. This is the old time "hobby horse," which is an animal's head at the end of a stick and wooden wheels at the other end so that the child can "ride" it.

NODDING HEAD NURSERY TOYS. In 1970 five different designs of animals were made with heads that would bobble or nod when the child handled it.

PULL-ALONG TOYS. These are various animals mounted on wheels so the child could pull them around.

PUSH-ALONG TOYS. These are large animals mounted on a heavy frame so the child could ride it while pushed along with a handle bar that was attached to the base of the toy.

TODDLE TOYS. Similar to the Push-Along Toys, except they are smaller and meant for smaller children to ride.

PUSH TOYS. These toys are the same as the Toddle Toys, except that they include foot rests for the child's feet.

RATTLES. An assortment of soft toys filled with rings and bells.

MERRYGO RIDING TOYS. This name was used for larger riding toys in 1938.

RIDING TOYS. These toys for children to ride are like the Push-Along Toys, except that they also include a rope so the child can be pulled on the animal.

ROCKING PULL-ALONG TOYS. This is a pull toy that has more animated movement in the animal so he looks like he is trying to propel the toy as it is pulled along.

ROCKING TOYS. These are large animals mounted on a curved frame so that they rock, like the old-fashioned "rocking horses."

SLIPPER TOYS. In 1932 an original concept was a small animal snuggled in a slipper, to make a cute presentation of the toy.

STAGE COACH WITH FOUR HORSES. In 1936 Merrythought presented one of the largest toys the company made, as it included four horses and a stage coach from the "Old West" of the United States.

STICKY TOYS. In 1971 three different toys included velcro patches to make them retain different positions.

TRICYCLE RIDING TOYS. These were ponies incorporated into a child's tricycle.

TROLLEY SCOOTER. These toys are like the Rocking Pull-Along Toys and the animal, whose arms are attached to a handlebar, looks like he is helping to propel the toy when it is pulled.

TROTTING TOYS. These are animals attached to a frame mounted on wheels. When pulled along, these toys move up and down as if they are trotting along.

WHEEL TOYS. In 1932 and 1933 animals mounted on frames with rubber-tired wheels also included a cord to pull the animal while the child rode it.

Stock No.	Type of Item	Name	Size inches	centimeter	Year
	Balls				
S1022/0		Play Balls	3½	(8.9)	1931
/1			4½	(11.5)	
/2			5½	(14.0)	
/3			6½	(16.5)	
/4			7½	(19.1)	
/5			9½	(24.2)	
S1024/1		Play Balls	4½	(11.5)	1931
/2			5½	(14.0)	
/3			6½	(16.5)	
/4			7½	(19.1)	
M1005/2		Play Balls	5	(12.7)	1932-1933
/3			6	(15.2)	
/4			7	(17.8)	
S1005/2		Play Balls	5	(12.7)	1932-1933
/3			6	(15.2)	
/4			7	(17.8)	
S1328/3½		Play Balls (with chimes)	3½	(8.9)	1935
/4½			4½	(11.5)	
/5½			5½	(14.0)	
/6½			6½	(16.5)	
/8			8	(20.3)	
1328/1		Nursery Ball	3½	(8.9)	1936-1938; 1947-1959
/2			4½	(11.5)	
/3			5½	(14.0)	1936-1938
/3			6	(15.2)	1953-1959
/4			6½	(16.5)	1936-1938
/5			8	(20.3)	
CS1395/3½		Play Balls	3½	(8.9)	1936-1938
/4½			4½	(11.5)	
/5½			5½	(14.0)	
/6½			6½	(16.5)	
/8			8	(20.3)	
183/1		Play Balls	3½	(8.9)	1960-1966
/2			4½	(11.5)	1960-1968
/3			6	(15.2)	
563/1		Patch Play Ball	6	(15.2)	1969-1981
/2			8	(20.3)	1969-1972
C13		Nursery Ball	6	(15.2)	1982-1983
D10		Chime Ball	4	(10.2)	1984
D10		Chime Ball	5	(12.7)	1985
	Cot Toys (Also called Baby and Cot Toys, Merry Toys, Merry Cot Toys and Nursery Toys.)				
S1034/0		Quacka (duck)	5	(12.7)	1931-1935; 1947-1948; 1950-1953
/1			6	(15.2)	1931-1938; 1947-1948; 1950-1954
/2			7½	(19.1)	1931-1938; 1947-1948; 1950-1953
/3			10½	(26.7)	1931-1938
/4			12½	(31.8)	
S1036/1		Pimpo (elephant)	5	(12.7)	1931
/2			6	(15.2)	
/3			7½	(19.1)	
/4			9	(22.9)	
S1120/1		Pimpo (elephant)	6½	(16.5)	1932-1933
/2			8	(20.3)	
/3			9½	(24.2)	
/4			11½	(29.2)	
/5			14	(35.6)	
/6			16	(40.6)	1933
COT/1		Various Puppies	9½	(24.2)	1932
/2			11	(27.9)	
/3			14	(35.6)	
1226		Bengie Bear	7½	(19.1)	1933
1227		Humpty Dumpty	7½	(19.1)	1933

Stock No.	Type of Item	Name	Size inches	centimeters	Year
1228		Monkey	7½	(19.1)	1933
1229		Twinkle Star	7½	(19.1)	1933
1230		Bunny	7½	(19.1)	1933
1231		Dowee Bird	7½	(19.1)	1933
S1031/0		Silk Bunny (rabbit)	6	(15.2)	1935-1938
/1			9	(22.9)	1935
/2			12	(30.5)	
S1332/5		Baby Rabbit	5	(12.7)	1935-1938
/6½			6½	(16.5)	
/8			8	(20.3)	
/10			10	(25.4)	
W1332/6½		Booby Rabbit	6½	(16.5)	1935
/8			8	(20.3)	
/10			10	(25.4)	
1332/5		Booby (rabbit)	5	(12.7)	1936-1938
/6			6	(15.2)	
/8			8	(20.3)	
/10			10	(25.4)	
1332/1		Booby (rabbit)	5¼	(13.4)	1947
/3			8	(20.3)	
1332/0		Booby (rabbit)	5	(12.7)	1953
/2			9½	(24.2)	1948; 1950-1956
/3			11½	(29.2)	1948; 1950-1955
/4			14	(35.6)	1948; 1950-1954
1267/2		Pimpo the Elephant	8	(20.3)	1936-1938
/3			9½	(24.2)	
/4			11½	(29.2)	
/5			14	(35.6)	1935
/5			14½	(36.9)	1936-1938
/6			16	(40.6)	1935
S1326/5½		Mary Ba-Ba (white lamb)	5½	(14.0)	1936-1938
1326/5½		Mary Ba-Ba (white lamb)	5½	(14.0)	1947
/8½			8½	(21.6)	1947-1948; 1950-1953
/11			11	(27.9)	1948
1406		Efelunt (elephant)	10½	(26.7)	1936-1938
1561/1		Bombardier Bruin (bear)	12	(30.5)	1937-1938
/2			13¼	(33.7)	
/3			15	(38.1)	
/4			17½	(44.5)	
/5			24	(61.0)	
1562/1		Military Mick (monkey)	12	(30.5)	1937-1938
/2			13¼	(33.7)	
/3			15	(38.1)	
/4			17½	(44.5)	
/5			24	(61.0)	
1482D/1		Black Spotted Pup (sitting)	7	(17.8)	1938
/2			10	(25.4)	
/3			12½	(31.8)	
1667D/1		Black Spotted Pup (standing)	9	(22.9)	1938
/2			11	(27.9)	
/3			13	(33.0)	
1734		Lamb	8¼	(21.0)	1939
1735		Rabbit	8¼	(21.0)	1939
1736		Bear	8¼	(21.0)	1939
1844/00		Panda	5½	(14.0)	1939
/0			7½	(19.1)	
1841		Panda	8	(20.3)	1939
1843		Cuddly Panda Doll	11½	(29.2)	1939
1728/1		Squatting Lamb	10	(25.4)	1947
/2			13	(33.0)	1947-1948
4915		Pampered Pets (pups)	3¼	(8.3)	1951-1954
1936		Cot Bear	7	(17.8)	1954-1958
Z2088		Panda	6	(15.2)	1958
Z2091		Cat	6	(15.2)	1958
158		Miniature Bear	4	(10.2)	1960-1975
609/1		Sitting Donkey	12	(30.5)	1970-1971
/3			24	(61.0)	
632		Dismal Dog	12	(30.5)	1971
659		Fish	14	(35.6)	1971-1972
661		Fox	12	(30.5)	1971-1973
700		Guinea Pig	10	(25.4)	1972-1976
719		Ferdinand Bull	11	(27.9)	1972-1981

Stock No.	Type of Item	Name	Size inches	centimeters	Year
801/1		Koala Bear	6	(15.2)	1974-1976
/2			8	(20.3)	
/3			10	(25.4)	
A14/1		Penguin	11½	(29.2)	1976-1977
/2			17	(43.2)	
A15		Baby Bear	7	(17.8)	1976-1981
	Jumpee Cot Toys Jumpee Toys on elastic string (Also called Cot Toys, Merry Jumpee Cot Toys and Nursery Pouffe Dolls.)				
2057		Jumpee Lamb	11	(27.9)	1958-1959
2058		Jumpee Horse	11	(27.9)	1958-1959
2059		Jumpee Rabbit	10	(25.4)	1958-1959
2060		Jumpee Pup	9	(22.9)	1958-1959
2061		Jumpee Bear	11	(27.9)	1958-1959
2116		Jumpee Hound	8	(20.3)	1959
2117		Jumpee Puss	8	(20.3)	1959
057		Jumpee Lamb	11	(27.9)	1960-1964
058		Jumpee Horse	11	(27.9)	1960-1962
059		Jumpee Rabbit	10	(25.4)	1960-1966
060		Jumpee Pup	9	(22.9)	1960-1962
061		Jumpee Bear	11	(27.9)	1960-1964
195		Jumpee Lambkin	7½	(19.1)	1961-1966
256		Jumpee Washable Rabbit	12	(30.5)	1963-1964
302		Jumpee Bun	12	(30.5)	1963-1967
261		Jumpee Washable Cat	12	(30.5)	1964
315/1		New Humpty Dumpty	10½	(26.7)	1964-1983
/2			15	(38.1)	1976-1979
/3			23	(58.4)	1964-1979
320		Owl	8	(20.3)	1964-1965
390		Jumpee Horse	8	(20.3)	1965-1967
392		Jumpee Donkey	8	(20.3)	1965-1967
393		Jumpee Honey Bun	11	(27.9)	1965-1966
394		Jumpee Sitting Bear	10	(25.4)	1965
394		Jumpee Sitting Bear	11	(27.9)	1966
401/1		Hedgehog	7	(17.8)	1965-1981
/3			18½	(47.0)	1966-1978
243		Jumpee Lamb	8	(20.3)	1967
394		Jumpee Bear	11	(27.9)	1967
496		Jumpee Honey Bun	11	(27.9)	1967
497		Jumpee Rabbit	10	(25.4)	1967
243		Merry Lamb	8	(20.3)	1968-1969
394		Merry Bear	11	(27.9)	1968-1969
394/0		Merry Bear	12	(30.5)	1970-1973
/2			24	(61.0)	1970-1971
/3			36	(91.4)	
534		Merry Dolphin	14	(35.6)	1968-1969
535		Merry Spaniel	9	(22.9)	1968
536		Merry Bun	8	(20.3)	1968
537		Merry Rabbit	11	(27.9)	1968
536		Cuddly Rabbit	12	(30.5)	1969-1970
538		Lying Rabbit	14	(35.6)	1969-1971
558/2		Sitting Rabbit	19	(48.3)	1969-1976
/3			27	(68.6)	
564		Merry Bun	8	(20.3)	1969-1970
325		Merry Elephant	9	(22.9)	1970-1975
622		Humpty Pouffe (Dumpty)	12 dia.	(30.5)	1970
668/1		Merry Chimp	16	(40.6)	1971-1981
/2			20	(50.8)	
/3			36	(91.4)	1972-1981
714/1		French Humpty	10	(25.4)	1972-1977
/2			14	(35.6)	1972-1974
778		Highland Humpty	11	(27.9)	1973-1977
827/1		Top Hat Humpty	12	(30.5)	1975-1977
/2			18	(45.7)	1976-1977
/3			26	(66.0)	1975-1977
A13/1		Merry Ann (doll)	18	(45.7)	1976
/3			30	(76.2)	
A84		Happy Humpty	11	(27.9)	1978
C14/1		Hedgehog	7	(17.8)	1984
/3			14	(35.6)	
C76/1		Merry Chimp	13	(33.0)	1984
/2			18	(45.7)	

Stock No.	Type of Item	Name	Size inches	centimeters	Year
	Cot Toy With Musical Chime				
1418/2		Cradle Dollie	8½	(21.6)	1936-1938; 1947
1464/1		Baby Jester (doll)	10	(25.4)	1936-1938
/2			14	(35.6)	
220		Chime Bear	9	(22.9)	1961-1966; 1968-1969
233		Chime Cat	9	(22.9)	1961-1964; 1968-1969
234		Chime Rabbit	9	(22.9)	1961-1966; 1968-1969
399		Chime Poodle	9	(22.9)	1965-1966
485		Chime Penguin	9	(22.9)	1968-1969
	Cushions				
Z2092		Panda	12	(30.5)	1958
Z2083		Cat	12	(30.5)	1958
Z2085		Clown	12	(30.5)	1958
	Flexi Toys (Safety wire frame; flexes into many positions)				
829/1		Flexi Rabbit Girl	15	(38.1)	1975
/2			22	(55.9)	
830/1		Flexi Rabbit Boy	15	(38.1)	1975
/2			22	(55.9)	
831/1		Flexi Puss Girl	12	(30.5)	1975-1976
/2			18	(45.7)	
832/1		Flexi Puss Boy	12	(30.5)	1975-1976
/2			18	(45.7)	
833/1		Flexi Dog Girl	12	(30.5)	1975-1976
/2			18	(45.7)	
834/1		Flexi Dog Boy	12	(30.5)	1975-1976
/2			18	(45.7)	
835/1		Flexi Bear Girl	11	(27.9)	1975
/2			17	(43.2)	
836/1		Flexi Bear Boy	11	(27.9)	1975
/2			17	(43.2)	
	Glove Toys				
1842		Panda	9	(22.9)	1939
1842		Panda	8½	(21.6)	1948; 1950-1952
5217		Cat	9½	(24.2)	1953-1955
5220		Kitten	9½	(24.2)	1953-1957
1917		Bobo Penguin	9½	(24.2)	1954
1930		Poodle	9½	(24.2)	1954-1959
1948		Lamb	9½	(24.2)	1955
1949		Dog	9½	(24.2)	1955-1956
2042		Cheshire Cat	9½	(24.2)	1957-1959
042		Cheshire Cat	9½	(24.2)	1960-1962
177		Poodle	9½	(24.2)	1960-1962
	Arm Length Glove Toys				
A27		Fox	16	(40.6)	1977-1979
A28		Leopard	16	(40.6)	1977-1980
A29		Lion	16	(40.6)	1977-1980
A30		Tiger	16	(40.6)	1977-1980
A50		Spaniel	16	(40.6)	1977
A62		Rabbit	16	(40.6)	1978-1980
A64		Elephant	16	(40.6)	1978
	Hobby Toys (A head at the end of a stick with wheels.)				
213		Donkey	36	(91.4)	1961-1973
214		Elephant	36	(91.4)	1961
222		Horse	36	(91.4)	1961-1962
303		Shetland Pony	36	(91.4)	1963-1967
615		Horse	36	(91.4)	1970-1972
A57		Horse	36	(91.4)	1977-1978
HBO2		Shire Horse	34	(86.4)	1982-1985
HBO4		Skewbald Shetland	34	(86.4)	1982-1985
HBO5		Dappled Grey	34	(86.4)	1982-1985
HBO7		Pedro (donkey)	34	(86.4)	1983-1984
HBO8		Zebra	34	(86.4)	1983
HBO9		Pancho Donkey	34	(86.4)	1985
	Nodding Head Nursery Toys				
624/1		Nodding Cat	11	(27.9)	1970
625/1		Nodding Rabbit	12	(30.5)	1970
626/1		Nodding Clown	11	(27.9)	1970

Stock No.	Type of Item	Name	Size inches	centimeters	Year
627/1		Nodding Elephant	11	(27.9)	1970
628/1		Nodding Mouse	11	(27.9)	1970
	Pull-Along Toys (Also called Tiny-Tots Pull-Along.)				
PA/S1031/0		Bunnikin	6	(15.2)	1936
PA1038/1		Robbie (Terrier)	11	(27.9)	1936-1938
/2			13½	(34.3)	
/3			14½	(36.9)	
/4			17½	(44.5)	
PA1333/9½		Old Faithful (horse)	9½	(24.2)	1936-1938
/11			11	(27.9)	
/12½			12½	(31.8)	
PA1335/10½		Towzer (Terrier)	10½	(26.7)	1936-1938
/12			12	(30.5)	
/14			14	(35.6)	
PA1326/8½		Lamb	8½	(21.6)	1936-1938
/9½			9½	(24.2)	
/11			11	(27.9)	
PA/S1326/5½		Lambkin	5½	(14.0)	1936
PA1327/11½		Running Hare	11½	(29.2)	1936-1938
/14			14	(35.6)	
PA1356/9		Airedale	9	(22.9)	1936-1938
/11			11	(27.9)	
/13½			13½	(34.3)	
/16½			16½	(41.9)	
PA1335/1		Towzer (Terrier)	11	(27.9)	1952-1959
PA1765/1		Angus (Terrier)	11	(27.9)	1952-1958
?		Neddy (donkey)	11	(27.9)	1952-1954
?		Old Faithful (horse)	11	(27.9)	1952-1954
?		Curly Lamb	11	(27.9)	1952-1954
PA1937/1		Honey Lamb	11	(27.9)	1955-1958
PA1968/2		Splasher Duck	11	(27.9)	1955
2002/1		Elephant	11	(27.9)	1956-1958
PA2119		Curly Poodle	11	(27.9)	1959
PA119		Curly Poodle	11	(27.9)	1960-1961
PA124		Towzer (Terrier)	11	(27.9)	1960-1961
PA150		Honey Lamb	11	(27.9)	1962-1981
PA149		Boxer Pup	11	(27.9)	1962-1983
PA246		Dalmatian	11	(27.9)	1962-1963
PA424		Road Hog (hedgehog)	11	(27.9)	1966-1981
PA467		Tortoise	11	(27.9)	1967-1976
PA468		Ladybird	11	(27.9)	1967-1984
PA561		Caterpillar	11	(27.9)	1969
PA325		Elephant	11	(27.9)	1970-1975
PA635		Snail	11	(27.9)	1971-1972
PA825		St. Bernard	11	(27.9)	1975-1977
PA.A42		Spaniel Pup	11	(27.9)	1977-1981
PA B17		Fox Terrier	11	(27.9)	1980-1981
PA849		Alsatian Pup	11	(27.9)	1980-1981
PA.C14		Squeaker Hog (hedgehog)	7	(17.8)	1982-1983
PA.C74/1		Tortoise	6	(15.2)	1984
PA.C84		Roller Bear	9	(22.9)	1984
C14/PA		Hedgehog	11	(27.9)	1985
C74/PA		Tortoise	11	(27.9)	1985
C86/PA		Camel	11	(27.9)	1985
D19/PA		Guinea Pig	11	(27.9)	1985
468/PA		Ladybird (ladybug)	11	(27.9)	1985
	Push-Along Toys (Y after number = enamel frame; Z after number = chromium frame)				
PRS1423/1Y		Bobtail Sheepdog	26½	(67.3)	1937-1938
/1Z			26½	(67.3)	1937
/3			31	(78.7)	1936
/3Z			31	(78.7)	1937-1938
PRS1424/1Y		Scots Grey (dapple) Pony	26½	(67.3)	1937
/1Z			26½	(67.3)	
/3			31	(78.7)	1936
/3Z			31	(78.7)	1937
PRS1425/3		Windsor Cream Pony	31	(78.7)	1936
PRS1426/3		Circus Pony	31	(78.7)	1936
PRS1427/1Y		Chestnut Pony	26½	(67.3)	1937-1938
/1Z			26½	(67.3)	1937
/3			31	(78.7)	1936

Stock No.	Type of Item	Name	Size inches	centimeters	Year
/3Z		Chestnut Pony, continued	31	(78.7)	1937-1938
PRS1428/1Y		Clydesdale Cart Horse	26½	(67.3)	1937-1938
/1Z			26½	(67.3)	1937
/3			31	(78.7)	1936
/3Z			31	(78.7)	1937-1938
PRS1429/3		Suffolk Punch Cart Horse	31	(78.7)	1936
PRS1430/3		Grizzly Bear	31	(78.7)	1936
PRS1431/1Y		St. Bernard	26½	(67.3)	1937-1938
/1Z			26½	(67.3)	1937
/3			31	(78.7)	1936
/3Z			31	(78.7)	1937-1938
PRS1423/1Y		Elephant	26½	(67.3)	1937-1938
/1Z			26½	(67.3)	1937
/3			31	(78.7)	1936
/3Z			31	(78.7)	1937-1938
PRS1433/1Y		Donkey	26½	(67.3)	1937-1938
/1Z			26½	(67.3)	1937
/3			31	(78.7)	1936
/3Z			31	(78.7)	1937-1938
PRS1434/1Y		Shetland Pony	26½	(67.3)	1937-1938
/1Z			26½	(67.3)	1937
/3			31	(78.7)	1936
/3Z			31	(78.7)	1937-1938
PRS1494/3		Piebald Pony	31	(78.7)	1936
PRS1494/1Y		Circus Pony (piebald)	26½	(67.3)	1937-1938
/1Z			26½	(67.3)	1937
/3Z			31	(78.7)	1937-1938
PRS1501/3		Piebald Cart Horse	31	(78.7)	1936
PRS1609/1Y		Donkey Cart	26½	(67.3)	1938
SPT01		St. Bernard	21	(53.3)	1981
SPT02		Shirehorse	22	(55.9)	1981
SPT03		Spaniel	22	(55.9)	1981
SPT04		Skewbald (pony)	21	(53.3)	1981
SPT05		Dappled Grey (horse)	22	(55.9)	1981
SPT06		Donkey	21	(53.3)	1981
PT01		St. Bernard	21	(53.3)	1985
PT02		Shirehorse	22	(55.9)	1985
PT04		Skewbald Pony	21	(53.3)	1985
PT05		Dappled Grey Horse	22	(55.9)	1985
PT09		Pancho Donkey	22	(55.9)	1985
PT10		Jumbo Elephant	22	(55.9)	1985
	Toddle Toys (These have an elevated handlebar to push a child riding the animal.) (Steel chasis and frame) Y = enamel frame Z = chromium frame				
1245/2		Terrier	24	(61.0)	1933
1246/2		Sheep Dog	24	(61.0)	1933
1247/2		Donkey	24	(61.0)	1933
1248/2		Donkey (special model)	24	(61.0)	1933
TT/0/1038/A		Robbie (Aberdeen Terrier)	17	(43.2)	1936
TT1038/0Y		Robbie	17	(43.2)	1937
/0Z			17	(43.2)	
TT1038/0Y		Robbie	19	(48.3)	1938
/0Z			19	(48.3)	
TT/0/1041/A		Bruce (Cairn Terrier)	17	(43.2)	1936
TT/1041/0Y		Bruce	17	(43.2)	1937
/0Z			17	(43.2)	
TT/1041/0Y		Bruce	19	(48.3)	1938
/0Z			19	(48.3)	
TT/0/1250/B		Airedale Pup	17	(43.2)	1936
TT/1250/0Y		Airedale Pup	17	(43.2)	1937
/0Z			17	(43.2)	
TT/1250/0Y		Airedale Pup	19	(48.3)	1938
/0Z			19	(48.3)	
TT/0/1310/A		Bobtail Sheepdog	17	(43.2)	1936
TT/1310/0Y		Bobtail Sheepdog	17	(43.2)	1937
/0Z			17	(43.2)	
TT/1310/0Y		Bobtail Sheepdog	19	(48.3)	1938
/0Z			19	(48.3)	
TT/0/1333/B		Old Faithful (horse)	17	(43.2)	1936
TT/1333/0Y		Old Faithful	17	(43.2)	1937
/0Z			17	(43.2)	

Stock No.	Type of Item	Name	Size inches	centimeters	Year
TT/1333/0Y		Old Faithful	19	(48.3)	1938
/0Z			19	(48.3)	
TT/0/1353/B		Collie Pup	17	(43.2)	1936
TT/1353/0Y		Collie Pup	17	(43.2)	1937
/0Z			17	(43.2)	
TT/1353/0Y		Collie Pup	19	(48.3)	1938
/0Z			19	(48.3)	
TT/0/1335/B		Towzer (Fox Terrier)	17	(43.2)	1936
TT/1335/0Y		Towzer	17	(43.2)	1937
/0Z			17	(43.2)	
TT/1335/0Y		Towzer	19	(48.3)	1938
/0Z			19	(48.3)	
TT/0/1451/B*		Donkey	17	(43.2)	1936
TT/0/1453/A		Donkey	17	(43.2)	1936
TT1451/0Y*		Donkey	17	(43.2)	1937
TT1453/0Y		Donkey	17	(43.2)	1937
/0Z			17	(43.2)	
TT1451/0Y*		Donkey	19	(48.3)	1938
TT1453/0Y		Donkey	19	(48.3)	1938
/0Z			19	(48.3)	
TT/0/1452/B*		Bay Horse	17	(43.2)	1936
TT/0/1454/A		Bay Horse	17	(43.2)	1936
TT/1452/0Y*		Bay Horse	17	(43.2)	1937
TT/1454/0Y		Bay Horse	17	(43.2)	1937
/0Z			17	(43.2)	
TT/1452/0Y*		Bay Horse	19	(48.3)	1938
TT /1454/0Y		Bay Horse	19	(48.3)	1938
/0Z			19	(48.3)	
TT/0/1455/AZ		Black Spaniel	17	(43.2)	1936
TT/1455/0Y		Black Spaniel	17	(43.2)	1937
/0Z			17	(43.2)	
TT/1455/0Y		Black Spaniel	19	(48.3)	1938
/0Z			19	(48.3)	
TT/0/1496/AZ		Piebald Pony	17	(43.2)	1936
TT/1496/0Y		Piebald Pony	17	(43.2)	1938
/0Z			17	(43.2)	
TT/1496/0Y		Piebald Pony	19	(48.3)	1938
/0Z			19	(48.3)	
TT/1608/0Y		Kid (donkey)	17	(43.2)	1937
/0Z			17	(43.2)	
TT1608/0Y		Kid	19	(48.3)	1938
/0Z			19	(48.3)	
/2Y			24	(61.0)	
/2Z			24	(61.0)	
TT1609/0Y		Donkey Colt	17	(43.2)	1937
/0Z			17	(43.2)	
TT1609/0Y		Donkey Colt	19	(48.3)	1938
/0Z			19	(48.3)	
TT1610/0Y		Pony Colt	17	(43.2)	1937
/0Z			17	(43.2)	
TT1610/0Y		Pony Colt	19	(48.3)	1938
/0Z			19	(48.3)	
/2Y			24	(61.0)	
/2Z			24	(61.0)	
TT/00/1659		Towzer (Terrier)	14¼	(36.9)	1938
TT/00/1660		Collie	14¼	(36.9)	1938
TT/00/1661		Donkey	14¼	(36.9)	1938
TT/00/1662		Bay Horse	14¼	(36.9)	1938
TT1792/0Y		Brindle (Bull Terrier)	19	(48.3)	1939
/0Z			19	(48.3)	
TT1815/0Y		Dalmatian	19	(48.3)	1939
/0Z			19	(48.3)	
TT1819/0Y		Prince (Chow)	19	(48.3)	1939
/0Z			19	(48.3)	
TT1820/0Y		Persian Cat	19	(48.3)	1939
/0Z			19	(48.3)	
TT/0/1828/Y		Panda	19	(48.3)	1939
/Z			19	(48.3)	
TT/1828/0Y		Panda	19	(48.3)	1939
/0Z			19	(48.3)	
TT1250/0		Airedale Pup	19	(48.3)	1950-1953
TT1310/0		Bob Tail (Sheep Dog)	19	(48.3)	1950-1956
TT1310		Bob Tail (Sheep Dog)	19	(48.3)	1957-1958

*Cheaper model

Stock No.	Type of Item	Name	Size inches	centimeters	Year
TT1310		Bob Tail (Sheep Dog)	18	(45.7)	1959
T823		Bob Tail (Sheep Dog)	18	(45.7)	1960-1965
TT1333/0		Old Faithful (horse)	19	(48.3)	1950-1953
TT1353/0		Collie Pup	19	(48.3)	1950-1956
TT1353		Collie Pup	19	(48.3)	1957-1958
TT1451/0		Donkey	19	(48.3)	1950-1956
TT1451		Donkey	19	(48.3)	1957-1958
TT1455/0		Black Spaniel	19	(48.3)	1950-1953
TT1610/0		Pony Colt	19	(48.3)	1954-1955
TT1335		Towzer (Terrier)	19	(48.3)	1957-1958
TT2131		Pablo Donkey	20	(50.8)	1959
T820		Pablo Donkey	20	(50.8)	1960-1969
BW820		Pablo Donkey	20	(50.8)	1970
TT820		Pablo Donkey	20	(50.8)	1971
TT2132		Nellie Elephant	22	(55.9)	1959
T821		Nellie Elephant	22	(55.9)	1960-1965
BW821		Nellie Elephant	22	(55.9)	1970
TT821		Nellie Elephant	22	(55.9)	1971
TT2133		Poodle	19	(48.3)	1959
T822		Poodle	19	(48.3)	1960-1963
T826		Horse	20	(50.8)	1962
T827		Shetland Pony	18	(45.7)	1963-1965
BW827		Shetland Pony	18	(45.7)	1970
TT827		Shetland Pony	18	(45.7)	1971
T829		Merrylegs Pony	19	(48.3)	1964
T831		Hunter (horse)	20	(50.8)	1966
T832		Connemara (Irish donkey)	20	(50.8)	1966-1967
T833		Panda	20	(50.8)	1966
T835		Taurus the Bull	20	(50.8)	1967-1968
T813		Bobtail (Sheep Dog)	20	(50.8)	1968-1969
BW813		Bobtail (Sheep Dog)	20	(50.8)	1970
TT813		Bobtail (Sheep Dog)	20	(50.8)	1971
T840		Bulldog	20	(50.8)	1969
T841		Poodle	20	(50.8)	1969
	Push Toys (These are the same as TOODLE TOYS, except they have foot rests.) Y = enamel frame Z = chrome frame				
1435/2		Fox Terrier	24	(61.0)	1936
PT/1435/2Y		Fox Terrier	24	(61.0)	1937-1938
/2Z			24	(61.0)	
PT1437/2		Airedale	24	(61.0)	1936
/2Y			24	(61.0)	1937-1938
/2Z			24	(61.0)	
PT1438/2Y		Brown Horse	24	(61.0)	1936-1938
PT1439/2		Bobtail Sheep Dog	24	(61.0)	1936
/2Y			24	(61.0)	1937-1938
/2Z			24	(61.0)	
PT1440/2		St. Bernard	24	(61.0)	1936
/2Y			24	(61.0)	1937-1938
/2Z			24	(61.0)	
PT1441/2Z		Circus Pony	24	(61.0)	1936
PT1442/2Y		Chestnut Pony	24	(61.0)	1937-1938
/2Z			24	(61.0)	1936-1938
PT1443/2		Windsor Cream Pony	24	(61.0)	1936
PT1444/2Z		Scots Grey Pony	24	(61.0)	1936
PT1445/2Y		Cart Horse (Clydesdale)	24	(61.0)	1937-1938
/2Z			24	(61.0)	1936-1938
PT1448/2Y		Elephant	24	(61.0)	1936-1938
/2Z			24	(61.0)	1937-1938
PT1436/2		Donkey	24	(61.0)	1936
PT1449/2		Donkey	24	(61.0)	1936
/2Y			24	(61.0)	1937-1938
/2Z			24	(61.0)	
PT1467/2Y		Donkey	24	(61.0)	1937-1938
PT1450/2		Shetland Pony	24	(61.0)	1936
PT1495/2		Piebald Circus Pony	24	(61.0)	1936
/2Y			24	(61.0)	1937
/2Z			24	(61.0)	
PT1500/2		Piebald Cart Horse	24	(61.0)	1936
PT1610/2Y		Pony Colt	24	(61.0)	1937-1938
/2Z			24	(61.0)	
PT1444/2Y		Windsor Grey Horse	24	(61.0)	1938

Stock No.	Type of Item	Name	Size inches	centimeters	Year
/2Z		Windsor Grey Horse, continued	24	(61.0)	
PT1446/2Y		Windsor Grey Horse	24	(61.0)	1937-1938
/2Z			24	(61.0)	
PT1608/2Y		Kid (donkey)	24	(61.0)	1937-1938
/2Z			24	(61.0)	
PT1609/2Y		Donkey Colt	24	(61.0)	1937-1938
/2Z			24	(61.0)	
PT1793/2Y		Bull Terrier	24	(61.0)	1939
/2Z			24	(61.0)	
PT1814/2Y		Dalmatian	24	(61.0)	1939
/2Z			24	(61.0)	
PT1818/2Y		Prince (Red Chow)	24	(61.0)	1939
/2Z			24	(61.0)	
PT1829/2Y		Panda	24	(61.0)	1939
/2Z			24	(61.0)	
PT12/2		Poodle	25	(63.5)	1959-1963
PT14/2		Pablo Donkey	25	(63.5)	1959-1969; 1971
BW14/2		Pablo Donkey	25	(63.5)	1970
P14/2		Pablo Donkey	25	(63.5)	1973-1974
PT15/2		Nellie Elephant	25	(63.5)	1959-1965; 1971
BW15/2		Nellie Elephant	25	(63.5)	1970
P15/2		Nellie Elephant	25	(63.5)	1973-1974
PT40/2		Bob Tail (Sheep Dog)	25	(63.5)	1959-1965; 1968-1969; 1971
BW40/2		Bob Tail (Sheep Dog)	25	(63.5)	1970
P40/2		Bob Tail (Sheep Dog)	25	(63.5)	1973-1974
P16/2		Horse	25	(63.5)	1962
P18/2		Shetland Pony	25	(63.5)	1963-1965; 1971
BW18/2		Shetland Pony	25	(63.5)	1970
P18/2		Shetland Pony	25	(63.5)	1973-1974
P20/2		Merrylegs Pony	25	(63.5)	1964
P25/2		Panda	25	(63.5)	1966
P27/2		Hunter (horse)	25	(63.5)	1966
P30/2		Connemara (Irish donkey)	25	(63.5)	1966-1967
P32/2		Taurus the Bull	25	(63.5)	1967-1968
P35/2		Donkey Colt	25	(63.5)	1968
P39/2		Bulldog	25	(63.5)	1969
P41/2		Poodle	25	(63.5)	1969
P48		Donkey	24	(61.0)	1976-1977
P49		Pablo Donkey	24	(61.0)	1976-1980
P50		Nellie Elephant	24	(61.0)	1976-1977
P51		Shetland Pony	24	(61.0)	1976-1980
P53		Shirehorse	24	(61.0)	1980
PT02		Shirehorse	22	(55.9)	1982-1984
PT01		St. Bernard	21	(53.3)	1982-1984
PT03		Welsh Dun (donkey)	22	(55.9)	1982
PT04		Skewbald (horse)	21	(53.3)	1982-1984
PT05		Dappled Grey (horse)	22	(55.9)	1982-1984
PT07		Pedro (donkey)	22	(55.9)	1983-1984
PT08		Zebra	21	(53.3)	1983
	Rattles				
1226		Bengie Bear	10	(25.4)	1933
1227		Humpty Dumpty	10	(25.4)	1933
1228		Monkey	10	(25.4)	1933
1229		Twinkle Star	10	(25.4)	1933
1230		Bunny	10	(25.4)	1933
1231		Oowee Bird	10	(25.4)	1933
1417/2		Jester	15	(38.1)	1936
1419/1		Little Tomtit	7¾	(19.8)	1936
/2			11	(27.9)	
1463/1		Joey	12	(30.5)	1936
	Merrygo Riding Toys (Mounted on a wheeled frame)				
1677/1		Bay Horse	16	(40.6)	1938
/2			20	(50.8)	
/3			23	(58.4)	
/4			26½	(67.3)	
1677/1		Bay Horse	17	(43.2)	1938*
/2			19½	(49.6)	
/3			23	(58.4)	
/4			27¾	(70.6)	
1678/1		Skewbald Pony	16	(40.6)	1938

*There were two different Merrythought Catalogs in 1938.

Stock No.	Type of Item	Name	Size inches	centimeters	Year
/2		Skewbald Pony, continued	20	(50.8)	
/3			23	(58.4)	
/4			26½	(67.3)	
1678/1		Skewbald Pony	17	(43.2)	1938*
/2			19½	(49.6)	
/3			23	(58.4)	
/4			27¾	(70.6)	
1679/1		Donkey	16	(40.6)	1938
/2			20	(50.8)	
/3			23	(58.4)	
/4			26½	(67.3)	
	Riding Toys (Mounted on a wheeled frame; have a pull rope)				
R1089/1		Shetland Pony	26	(66.0)	1935
/3			31½	(80.0)	
/5			39	(99.0)	
R1091/1		Circus Pony (piebald)	23	(58.4)	1935-1937
/3			27	(68.6)	
/5			38	(96.5)	
R1092/1		Circus Pony (cream)	23	(58.4)	1935
/3			27	(68.6)	
/5			38	(96.5)	
R1093/1		Chestnut Pony	23	(58.4)	1935; 1937
/3			27	(68.6)	
/5			38	(96.5)	
R1094/1		Clydesdale Cart Horse	25	(63.5)	1935
/3			30	(76.2)	
/5			37	(93.9)	
R1094/1		Clydesdale Cart Horse	21½	(54.6)	1936-1938
/3			30	(76.2)	
/5			37	(93.9)	
R1079/1		Riding Grizzly Bear	18	(45.7)	1936-1938
/3			21	(53.3)	
/5			31½	(80.0)	
R1086/1		Riding Donkey	23	(58.4)	1936-1938
/3			29	(73.7)	
/5			40	(101.6)	
R1089/1		Shetland Pony	26	(66.0)	1936-1938
/3			31½	(80.0)	
/5			39	(99.0)	
R1090/1		Camel	25	(63.5)	1936-1937
/3			29	(73.7)	
R1092/1		Windsor Cream Pony	23	(58.4)	1936-1937
/3			27	(68.6)	
/5			38	(96.5)	
R1358/1		Riding St. Bernard	22	(55.9)	1936-1937
/3			26	(66.0)	
R1359/1		Riding Bobtail Sheepdog	22	(55.9)	1936-1937
/3			26	(66.0)	
R1366/1		Riding Elephant	16	(40.6)	1936-1937
/3			21	(53.3)	
R1377/1		Scots Grey (pony)	23	(58.4)	1936-1937
/3			27	(68.6)	
/5			38	(96.5)	
R1460/1		Suffolk Punch Cart Horse	21½	(54.6)	1936-1938
/3			30	(76.2)	
/5			37	(93.9)	
R1502/1		Piebald Cart Horse	21½	(54.6)	1936-1938
/3			30	(76.2)	
/5			37	(93.9)	
R1503/1		Piebald Pony	23	(58.4)	1936-1937
/3			27	(68.6)	
/5			38	(96.5)	
R1642/1		Riding Panda Bear	18	(45.7)	1937
R1642		Riding Panda Bear	16	(40.6)	1939
	Rocking Pull-Along Toys				
RPA1470/3		Jacko (monkey)	11½	(29.2)	1952-1956
RPA1963		Trolley Bun (rabbit)	11½	(29.2)	1955-1956
	Rocking Toys				
185		Rocking Pablo Donkey	36	(91.4)	1961-1962
185/1			23	(58.4)	1963-1968
/3			36	(91.4)	1963-1980
215		Rocking Horse	39	(99.0)	1961-1962
298/1		Rocking Shetland Pony	23	(58.4)	1963-1968
/3			32	(81.3)	1963-1980

*There were two different Merrythought Catalogs in 1938.

Stock No.	Type of Item	Name	Size inches	centimeters	Year
329/1		Rocking Nellie Elephant	21	(53.3)	1964
352/1		Rocking Merrylegs Pony	24	(61.0)	1964
451/2		Rocking Connemara Donkey	24	(61.0)	1967-1968
/3			32	(81.3)	1967-1969
640/3		Show Pony	32	(81.3)	1971
819/3		Rocker Donkey	32	(81.3)	1975-1978
A97		Rocking Shirehorse	32	(81.3)	1979-1981
B47/3		Rocking Skewbald Pony	29	(73.7)	1981
B56/3		Rocking Dappled Grey Horse	30	(76.2)	1981
RH02		Rocking Shirehorse	30	(76.2)	1982-1985
RH03		Rocking Welsh Dun	30	(76.2)	1982
RH04		Rocking Skewbald Pony	29	(73.7)	1982-1985
RH05		Rocking Dappled Grey Horse	30	(76.2)	1982-1985
RH07		Rocker Pedro	30	(76.2)	1983-1984
RH08		Rocking Zebra	29	(73.7)	1983
RH09		Rocking Pancho Donkey	30	(76.2)	1985
	Slipper Toys (The animal is snuggled in a slipper or boot.)				
A.		Child's Slipper w/ lying pup	Size 0		1932
B.		Ladies' Felt Slipper w/ pup	Size 0		1932
C.		Ladies' Blanket Slipper w/ pup	Size 1		1932
D.		Gentleman's Slipper w/ pup	Size 1		1932
S1157/2		Puss in Boots	10½	(26.7)	1932
S1158/2		Bunny in Boots	10½	(26.7)	1932
	Stage Coach with Four Horses	American Stage Coach	18	(45.7)	1936
			7½ ft. long	(228.7)	
	Sticky Toys (Arms, legs and/or tails will stick to other parts of toys.)				
656		Sticky Monkey	17	(43.2)	1971
665		Sticky Bear	14	(35.6)	1971
676		Sticky Doll	19	(48.3)	1971
	Tricycle Riding Toys				
TRIK/1628/1Y /1Z		Piebald Circus Pony	19½	(49.6)	1937-1938
TRIK/1629/1Y /1Z		Chestnut Horse	19½	(49.6)	1937-1938
	Trolley Scooter				
1469/1		'Andsome (dog)	10¼	(26.1)	1936-1938
/2			11	(27.9)	
/3			13	(33.0)	
1470/1		Jacko (monkey)	10¼	(26.1)	1936-1938
/2			11	(27.9)	
/3			13	(33.0)	
1471/1		Jumbo (elephant)	10¼	(26.1)	1936
/2			11	(27.9)	
/3			13	(33.0)	
1472/1		Dollie (doll)	10¼	(26.1)	1936-1938
/2			11	(27.9)	
/3			13	(33.0)	
1473/1		Puppy	10¼	(26.1)	1936-1938
/2			11	(27.9)	
/3			13	(33.0)	
	Trotting Toys				
RPA1038/2		Robbie (Aberdeen)	10¾	(27.4)	1936; 1938
/3			11	(27.9)	
RPA1041/2		Bruce (Cairn)	10¾	(27.4)	1936-1938
/3			11	(27.9)	
RPA1267/2		Elephant	8½	(21.6)	1936-1938
/4			11½	(29.2)	
RPA1326/11½		Lamb	13	(33.0)	1936; 1938
RPA1333/11		Old Faithful (horse)	13	(33.0)	1936-1938
/12½			12½	(31.8)	
RPA1335/10½		Towzer (dog)	11½	(29.2)	1936-1938
/14			14½	(36.9)	
RPA1394/11		Jack (dog)	11¼	(28.6)	1936-1938
/12			12	(30.5)	
RPA1608/2		Kid (donkey)	11½	(29.2)	1937
/3			13	(33.0)	
RPA1609/3		Donkey Colt	13½	(34.3)	1937-1938
RPA1610/3		Pony Colt	13½	(34.3)	1937-1938
1608/1		Kid (donkey)	12	(30.5)	1938
/2			15½	(39.4)	
/3			22	(55.9)	

Stock No.	Type of Item	Name	Size inches	centimeters	Year
1609/1		Donkey Colt	16½	(41.9)	1938
/2			19	(48.3)	
/3			24	(61.0)	
	Wheel Toys				

In 1931 the following animals could be ordered as Wheel Toys, by adding a "W" in front of the stock number of the item:

Stock No.	Name	inches	centimeters	Year
S1033/1	Cutie Rabbit	13½	(34.3)	
/2		17	(43.2)	
/3		21	(53.3)	
S1032/1	Running Rabbit	9½	(24.2)	
/2		11	(27.9)	
/3		14	(35.6)	
S1031/1	Sitting Rabbit	9	(22.9)	
/2		10½	(26.7)	
/3		13	(33.0)	
B1044/1	Greyfriars Bobby (standing)	10	(25.4)	
/2		12	(30.5)	
B1043/1	Greyfriars Bobby (sitting)	7½	(19.1)	
/2		8½	(21.6)	
C1055/2	Foo-Foo (dog)	10	(25.4)	
S1045/1	Patch (Sealyham)	9	(22.9)	
/2		12	(30.5)	
/3		14	(35.6)	
A1045/3	Patch (Sealyham)	14	(35.6)	
S1037/1	Jerry (Dachshund)	9	(22.9)	
/2		12	(30.5)	
/3		15	(38.1)	
S1025/2	Gary (Irish Terrier) (standing)	8½	(21.6)	
/3		10	(26.7)	
/4		12	(30.5)	
S1026/2	Gary (sitting)	8½	(21.6)	
/3		10	(26.7)	
/4		12	(30.5)	
A1049/2	Spot (Terrier pup) (standing)	9	(22.9)	
/3		11	(27.9)	
A1048/2	Spot (sitting)	9	(22.9)	
/3		11	(27.9)	
S1036/1	Pimpo (elephant)	5	(12.7)	
/2		6	(15.2)	
/3		7½	(19.1)	
/4		9	(22.9)	
S1029/2	Mary (baby lamb)	7½	(19.1)	
/3		9	(22.9)	
S1034/2	Quacka (duck)	7½	(19.1)	
/3		10½	(26.7)	
B1038/1	Robbie (Highland Terrier)	11	(27.9)	
/2		12½	(31.8)	
B1041/1	Bruce (Cairn Terrier)	11	(27.9)	
/2		12½	(31.8)	
R1075/2	Robbie (Aberdeen Terrier)	16	(40.6)	1932-1933
/3		17½	(44.5)	
/4		22	(55.9)	
R1076/2	Bruce (Cairn Terrier)	16	(40.6)	1932-1933
/3		17½	(44.5)	
/4		22	(55.9)	
R1077/2	Mac (West Highland Terrier)	16	(40.6)	1932-1933
/3		17½	(44.5)	
/4		22	(55.9)	
R1079/1	Brown Bear or Polar Bear	14	(35.6)	1932-1933
/2		18	(45.7)	
/3		21	(53.3)	
/4		23	(58.4)	
/5		31½	(80.0)	
R1081/2	Tiger or Leopard	16½	(41.9)	1932-1933
/3		18	(45.7)	
/4		23	(58.4)	
R1086/1	Donkey	15½	(39.4)	1932-1933
/2		19½	(49.6)	
/3		26	(66.0)	
/4		29	(73.7)	
/5		36	(91.4)	
R1087/3	Zebra	26	(66.0)	1932-1933
/4		29	(73.7)	
/5		36	(91.4)	

Stock No.	Type of Item	Name	Size inches	centimeters	Year
R1088/1		*Pony*	16½	(41.9)	1932
/2			20½	(52.1)	
/3			27	(68.6)	1932-1933
/4			31	(78.7)	1932
/5			39	(99.0)	

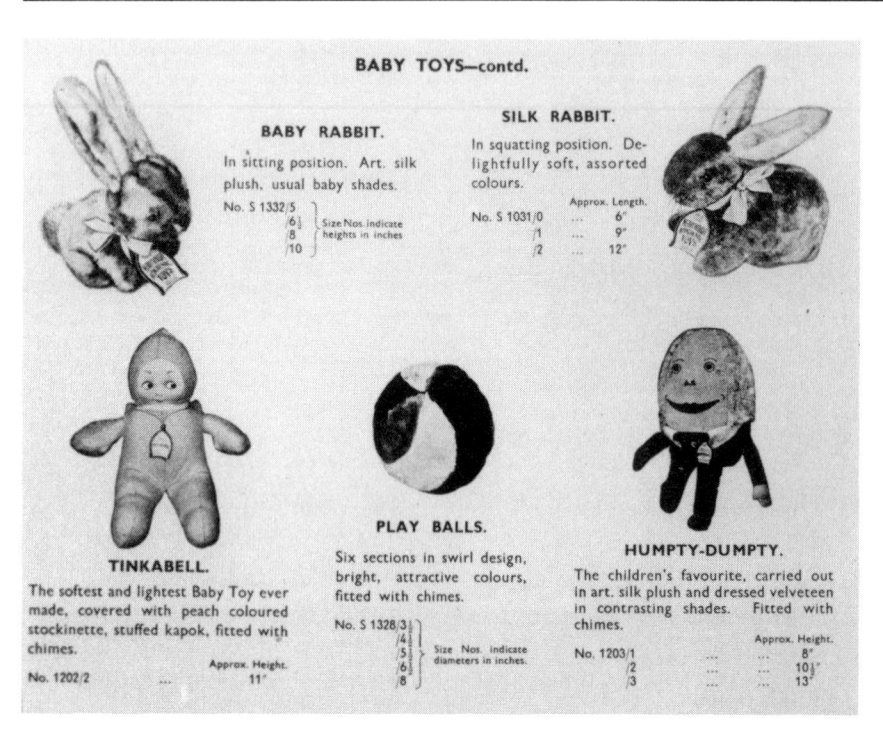

Illustration 180. A selection of "Baby Toys" from the 1935 Merrythought catalog. Except for the balls, the other items are listed in their respective categories. (*Baby Rabbit* is listed under "Cot Toys.")

Illustration 181. "Cot Toys" and "Cot Toys with Musical Chime" from the 1937 Merrythought catalog.

Illustration 182. "Jumpee Cot Toys" from the 1975 Merrythought catalog. They are No. 827, *Top Hat Humpty;* No. 778, *Highland Humpty;* No. 401, *Hedgehog;* No. 714, *French Humpty;* and No. 315, *New Humpty Dumpty.*

Illustration 183. "Glove Toys," or "Glove Puppets" from the 1954 Merrythought catalog, including some licensed characters. Each is 9½ inches (24.2cm) tall. Top row: No. 1930 *Poodle* with a wool plush head and a felt body; *Gran'pop,* No. 5218, in mohair with a velveteen face; and No. 1929 *Doc Dwarf* with a felt mask face and felt jacket. Bottom row: No. 1931 *Jerry Mouse* in velveteen; No. 1919 *Pluto* in art silk plush; and No. 5217 *Cat* in mohair plush. *Merrythought photograph.*

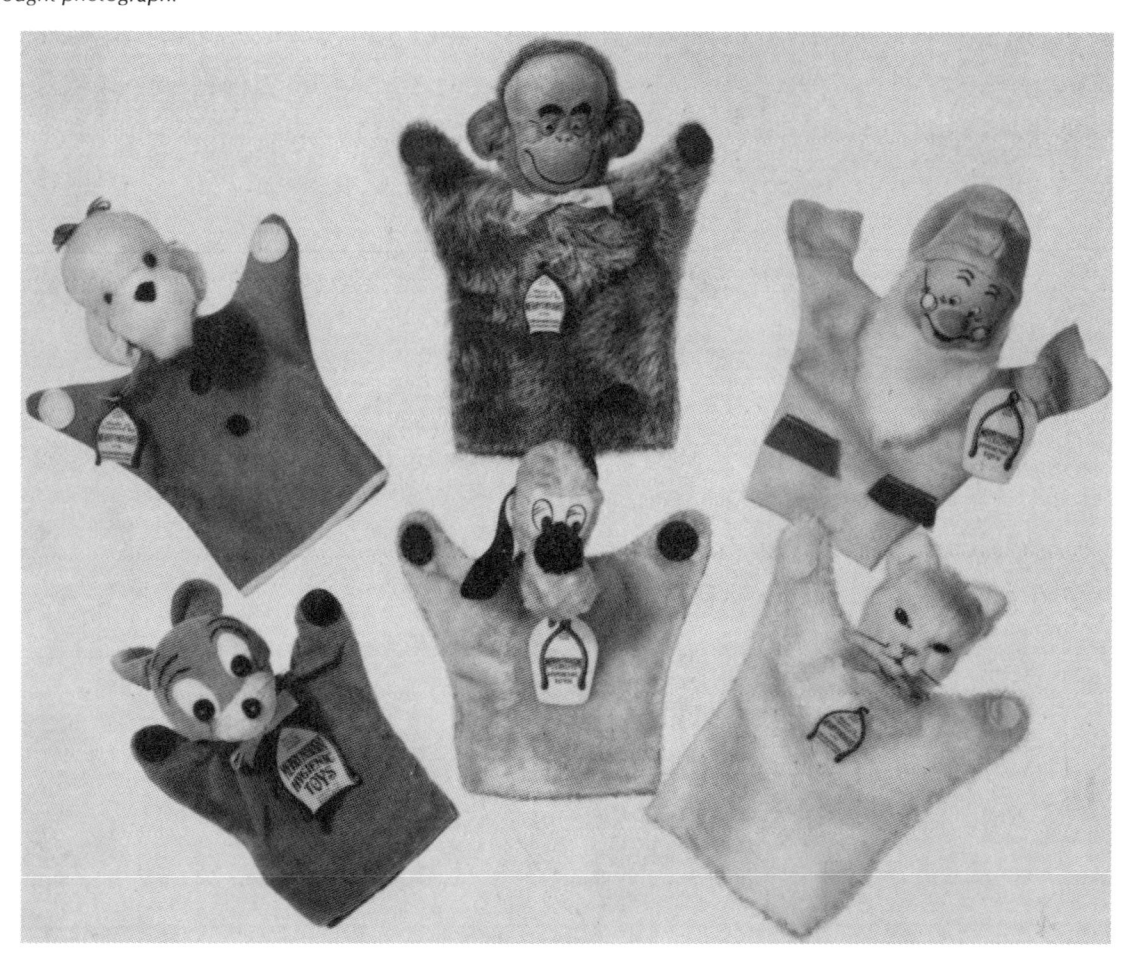

177

Illustration 184. From the 1977 Merrythought catalog. The *Hobby Horse* is No. A57 and he is 36 inches (91.4cm) long. The other toys are *Duck*, No. 494, 8 inches (20.3cm) high in yellow nylon plush; *Penguin*, No. A14; *Bed-Time Bear*, No. A46, 17 inches (43.2cm) high; and *Baby Bear*, No. A15, in mohair plush.

Illustration 185. "Pull-Along Toys" from the 1937 Merrythought catalog. Each animal is on a steel chasis and has wooden wheels.

178

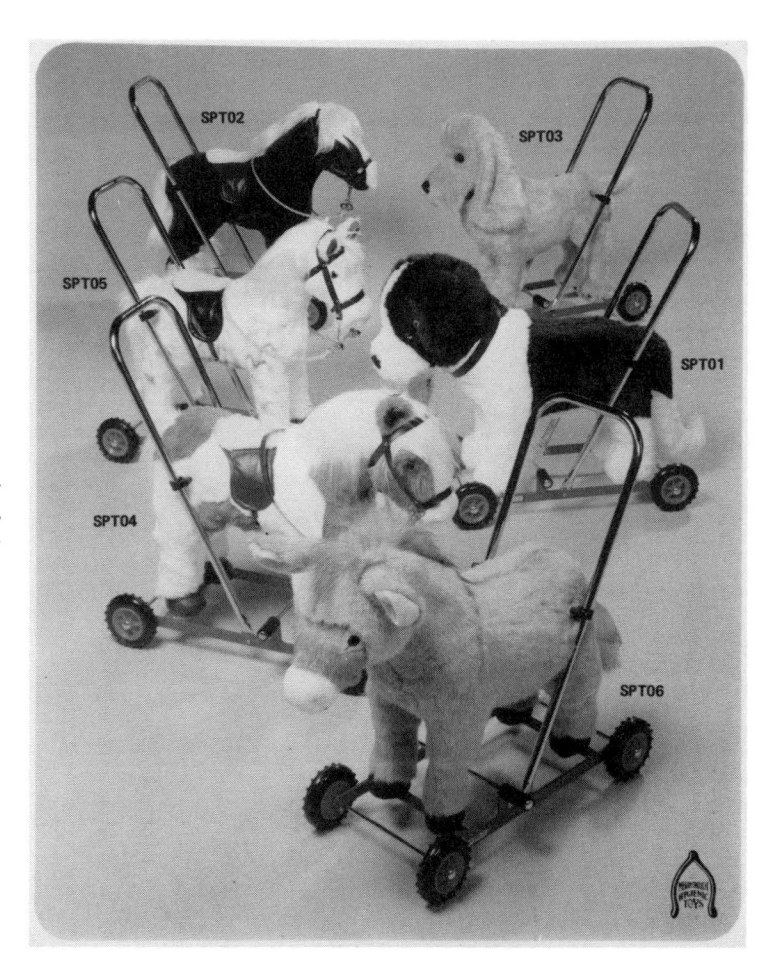

Illustration 186. "Super Push Along Toys" from the 1981 Merrythought catalog. Note that each toy has a foot rest for the child's feet. They are No. SPT01, *St. Bernard;* No. SPT02, *Shirehorse;* No. SPT03, *Spaniel;* No. SPT04 *Skewbald;* No. SPT05 *Dappled Grey;* and No. SPT06 *Donkey.*

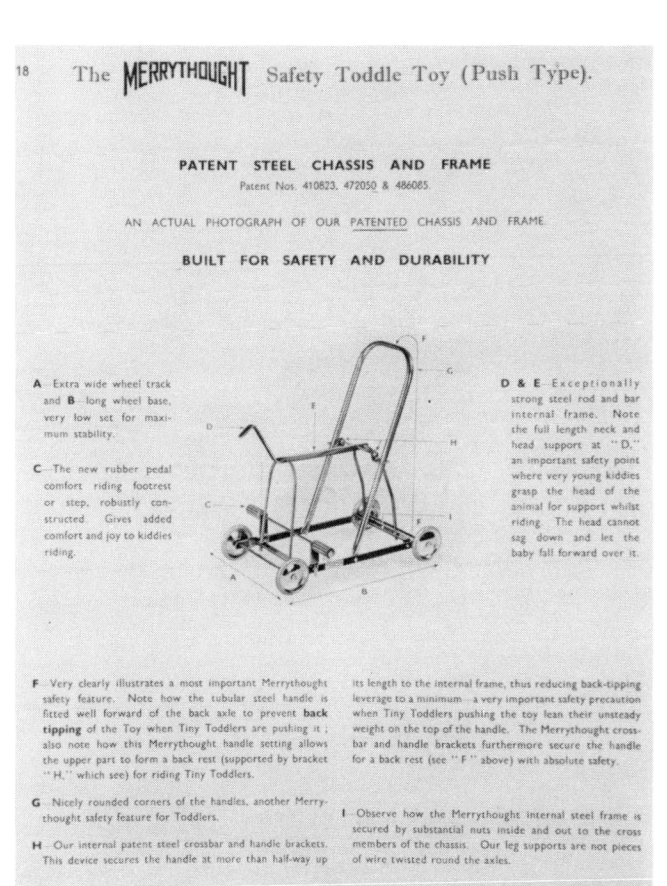

Illustration 187. The Patent Steel Chassis and Frame for the Merrythought Safety Toddle Toy. Illustration from the 1950 Merrythought catalog.

179

Illustration 188. "Safety Toddle Toys, Push Type." From left to right they are, *Bobtail*, No. TT/0/1310/A; *Collie Pup*, No. TT/0/1353/B; and *Old Faithful*, No. TT/0/1333/B. All are from 1936. The size is 17 inches high (43.2cm), 18 inches long (45.7cm), 8¾ inches wide (22.3cm). Each animal is made of mohair and is constructed with the internal frame shown in the previous photograph. Note the wishbone, which is the Merrythought symbol. This photograph is from the 1936 Merrythought catalog.

Illustration 189. *Bobtail Sheepdog*, Toddle Toy, from 1936. *Merrythought photograph.*

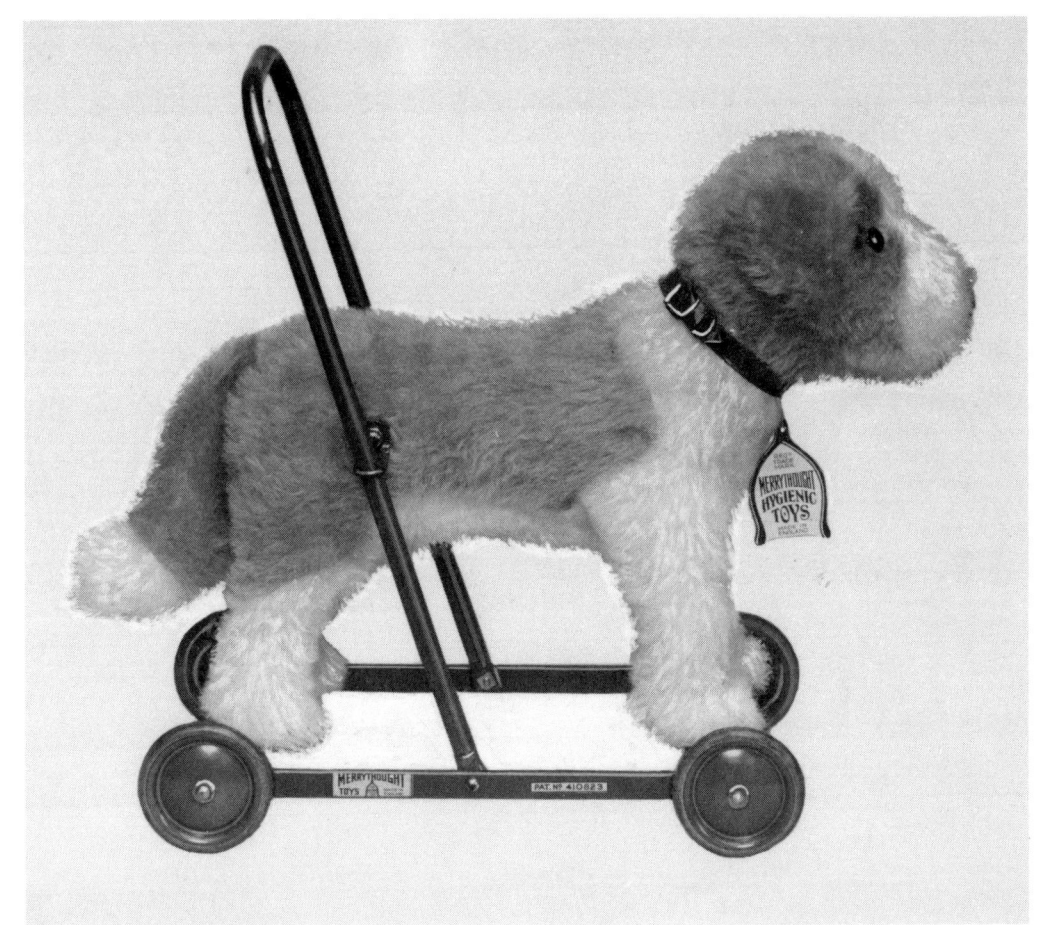

Illustration 190. Collie Pup, Toddle Toy, 1936. Merrythought photograph.

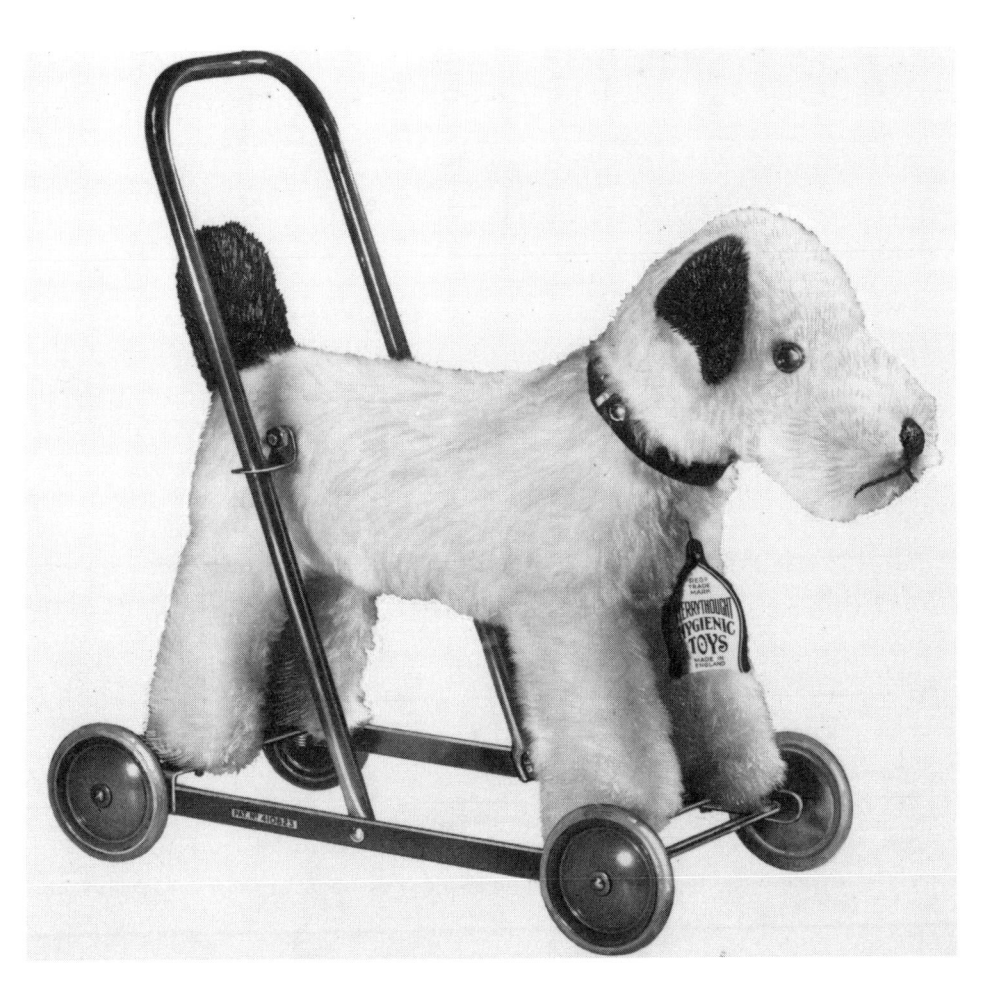

Illustration 191. Towzer, No. TT/0/1335/B, 1936, another Toddle Toy on rubber tires. Merrythought photograph.

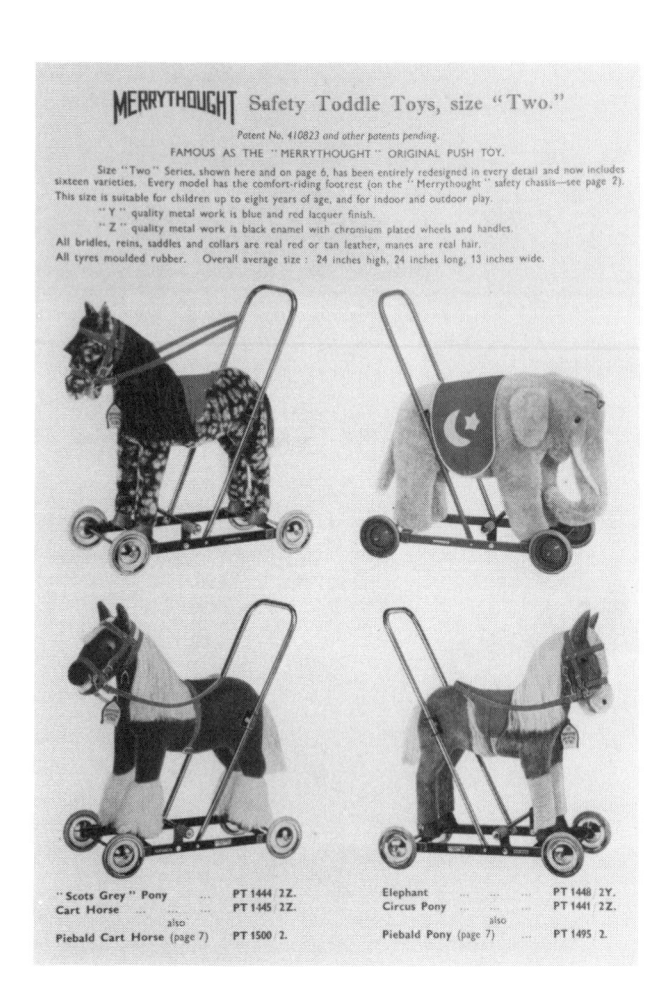

Illustration 192. The "Push Toys" are the same as the "Toddle Toys," except that they have a foot rest. From the 1936 Merrythought catalog: *Scots Grey Pony, Cart Horse, Elephant* and *Circus Pony.*

Illustration 193. *Poodle,* No. PT12/2, from 1959 to 1963, a "Push Toy." *Merrythought photograph.*

Illustration 194. The "Riding Toys" are similar to the "Toddle Toys" and the "Push Toys," except that they have a rope for pulling the animal along as the child sits on it. These, the *Cart Horse, Shetland Pony, Riding Grizzly Bear* and *Riding Panda Bear,* are from the 1937 Merrythought catalog.

Illustration 195. This is a "Rocking Pull-Along Toy" from 1952-1956. When pulled along, *Jacko* (No. RPA 1470/3) moves his arms and body backwards and forwards as if propelling himself. The wheels have rubber tires. 11½ inches (29.2cm). *Merrythought photograph.*

Illustration 196. *Trolley Bun* is another "Rocking Pull-Along Toy" from 1955-1956, and is similar to *Jacko*. Merrythought sample.

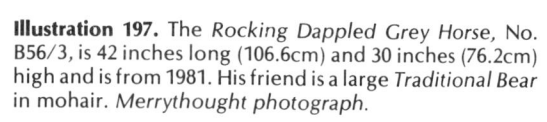

Illustration 197. The *Rocking Dappled Grey Horse*, No. B56/3, is 42 inches long (106.6cm) and 30 inches (76.2cm) high and is from 1981. His friend is a large *Traditional Bear* in mohair. *Merrythought photograph.*

ABOVE: Illustration 198. The old-fashioned *American Stage Coach* with four horses "in hand" was a show-piece shown in the 1936 Merrythought catalog. It is 7½ feet long. The doll is *Buddy*, No. 1413; the horses are *Windsor Cream Pony*, No. R1092, 1936-1937, used as a "Riding Toy."

BELOW: Illustration 199. "Wheel Toys" from the first Merrythought catalog, 1931. Many of the regular Merrythought animals could also be supplied this way for purchasers if they added a "W" in front of the stock number of the animal. For example *Pimpo*, No. S1036, was *Pimpo*, the Elephant on Wheels, if he was ordered as WS1036. The other animals are *Patch*, the Sealyham puppy, No. WS1045; *Cutie Rabbit*, No. WS1033; and *Running Rabbit*, No. WS1032. After 1931 the "Wheel Toys" were advertised separately.

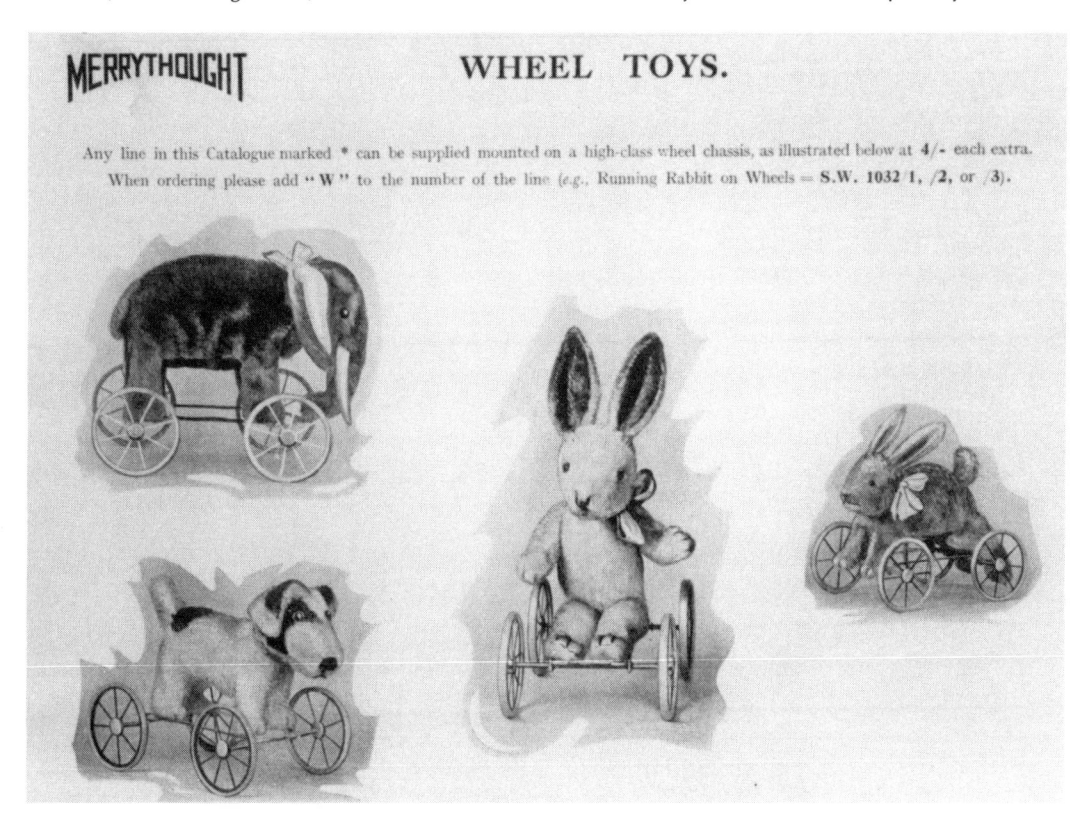

XVI. NIGHTDRESS CASES

The nightdress cases, of which Merrythought made a great variety, are animals, dolls and other figures that have body portions that are not stuffed so that it makes a hidden pocket for storing a child's pajamas or nightgown and can be displayed on the bed. These compartments for storage are usually closed with a zipper.

The nightdress cases are as desirable as collectibles as are all Merrythought toys. They can be made more practical for display if the pocket compartment is filled with cotton or polyester stuffing to make the piece retain its shape. Most of the earlier nightdress cases that are animals were made of mohair cloth.

The Merrythought production of nightdress cases are grouped within three categories: A. *Nightdress Cases*; B. *Sachets*, which are smaller cases that are usually round in shape; and C. *Super Nightdress Cases*, the term used for these items since the late 1960s.

Within the three categories, the nightdress cases are listed in the same manner as Chapters Two through Eleven. This begins with the bears in chronological order; Dogs are listed in alphabetical order and by year; Cats are listed by year; Rabbits are listed by year; Domestic Animals are in alphabetical order and then by year; Wild Animals and Jungle Animals are the same way; Birds and Insects are listed in alphabetical order and then in chronological sequence; Dolls are listed in the order in which they appeared in the catalogs.

A. NIGHTDRESS CASES

Stock No.	Name	Size inches	centimeter	Year
ZNC1637	Noah's Ark	17½	(44.5)	1938
1617	Teddies	15½	(39.4)	1938
ZNC1835/1	Panda	16	(40.6)	1939
/2		21	(53.3)	
ZNC1836/1	Panda	16	(40.6)	1939
/2		21	(53.3)	
Z2093	Panda	12	(30.5)	1958
951	Sitting Panda	16	(40.6)	1966-1967
998	Standing Panda	18	(45.7)	1969-1970
965	Koala Bear	16	(40.6)	1967-1968
ZIP1038/2	Doggie Bag Aberdeen	12½	(31.8)	1935-1936
ZNC1341/3½	Robbie (Aberdeen Terrier)	16	(40.6)	1935-1936; 1938
ZNC1489/2	Aberdeen Terrier	20	(50.8)	1936; 1938; 1954-1955; 1957-1959
ND1614	Aberdeen	15½	(39.4)	1938
ZNC1883	Aberdeen "Tiggle Tummy"	18	(45.7)	1949-1952
ZNC1341/3½	Scottie (Aberdeen)	16	(40.6)	1955-1956
933/2	Tiggle-Tummy Aberdeen	20	(50.8)	1964-1965
982	Bassett Hound	22	(55.9)	1968
888/2	Boxer	21	(53.3)	1961-1963
999	Bulldog	18	(45.7)	1969-1973
ZNC1488/2	Bull Mastiff Pup	20	(50.8)	1936; 1938
ZNC1497/2	Bull Puppy	20	(50.8)	1936; 1938
ZNC1498/2	Bull Terrier Pup	20	(50.8)	1936; 1938
ZNC1340/3½	Robbie (Cairn Terrier)	16	(40.6)	1935-1936; 1938
ZIP1041/2	Doggie Bag (Cairn Terrier)	12½	(31.8)	1935-1936
ZNC1490/2	Cairn Terrier	20	(50.8)	1936; 1938
ZNC1490/2	Cairn Terrier	22	(55.9)	1948; 1950-1959
ND1619/2	Cairn Terrier	15½	(39.4)	1938
ZNC1884	Cairn "Tiggletummy"	18	(45.7)	1949-1952
850/2	Cairn Terrier	22	(55.9)	1960-1972
931/2	Tiggle-Tummy Cairn	20	(50.8)	1964-1965
ZNC1492/2	Chow Puppy	20	(50.8)	1936; 1938
ZNC1339/3½	Cocker Spaniel	16	(40.6)	1935; 1938; 1953-1956
ZNC1506/2	Black Cocker	20	(50.8)	1938
ZNC4629/2	Golden Cocker Spaniel	22	(55.9)	1949-1959
ZNC4630/2	Black Cocker Spaniel	22	(55.9)	1949-1959
862/2	Golden Cocker Spaniel	22	(55.9)	1960-1972
863/2	Black Cocker Spaniel	22	(55.9)	1960-1967
Z2046	Floppy Corgi	14	(35.6)	1957
880	Dachshund	21	(53.3)	1961-1963
987	Bedtime Daxi	22	(55.9)	1968

Stock No.	Name	Size inches	centimeters	Year
ZNC1484/2	Dalmatian (Puppy)	20	(50.8)	1936; 1938; 1954-1959
866/2	Dalmatian Puppy	20	(50.8)	1960-1965
Z209	Floppy Alsatian (German Shepherd)	14	(35.6)	1958
ZNC 1337/3½	Peke	16	(40.6)	1935-1936; 1938; 1953-1957
ZNC1487/2	Pekingese	20	(50.8)	1936; 1938; 1948; 1950-1957
ZNC1882	Peke "Tiggletummy"	18	(45.7)	1949-1952
Z2027	Floppy Peke	14	(35.6)	1957-1958
927/2	Tiggle-Tummy Peke	20	(50.8)	1964-1965
ZNC1978	Poodle (black or white)	24	(61.0)	1956-1959
Z2029	Floppy Poodle	14	(35.6)	1957-1959
852/2	Poodle (black or white)	24	(61.0)	1960-1966
864/3	Poodle (black or white)	18	(45.7)	1960-1966
869	Miss Poodle	18	(45.7)	1960-1961
889	Dutch Poodle	19	(48.3)	1961-1962
906	Sleepytime Poodle	23	(58.4)	1963
995	Poodle	22	(55.9)	1969-1980
ZNC1486/2	Sealyham	20	(50.8)	1936; 1938
ZNC1486/2	Sealyham	22	(55.9)	1948; 1950-1959
ZNC1881	Sealyham "Tiggle Tummy"	18	(45.7)	1949-1952
ZNC1881	Sealyham "Tiggle Tummy"	22	(55.9)	1953-1956
853/2	Sealyham	22	(55.9)	1960-1972
894/4	Sealyham	15	(38.1)	1961-1966
ZNC1995	Sheepdog	22	(55.9)	1956-1958
ZNC1336/3½	Black and White Spaniel	16	(40.6)	1935; 1938; 1953-1959
ZNC1485/2	Black and White Spaniel	20	(50.8)	1936; 1938
ZNC1506/2	Black Spaniel	20	(50.8)	1936
ZNC1485/2	Black and White Spaniel	22	(55.9)	1948; 1950-1959
851/2	Black and White Spaniel	22	(55.9)	1960-1972
859/3	Black and White Spaniel	16	(40.6)	1960-1963
893/4	Black and White Spaniel	15	(38.1)	1961-1966
918/2	Doleful Spaniel	22	(55.9)	1964-1979
948	Sitting Doleful (Spaniel)	16	(40.6)	1966
ZNC1338/3½	Robbie (White Highland)	16	(40.6)	1935-1936; 1938
ZNC1491/2	West Highland Terrier	20	(50.8)	1936; 1938
?	Sleeping Pup	18	(45.7)	1932
?	Sleeping Pup	10	(25.4)	1933
ZNC1098/3½	Fawn Pup	16	(40.6)	1935-1936; 1938
ZNC1342/3½	White Curly Dog	16	(40.6)	1935-1936; 1938
ZNC1343/3½	Black Curly Dog	16	(40.6)	1935-1936; 1938
ZNC1480	'Andsome	23	(58.4)	1936; 1938
ND1613	Puppies	15½	(39.4)	1938
ND1618	Puppies	15½	(39.4)	1938
Z2097	Sandy	24	(61.0)	1958-1959
865/2	Whiskers	20	(50.8)	1960
941	Toggles	22	(55.9)	1965
ZNC1684/4	Persian Cat	17	(43.2)	1938
/5		19	(48.3)	
/6		22	(55.9)	
/6		23	(58.4)	1949-1959
ZNC1731	Pussy	21	(53.3)	1939; 1952-1957
ZNC2003	Cheshire Cat	21	(53.3)	1956-1957
Z2028	Floppy Puss	14	(35.6)	1957-1959
Z2084	Cat	12	(30.5)	1958
860/6	Cat	23	(58.4)	1960-1963
ND1620	Bunnies	15½	(39.4)	1938
ZNC1970	Rabbit	21	(53.3)	1956
Z2038	Rabbit	16	(40.6)	1957-1959
868	Rabbit	16	(40.6)	1960
905	Sleepytime Rabbit	18	(45.7)	1963-1966
980	Taurus the Bull (Hereford)	18	(45.7)	1967-1970
962	Sitting Connemara (donkey)	18	(45.7)	1966-1981
935	Horse	15	(38.1)	1965
Z2129	Sleepy Lamb	18	(45.7)	1959
991	Dolfin (dolphin)	24	(61.0)	1968-1973
946	Hedgehog	18	(45.7)	1965-1966
968/3	Hedgehog	18	(45.7)	1967
973	Hedgie (hedgehog)	18	(45.7)	1968-1981

Stock No.	Name	Size inches	centimeters	Year
938	Octopus	24 dia.	(61.0)	1965
924/2	Elephant	18	(45.7)	1964-1966
949	Sitting Elephant	16	(40.6)	1966-1967
983	Hippo	18	(45.7)	1968-1985
ZNC1483/1	Lion	17	(43.2)	1936; 1938
Z2041	Lion	16	(40.6)	1957-1959
867/2	Lion	16	(40.6)	1960-1973
ND1618	Monkeys	15½	(39.4)	1938
963	Chick	21	(53.3)	1966-1967
Z2021	Duck	14	(35.6)	1957-1958
904	Sleepytime Duck	22	(55.9)	1963
992	Duck	10	(25.4)	1968-1969
950	Penguin	20	(50.8)	1966-1971; 1974-1979
1576	Purple Hairstreak (butterfly)	18	(45.7)	1938
1577	Emerald Moth	18	(45.7)	1938
1578	Clouded Yellow (butterfly)	18	(45.7)	1938
1579	Camberwell Beauty (butterfly)	18	(45.7)	1938
1580	Actias Selene (butterfly)	22	(55.9)	1938
1581	Red Admiral (butterfly)	18	(45.7)	1938
1583	Junania (butterfly)	18	(45.7)	1938
1584	Privet Hawk (butterfly)	18	(45.7)	1938
1587	Burnished Brass (butterfly)	18	(45.7)	1938
1588	Peacock (butterfly)	18	(45.7)	1938
ZNC1235/2	Pixie Doll	20	(50.8)	1935-1936; 1938
/3		26	(66.0)	
ZNC1318/30	Sleeping Pixie Doll	30	(76.2)	1935-1936; 1938
ZNC1521	Cowboy Bill (doll)	25	(63.5)	1938
ZNC1522	Joey (doll)	24½	(62.3)	1938
ZNC1523	Harlequin (doll)	22	(55.9)	1938
ZNC1524	Bo'sun Bill (doll)	22	(55.9)	1938
ZNC1572	Turkish Delight (doll)	24	(61.0)	1938
ND1615	Dollies	15½	(39.4)	1938
ND1616	Gollies (doll)	15½	(39.4)	1938
ZNC1638	Little Goldilocks and the Three Bears	16	(40.6)	1938
ZNC1639	Mary, Mary, Quite Contrary	15	(38.1)	1938
1640	Old Woman in a Shoe	15	(38.1)	1938
ZNC1723	Josephine (doll)	21	(53.3)	1938; 1950-1953
ZNC1726/1727	Snow White	?		1939
ZNC1760	Dutch Doll (composition head)	?		1939
ZNC4809	Dutch Girl	21	(53.3)	1951-1953
ZNC4810	Dutch Boy	21	(53.3)	1951-1953
Z2086	Clown	12	(30.5)	1958
Z2128	Clown	24	(61.0)	1959
945	Humpty Dumpty	18	(45.7)	1965-1966
981	Choir Boy	21	(53.3)	1967
984	Eskie Boy	16	(40.6)	1968
985	Eskie Girl	16	(40.6)	1968

B. SACHETS

Stock No.	Name	Size inches	centimeters	Year
?	Sleeping Pup	?		1932
854	Rabbit Sachet	12½ dia.	(31.8)	1960-1961
857	Puss Sachet	12½ dia.	(31.8)	1960-1964
932	Doleful Sachet (Spaniel)	12½ dia.	(31.8)	1964-1975
X41	Goose Sachet	21 dia.	(53.3)	1972-1973
959	Hankie Hog Hankie Sachet	8	(20.3)	1966-1981
964	Chick Hankie Sachet	8	(20.3)	1966-1967
978	Ladybird Hankie Sachet	8	(20.3)	1967-1971
990	Hippo Hankie Sachet	9	(22.9)	1968-1971
993	Duck Hankie Sachet	16	(40.6)	1968-1969

C. SUPER NIGHTDRESS CASES

Stock No.	Name	Size inches	centimeters	Year
926/21	Super Bear	21	(53.3)	1964-1969
947/2	London Gold Bear	21	(53.3)	1965-1966
XC9	Bear	22	(55.9)	1970-1980
X74	Polar Bear-Floppy	27	(68.6)	1976-1981
X56	Panda	22	(55.9)	1973
Y10	Panda	15	(38.1)	1980-1985
X97	Koala Bear	17	(43.2)	1979-1980
Y73	Koala Bear	13	(33.0)	1984-1985
928/2	Super Aberdeen	23	(58.4)	1964-1966
X42	Bloodhound	19	(48.3)	1972-1976
Y69	Border Collie	16	(40.6)	1983-1985
920/2	Super Cairn	23	(58.4)	1964-1969
X31	Collie	21	(53.3)	1972-1976
Y32	Collie	20	(50.8)	1981-1985
Y81	Dalmatian	24	(61.0)	1984-1985
Y70	Old English Sheepdog	24	(61.0)	1983-1985
922/2	Super Peke	23	(58.4)	1964-1965
901/2	Super Poodle (white)	23	(58.4)	1963-1969
X69	St. Bernard - Floppy	24	(61.0)	1976-1981
X99	Sitting St. Bernard	24	(61.0)	1980-1981
Y58	Lying St. Bernard	24	(61.0)	1982-1985
Y80	Scottie	16	(40.6)	1984-1985
944/2	Super Sealyham	23	(58.4)	1965-1966
919/2	Super Black and White Spaniel	23	(58.4)	1964-1969
X84	Doleful - Floppy (Spaniel)	24	(61.0)	1977-1978
X83	Spaniel - Floppy	24	(61.0)	1977-1980
Y21	Spaniel	18	(45.7)	1981
Y82	Spaniel	24	(61.0)	1984-1985
Y14	Westie	20	(50.8)	1980-1983
Y79	Westie	16	(40.6)	1984-1985
X54	Yorkshire Terrier	18	(45.7)	1973-1981
923/5	Super Cat	23	(58.4)	1964-1980
X78	Siamese Cat	22	(55.9)	1976-1980
Y11	Kitten	19	(48.3)	1980-1981
Y20	Tabby	19	(48.3)	1981
X63	Hare	18	(45.7)	1974-1979
X77	White Rabbit	20	(50.8)	1976-1979
Y60	Mother Rabbit	16	(40.6)	1983
X60	Ferdinand Bull	17	(43.2)	1974-1981
Y77	Camel	18	(45.7)	1984-1985
X13	Cow	17	(43.2)	1970-1971
X70	Donkey - Floppy	24	(61.0)	1976-1977
Y37	Donkey	19	(48.3)	1981
Y54	Lying Welsh Dun (donkey)	24	(61.0)	1982
Y67	Pedro (donkey)	24	(61.0)	1983
X92	Lamb - Floppy	27	(68.6)	1979-1980
X85	Shetland - Floppy	24	(61.0)	1977
Y19	Shirehorse	18	(45.7)	1981
Y35	Skewbald Pony	18	(45.7)	1981
Y36	Dappled Grey Horse	18	(45.7)	1981
Y39	Lying Dappled Grey (horse)	24	(61.0)	1982-1983
Y40	Lying Shirehorse	24	(61.0)	1982-1983
Y41	Lying Skewbald	24	(61.0)	1982-1983
X55	Pig	18	(45.7)	1973
Y64	Piglet	18	(45.7)	1983-1985
X14	Ram	20	(50.8)	1970-1971
X96	Chipmunk	18	(45.7)	1979-1985
Y18	Fawn - Floppy	27	(68.6)	1980
X79	Miss Fox	17	(43.2)	1977
X81	Fox - Floppy	24	(61.0)	1977-1980
Y59	Hedgehog	14	(35.6)	1983-1985
X90	Mountain Lion - Floppy	27	(68.6)	1978-1979
Y65	Seal	22	(55.9)	1983-1985
X1	Flower Tortoise	16	(40.6)	1970-1971
X98	Tortoise	22	(55.9)	1979-1980
Y72	Tortoise	13	(33.0)	1984-1985
X66	Crocodile	30	(76.2)	1975
Y34	Crocodile	24	(61.0)	1981-1983
X89	Elephant - Floppy	24	(61.0)	1978
Y38	Pink Elephant	26	(66.0)	1982
Y75	Elephant	18	(45.7)	1984
Y76	Gorilla	14	(35.6)	1984

Stock No.	Name	Size inches	centimeters	Year
X82	Leopard - Floppy	24	(61.0)	1977-1981
Y56	Lying Leopard	24	(61.0)	1982-1985
X64	Lion	21	(53.3)	1974-1975
X75	Lion - Floppy	27	(68.6)	1976-1981
Y55	Lying Lion	24	(61.0)	1982-1985
925/2	Super Monkey	23	(58.4)	1964-1965
X25	Monkey	21	(53.3)	1971-1980
Y78	Rhino	18	(45.7)	1984-1985
X58	Tiger	21	(53.3)	1974-1975
X76	Tiger - Floppy	27	(68.6)	1976-1981
Y53	Lying Tiger	24	(61.0)	1982-1985
Y68	Zebra Foal	24	(61.0)	1983
Y17	Duckling	16	(40.6)	1980-1981
X80	Mallard	16	(40.6)	1977-1980
X57	Owl	20	(50.8)	1973-1974
X91	Owl	15	(38.1)	1978-1981
Y57	Owl	14	(35.6)	1982-1985
X43	Baby Penguin	18	(45.7)	1972-1973
Y16	King Penguin	18	(45.7)	1980-1985
Y33	Swan	21	(53.3)	1981-1983
Y74	Humpty Dumpty	14	(35.6)	1984-1985

Illustration 200. *Cairn Terrier* nightdress case, No. ZNC1490/2, 1936-1959. This model is 20 inches (50.8cm) long and is in "natural cairn grey" mohair. He has a zipper in the stomach and a quilted silk lining inside for storing night clothing. *Merrythought photograph.*

Illustration 201. Puppy nightdress cases from 1936 to 1938. From left to right: *Dalmatian*, No. ZNC1484/2; *Sealyham*, No. ZNC1486/2; and *Black and White Spaniel*, No. ZNC1485/2. Each is 20 inches (50.8cm) long. *Merrythought photograph.*

Illustration 202. *Poodle* nightdress case, No. ZNC1978, 1956-1959. This item is 24 inches (61cm) and is of white plush with a wired head. *Merrythought photograph.*

191

Illustration 203. *Sheepdog* (Border Collie) nightdress case, No. ZNC1995, 1956-1958. *Merrythought photograph.*

Illustration 204. *Sleepy Lamb* nightdress case, No. Z2129, 1959. He has a flower in his mouth and he is 18 inches long (45.7cm) and made of curly white plush. *Merrythought photograph.*

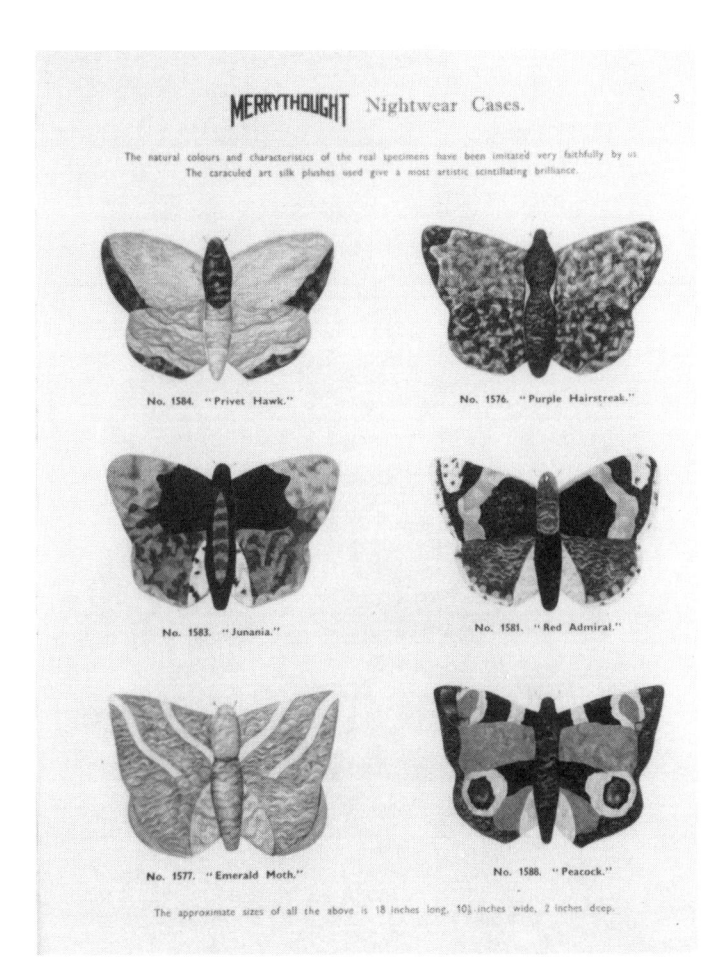

Illustration 205. Nightdress cases that are butterflies and moths. Each one is made of caraculed art silk plush. The back is rich silk, covering a quilted silk pocket or container closed with a zipper. They were packaged in a decorated box. The approximate sizes were 18 inches long (45.7cm), 10½ inches high (26.7cm) and 2 inches deep (5.1cm). From the 1938 Merrythought "Nightdress & Pyjama Case Catalogue No. 8 NDC."

Illustration 206. Nightdress cases from the 1938 Merrythought catalog. They are *Dollies, Robbie, Josephine, Cowboy Bill,* and Mabel Lucie Atwell's *Vanity Jane.*

Illustration 207. *Josephine* nightdress case, No. ZNC1723, 1938; 1950-1953. She is 21 inches (53.3cm) tall and wears a red and white dotted dress. Her skirt is the case portion and it is closed with a zipper. The head and arms are dark colored velveteen. *Merrythought photograph.*

Illustration 208. *Dutch Girl* nightdress case, No. ZNC4809, 1951-1953. She is 21 inches (53.3cm) tall with a felt mask face. *Merrythought photograph.*

Illustration 209. *Clown* nightdress case, No. Z2128, 1959. He wore bright red, blue or yellow and white striped cottons with a large zip pocket in the back. Size is 24 inches (61cm) high. *Merrythought photograph.*

XVII. MISCELLANEOUS

This chapter includes other items that Merrythought made over the years that incorporates Merrythought animals, two display pieces made in 1985 that are accessories for Merrythought animals, baskets for puppies and artificial Christmas trees.

The artificial Christmas trees were made with wire branches covered with a green synthetic material that simulated real foilage. They were made in four different sizes from 1948 to 1954. Many of these Christmas trees are still in use during the holiday season.

Stock No.	Type of Item	Name	Size inches	centimeters	Year
?	**Basket for Puppies**		12½ dia.	(31.8)	1932-1933
CN/T/23	**Artificial Christmas Trees**		23	(58.4)	1948-1954
/29			29½	(75.0)	
/32			32	(81.3)	
/36			36	(91.4)	
T/23			23	(58.4)	1950-1954
/29			29½	(75.0)	
/32			32	(81.3)	
/36			36	(91.4)	
1724/11½	**Handbag Novelty**	Aberdeen	11½	(29.2)	1938
/14½			14½	(36.9)	
1721/11½		Cairn	11½	(29.2)	1938
/14½			14½	(36.9)	
A56		Handbag Cat	9	(22.9)	1977
165	**Children's Muffs**	Muff Bear (nylon)	13	(33.0)	1960-1961
165		Muff Bear (nylon)	12	(30.5)	1970-1976
173		Muff Rabbit	14	(35.6)	1960-1961
219		Muff Lamb	14	(35.6)	1961
297	**Nursery Stools**	Pablo Hassock (donkey)	12	(30.5)	1966-1970
437		Pablo Stool (donkey)	12	(30.5)	1966-1967
430		Hassock Hog	15	(38.1)	1966-1967
A75		Tortoise Hassock	21	(53.3)	1978-1979
A82		Hippo Hassock	21	(53.3)	1978-1979
583		Tawny Owl Stool	12	(30.5)	1969-1970
	Display Items	Mole Manor Display Mushroom	22	(55.9)	1985
		Mouse Cottage Display Toadstool	28	(71.1)	1985

Note: The above lists consist only of toys and toy-related items; they do not include non-toy pieces, such as the children's respirator cases made during World War II.

Illustration 210. *Merrythought Artificial Christmas Trees, 1948-1954. Their description is included in the photograph from the 1948 catalog.*

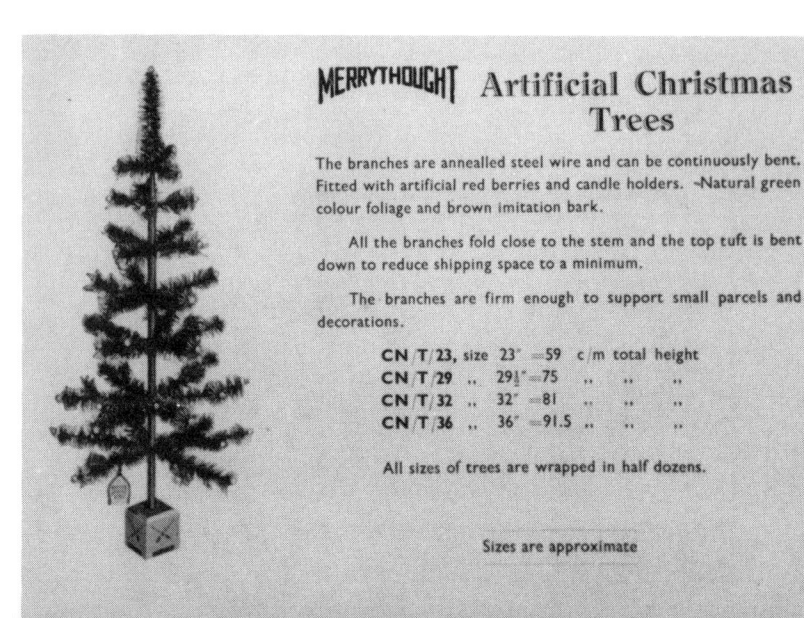

MERRYTHOUGHT Artificial Christmas Trees

The branches are annealled steel wire and can be continuously bent. Fitted with artificial red berries and candle holders. Natural green colour foliage and brown imitation bark.

All the branches fold close to the stem and the top tuft is bent down to reduce shipping space to a minimum.

The branches are firm enough to support small parcels and decorations.

CN/T/23, size 23" =59 c/m total height
CN/T/29 „ 29½" =75 „ „ „
CN/T/32 „ 32" =81 „ „ „
CN/T/36 „ 36" =91.5 „ „ „

All sizes of trees are wrapped in half dozens.

Sizes are approximate

Illustration 211. Handbags were made of Cairns and Aberdeens by Merrythought in 1938. Both dogs are illustrated in this page from the 1938 catalog. They were probably mohair and were in sizes of 11½ inches (29.2cm) and 14½ inches (36.9cm).

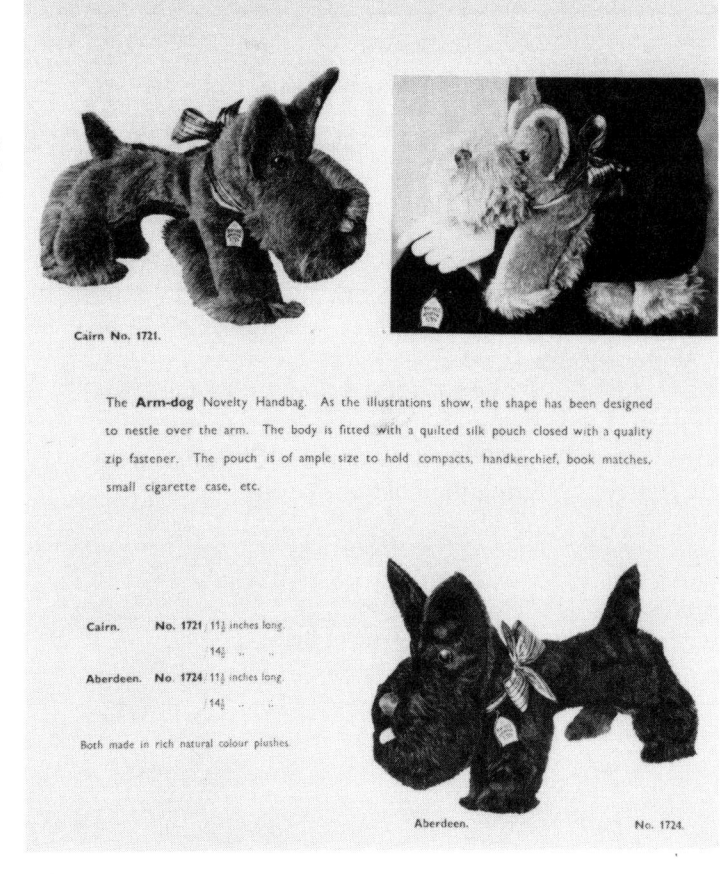

Illustration 212. The *Muff Rabbit* from 1960 to 1961 is 14 inches (35.6cm) long and came in pink or blue nylon plush. *Merrythought photograph.*

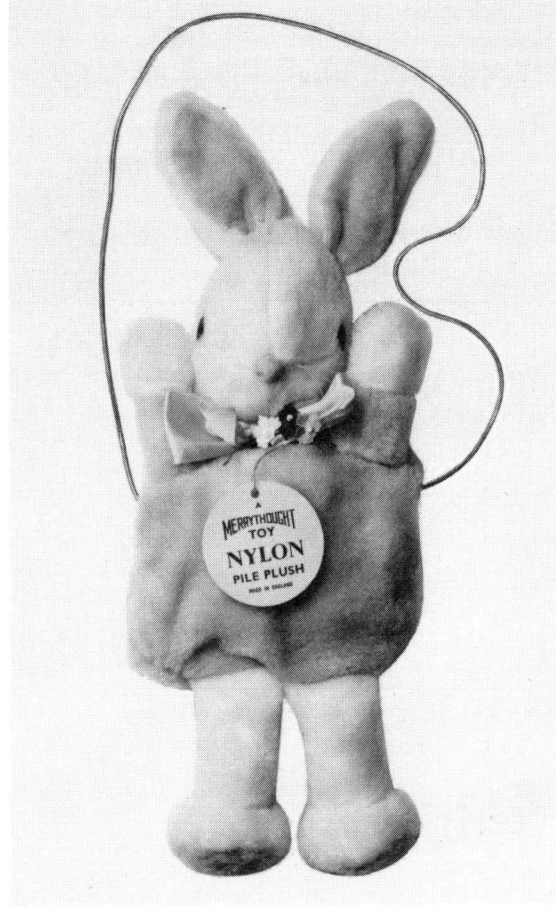

Illustration 213. Nursery Stools incorporating animals. No. 437 is *Pablo Stool*, a donkey that has a seat 12 inches (30.5cm) in diameter and made from 1966 to 1967. No. 297 is *Pablo Hassock*, with a seat the same size and made from 1966 to 1970. No. 430 is *Hassock Hog*, a Hedgehog which is 15 inches (38.1cm) long and made from 1966 to 1967. These stools are covered with synthetic plush and the photograph is from the 1966 Merrythought catalog.

APPENDIX

The "Magic of Merrythought" continues: For 1986 Merrythought Limited will present for the 55th time its fabulous toys that feature animals which children and collectors have loved since 1931. The samples featured here are some of the new ones that will be added to the line.

Merrythought Teddy Bears are as charming and lovable as they ever were. One exciting concept is the *Bear in Balloon,* which is a 5in (12.7cm) miniature bear who rides in a replica of the Merrythought hot air balloon. (See *Illustrations 4, 5,* and *6* in Chapter I.) The new 5in (12.7cm) bears are the smallest that Merrythought has produced, and all are fully-jointed of pure mohair. There is also a *Highlander* and *Policeman* who make the *Guardsman* and the *Beefeater* of 1985 good companions to form a British quartet of bears. The *Merrythought Muff and Purse Bear* is a fun item for children, but collectors will need him, too!

For 1986 there will be a new *Golliwog,* the Teddy Bear's "best friend." Other new animal friends are a dolphin, a duck, a penguin and others that are pictured here.

The most exciting new item of all for this author is the Limited Edition *Greyfriars Bobby* from Merrythought. This is the little Skye Terrier who was the first animal shown in the very first Merrythought Catalog of 1931. I remember as a child how much I liked the story of the devoted terrier who stayed at his master's grave in Edinburgh, Scotland, for the last 14 years of his life. I was given the privilege of re-designing *Greyfriars Bobby* so that he has a jointed head and a perky tail. Merrythought Limited has made him look just like John Gray's pet must have when he lived in Edinburgh in the 1860s, remaining close to his master's grave site in Greyfriars Churchyard.

It is a special privilege for me to have designed the *Greyfriars Bobby* that Merrythought will produce. But all of my associations with Merrythought are special privileges and they have added magic and enjoyment to my life.

Illustration 214. The new Merrythought *Miniature Teddy Bear* is 5 inches (12.7cm) tall and he will be available in pure mohair in a London gold shade as a part of the regular 1986 line. He is fully-jointed. *Merrythought photograph.*

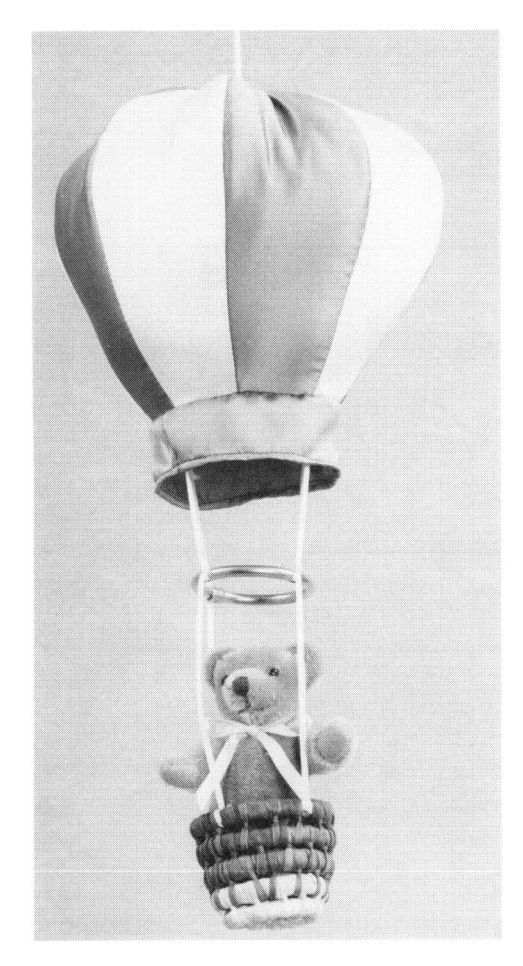

ABOVE: Illustration 215. A Limited Edition of only 500 sets of three of the 5 inch (12.7cm) bears will be produced to celebrate the addition to Merrythought's line of their smallest bears ever. Each Teddy Bear is fully-jointed and is of pure mohair pile. The colors are Ironbridge grey, cinnamon and spicy brown. *Merrythought photograph.*

LEFT: Illustration 216. The Merrythought *Bear in Balloon* is a 5 inch (12.7cm) miniature Teddy Bear of mohair and he is fully-jointed. He rides in a wicker basket suspended from a satin replica of the Merrythought hot air balloon. The overall height is 17 inches (43.2cm). *Merrythought photograph.*

RIGHT: Illustration 217. 18 inch (45.7cm) *Highlander* is a new Merrythought character Teddy Bear to compliment the *Guardsman* and the *Beefeater* of 1985. The head is jointed and is mohair. The clothing is a dress Stewart kilt and plaid with a green velvet hat and jacket, trimmed with white silky Russian braid and silver colored studs. *Merrythought photograph.*

Illustration 218. A brand new Merrythought design for 1986 is *The Elizabethan Bear* who comes in two colors, London gold and spicy brown. He is 12 inches (30.5cm) and 14 inches (35.6cm) tall, and the larger size is fitted with a growler. *Merrythought photograph.*

Illustration 219. One of the crew of the "H.M.S. Merrythought" is *Sailor Boy Bear,* a fully-jointed mohair *Elizabethan Bear* who is 12 inches (30.5cm) tall. His outfit is blue felt. *Merrythought photograph.*

ABOVE: Illustration 220. The *Merrythought Muff and Purse Teddy Bear* is a clever and useful combination that was designed for the younger Teddy Bear lover. This rascal is 12 inches (30.5cm) long and his body includes a purse that is lined and fitted with a zipper; the furry body also incorporates a muff for warming hands. *Merrythought photograph.*

BELOW: Illustration 221. The Merrythought *Bearington Family* of 1985 was such a success as a Limited Edition of 1000 sets that they are joined in 1986 by their *Country Cousins*. The *Country Cousins*, *Henry* and *Alma*, and their daughter, *Sadie*, are of pure mohair in a spicy brown color and are 16 inches (40.6cm), 15 inches (38.1cm) and 11 inches (27.9cm) tall. The *Country Cousins* are the "Newbeary Family" and will only be 1000 sets also. They arrive packaged in a hand-made display box with a hinged lid and a front flap that opens to show them off. *Merrythought photograph.*

Illustration 222. The fore-father of *Cheeky Bear*, which is now discontinued by Merrythought. Merrythought delved into the archives to re-create the ancestor of *Cheeky Bear* in a Limited Edition of 1000 pure mohair, 10 inch (25.4cm) characters. With a striking brown body, a flesh color muzzle and pads, a light gold tummy patch, and a blonde top knot, he is fully-jointed and he wears blue felt shorts. *Merrythought photograph.*

Illustration 223. The cutest of all the *Koalas* made by Merrythought is the 1986 one who is made from a synthetic pile cloth. He is 10 inches (25.4cm) tall.

Illustration 224. The 10 inch (25.4cm) *Pouncing Kittens* are one with a jet black coat and white paws and muzzle and one who is a genuine tabby with appropriate markings. *Merrythought photograph.*

Illustration 225. The *Crocodile* is 19 inches (48.3cm) long and is devious looking with his sly eyes. He is made of high quality green plush. *Merrythought photograph.*

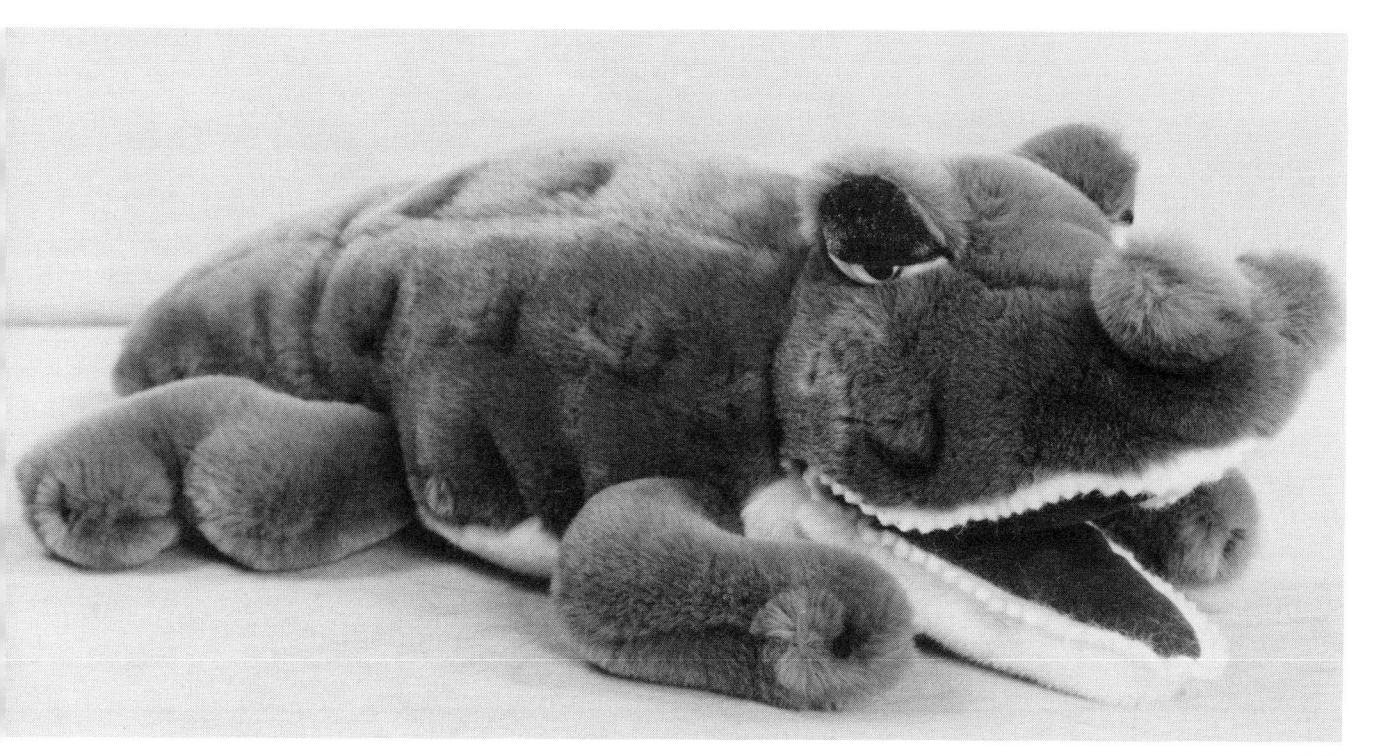

ABOVE: Illustration 226. The 9 inch (22.9cm) *Mallard* is made of the finest quality woven plush and he is colorful and characteristic looking. *Merrythought photograph.*

RIGHT: Illustration 227. The 1986 *Penguin* is 9 inches (22.9cm) tall and he has an open mouth, giving him a cute expression. *Merrythought photograph.*

BELOW: Illustration 228. The hand-made *Dolphin* is 12 inches (30.5cm) long. He has a colorful contrast of sky blue and midnight blue plush cloths. *Merrythought photograph.*

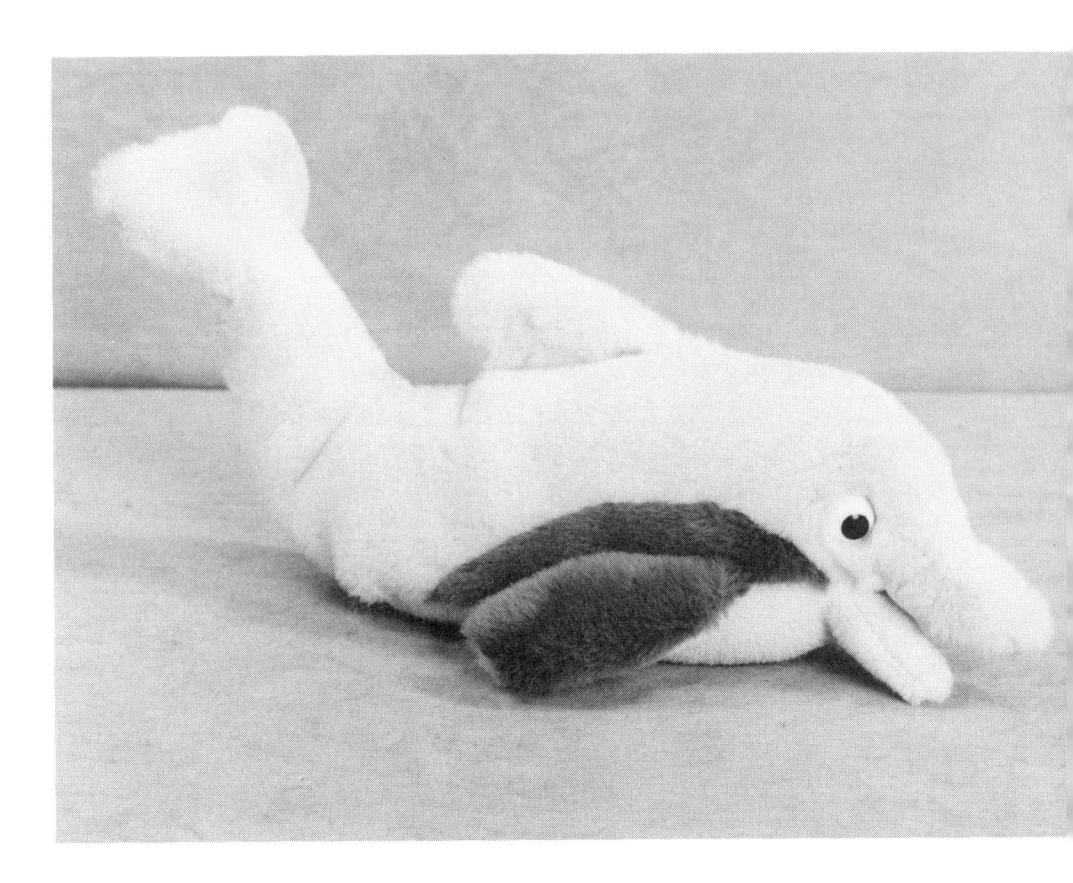

Illustration 229. The *New Merrythought Golliwog* of 1986 is 19 inches (48.3cm) tall. He is made of the finest cotton velvets in contrasting blue and red. The bright blue trousers are braided at the side seam with black and white silk cording. The red jacket lapels and cuffs are trimmed with blue velvet. The jacket is removable and is trimmed with brass buttons that match those on the shirt. *Merrythought photograph.*

Illustration 230. While researching the archives of Merrythought Limited for this book I discovered that the first toy shown on the first page of the first Merrythought catalog of 1931 was *Greyfrairs Bobby.* (See Illustration 45 and the Color Plates on page 99.) The true story of Greyfrairs Bobby was always one of my favorite books. I have re-designed *Greyfrairs Bobby* for Merrythought so that he has a jointed head to allow him to assume many different poses and expressions; he also has a perky little tail. This famous Skye Terrier who lived in Edinburgh, Scotland, in the 19th century will be a Limited Edition by Merrythought, made of a specially loomed long pile plush of silver gray with a dark undercoat. *Bobby* is 12 inches (30.5cm) tall. Merrythought's *Greyfrairs Bobby* of 1986 is packaged in a display box which includes a full-color booklet that tells his history. *Merrythought photograph.*

INDEX

All numbers refer to page numbers. The numbers in bold type refer to a photograph on that page.

A

Aaker, Lee, **158**
abominable snowman, **111**
Aldin, Cecil, 147
alligator, 105
Aristocrat Bears, 28
Arm Length Glove Toy, 163, 167
armadillo, 91
Artist, SEE Famous Artist
Attwell, Mable Lucie, 147, 193
Atwood, Florence, 7, 10, 11

B

badger, 91
ball, 163, 164, **176**
Bambi, 126, 127, 132, **140**
basket for puppies, 196
bear, 156, 157, **160**, 165, 169, 173, 175, **183**
bee, 113
Bingie Family, 27, **32**, 36
bird, 13, 112-113, **114, 115**, 126, 127, **128, 129, 139, 140,** 147, **150, 151,** 156, 158, 164, 165, 166, 167, 168, 172, 175, **178,** 188, 190, 196, 198, **204**
bird of paradise, 112
Blyton, Enid, 125, 147, 149
Bonzo, **97, 144,** 148, **153**
Bransky, Kay, 130, 144
Brown, James, **158**
buffalo, 91
bull, 84, **87, 90, 96,** 165, 171, 172, 187, 189
bunny, SEE rabbit
bush baby, 105
butterfly, 188, **193**

C

camel, 84, 168, 173, 183, 189
cat, 12, 13, 70-72, **73, 74, 75, 82, 102, 103, 104, 143,** 147, 156, 157, **157, 161, 162,** 165, 166, 167, 170, 174, **177,** 187, 188, 189, 196, **203**
caterpillar, 113, 168
Chad Valley, 7, 11, 134, 135
Prince Charles, **6, 22**
Cheeky, 27-28, 31, **33, 34, 38, 43, 44, 46, 48, 178, 202**
cheetah, 105
chicken, 112, 188
chipmunk, 91, 189
Christmas trees, 13, 196, **196**
cockatoo, 112, **114, 115**
Corbett, Harry, 147
Cot Toy, 163, 164, **176**
Cot Toy with Musical Chime, 163, 167
cougar, 91
cow, 84, **90,** 189
crocodile, 105, 189, **203**
crow, 112
cushion, 163, 167

D

Davis, Fanny Elizabeth, **8,** 9
Dean and Son Ltd., 9, 10
deer, 91, 126, **132, 140,** 147, 189

Deputy Dawg and Friends, **143**
dinosaur, 91
Disney, Walt, SEE Walt Disney
display items, 196
dog, 11, 12, 13, 51-56, **56, 57, 58, 59, 60,** 61-63, **63, 64, 65, 66, 67, 68, 69, 75, 96, 97, 98, 99, 100, 101, 103,** 126, 127, **129, 130, 131, 132, 133, 134, 143, 144,** 147, 148, **152, 153,** 156, 157, **157, 159, 162,** 164, 165, 166, 167, 168, 169, 170, 171, 172, 173, 174, 175, **177, 178, 179, 180, 181, 182, 185,** 186-187, 188, 189, **190, 191, 192,** 196, **197,** 198, **205**
doll, 13, 116-120, **120, 121, 122, 123, 124, 125,** 127, **134, 135, 136, 139, 141, 145,** 147, 148, **149, 152,** 164, 166, 167, 172, 174, **176, 177, 185,** 188, 190, **193, 194, 195,** 198, **205**
dolphin, 166, 187, 198, **204**
domestic animals, 13, **31,** 84-90, **88, 87, 89, 90, 96,** 126-127, **131, 146,** 148, **162,** 165, 166, 167, 168, 169, 170, 171, 172, 173, 174, 175, **176, 178, 179, 180, 182,** 183, **183, 184, 185,** 187, 189, **192,** 196, **197**
Donald Duck, **98,** 126, **128, 129, 139, 140**
donkey, 84, **87, 90, 96,** 126, **131, 162,** 165, 166, 167, 168, 169, 170, 171, 172, 173, 174, 175, **179,** 187, 189, 196, **197**
dragon, 111
duck, **98,** 112, 126, **128, 129, 139, 140,** 147, **150, 151,** 164, 168, 175, **178,** 188, 190, 198, **204**
Duddell, Elsie, 10
Dumbo, 126

E

Earnshaw, Peggy, 147
Eeyore, 126, **131**
elephant, 105, **108,** 126, **144,** 164, 165, 166, 167, 168, 169, 171, 172, 173, 174, 175, **182, 185,** 188, 189
Queen Elizabeth II, **20**
Queen Mother Elizabeth, **21**

F

Famous Artist, 7, 101, 125, 142, 144, 146-155, **150,** 162, 177, 193
fantastic animals, 13, 111
Farnell, J.K., 7
fish, 165
Flexi Toys, 163, 167
fox, 91, **93, 94,** 126, **143,** 165, 167, 189
frog, 91
Funicello, Annette, **20**

G

giraffe, **20,** 105
Glove Puppet Toys, 127, **161,** 163, 167, **177**
goat, 85, **90**
Golliwog, 116, 119, 120, **123, 124, 125, 141,** 198, **205**
goose, 112, 188

gopher, 91
gorilla, 105, 189
Greyfriars Bobby, 11, 55, **56,** 99, 175, 198, **205**
Groom, Arthur, 147, **150,** 151
Guest, Dorothy, **8,** 10, 44, 46, 74, 75, 97, 98, 125, 130, 159
guinea pig, 85, 165, 168

H

handbag, 196, **197**
Harrington, John, **13,** 97, 98
Harrods Department Store, **19**
Hassall, Ian, 147
hassock, 13, 196, **197**
hedgehog, 91, 166, 168, **177,** 187, 188, 189, 196, **197**
hippopotamus, 105, 188, 196
Hobby Toys, 163, 167, **178**
Holmes, B.T. (Trayton), **4,** 5, 9, **17, 22,** 42
Holmes, Oliver, **4,** 5, 10, **16, 17**
Holmes, W.G., 7
horse, **31,** 85, **88,** 148, 166, 167, 168, 169, 170, 171, 172, 173, 174, 176, **178, 179, 180, 182, 183, 184, 185,** 187, 189

I

insect, 13, 113, 168, 188, **193**
Ironbridge, 7, **14**

J

Janisch, A.C., 7
Jerry Mouse, 7, 13, **98, 140, 144, 160, 161, 162,** 177
Jumpee Cot Toys, 163, 166, **177**
jungle animals, 13, **97,** 105-110, **109, 110,** 126, 127, **142, 144,** 148, **154, 155,** 156, 157, **159,** 164, 165, 166, 167, 168, 169, 171, 172, 173, 174, 175, **177, 182, 183, 185,** 188, 189-190, 196, **203**

K

Kanga-&-Roo, 126, **131, 146**
Kangaroo, 92, **96,** 126, **131, 146**
kingfisher, 113
koala, 12, 49, **49, 50,** 166, 186, 189, **202**

L

Lady, 126, **130, 131, 132, 133**
Lady and the Tramp, 126, 127, **130,** 132, **133**
ladybug, 113, 168, 188
lamb, 85, **89, 90,** 165, 166, 167, 168, 174, 175, **176, 178,** 187, 189, **192,** 196
Laxton, G.H., 7
leopard, 106, **110,** 167, 175, 190
lion, 106, **109, 110,** 156, 157, **159,** 167, 188, 190
London Bears, 28, **34, 35, 41**
love bird, 113

M

magpie, 113
Princess Margaret Rose, **21**
Matthews, Jimmy, 9-10, **20, 21, 22**
Merrygo Riding Toys, 163, 172-173

Merrythought Balloon, **16, 17**
Merrythought Factory, 7, 9-11, **14, 15, 19**
Mickey Mouse, **98,** 126, **128, 129, 140**
Minnie Mouse, 126, **140**
mole, 92
Mole Manor Display Mushroom, 196
monkey, **97,** 106, **110, 142,** 148, **154, 155,** 165, 166, 172, 173, 174, **177, 183,** 188, 190
Morris, Doris, 10, 140
moth, 188, **193**
mountain lion, 189
mouse, 7, 13, 92, **98,** 126, **128, 129,** 140, **144,** 147, **151,** 156, 157, **160, 161, 162,** 168, **177**
Mouse Cottage Display Toadstool, 196
muff toy, 126, **129,** 147, 196, **197,** 198, **201**

N
nightdress case, 13, **101,** 126, 127, **128, 129,** 154, 186-195, **190, 191, 192, 193, 194, 195**
Noah's Ark, 186
Nodding Head Nursery Toys, 163, 167
Nursery Stool, 196, **197**

O
octopus, 92, 188
Old Yeller, 126, **134**
Oliver, Martin, **8**
101 Dalmatians, 126, **132**
otter, 92
owl, 113, 127, 166, 190, 196

P
panda, 12, 39, **40, 46, 162,** 165, 167, 170, 171, 172, 173, **183,** 186, 189
panther, 157
parakeet, 113, **115**
Parkes, John, 6
parrot, 113, **115**
pelican, 113
penguin, 113, 156, 158, 166, 167, **178,** 188, 190, 198, **204**
Perego, Maria, 147, 151, 162
pig, 86, 126-127, **146,** 148, 189
Piglet, 126-127, **146**
Pluto, 127, **129, 177**
polar bears, 12, 30, **38, 110,** 175, 189
pony, SEE Horse

Preston, Cloé (Chlöe), 7, 101, 147, 152
puffin, 113
Pull-Along Toys, 163, 168, **178**
Punkinhead, 29, 43, **48**
purse, 13, 198, **201**
Push Toy, 126, 163, 171-172
Push-Along Toys, 163, 168-169, **179, 182**

R
rabbit, 12, **59,** 76-79, **79, 80, 81, 82, 83, 97,** 127, **131, 133, 137, 138, 145,** 147, 156, 165, 166, 167, 168, 172, 173, 174, 175, **176, 178, 184, 185,** 187, 188, 189, 196, **197**
raccoon, 92, 127
ram, 86, **90,** 189
rattles, 163, 172
reindeer, 92, **95**
Rendle, C.J., 7, 9
Revitt, Jacqueline, **6,** 10-11
rhinoceros, 107, 190
Richard, Cliff, **20**
Riding Toys, 163, 173, **183**
Rin Tin Tin, 13, 157, **158, 159**
robin, 147
Rocking Pull-Along Toys, 163, 173, **183, 184**
Rocking Toys, 163, 173-174, **184**
Roundtree, Harry, 147
Rowan, Jane Holmes, 48
Rowles, Lilian, 148, 152

S
sachet, **137,** 188
Scamp, 127, **130, 131**
seal, 92, 189
Sieverling, Glenn, 142
Sieverling, Helen, 46, 142
skunk, 92, **96**
Slipper Toys, 163, 174
snail, 92, 168
snake, 92
Snow White and the Seven Dwarfs, 127, **134, 135, 136, 139. 145, 177**
squirrel, 92
Stage Coach with Four Horses, 163, 174, **185**
Sticky Toys, 163, 174
stools, SEE nursery stools
Studdy, G.E., 7, 144, 148, 153
Super Nightdress Cases, 189-190
swan, 113, 190

T
Taylor Phyllis, **8,** 10, 30, 35, 44, 65, 125, 129, 136, 139
Teddy Bears, 12, **19,** 23-29, **30, 31, 31, 32, 33, 34, 35,** 36, **36, 37, 38, 41, 42, 43, 43, 44, 45, 46, 47, 48,** 69, **97, 98,** 127, **131,** 146, 147, 162, 164, 165, 166, 167, 168, 172, 174, **176, 178, 184,** 186, 189, 196, 198, **198, 199, 200, 201, 202**
Thumper, 127, **131, 133, 145**
Tide-Rider, Inc., 10, 11, 29, 38, 42, 45
tiger, 107, **109, 110,** 127, 167, 175, 190
Tigger, 127
Toddle Toys, 126, 127, 163, 169-171, **180, 181, 182**
Tom Cat, 13, **161, 162**
tortoise, 92, 168, 189, 196
toucan, 113
Toys, 13, 163-185
Tramp, 127, **130, 133**
Tricycle Riding Toys, 163, 174
Trolley Scooter, 163, 174
Trotting Toys, 163, 174-175

W
Walt Disney characters, 11, 13, **98,** 116, 126-136, **128, 129, 130, 131, 132, 133, 134, 135, 136,** 139-140, **139, 140,** 145-146, **145, 146,** 162, **162, 177**
Walters, Esther, 10, **18**
Wellings, Norah, 7
Wheel Toys, 163, 175-176, **185**
White, Brian, 148
wild animals, 7, 13, 91-96, **92, 93, 94, 95, 96, 98,** 126, 127, **128, 129, 131, 132,** 140, **143, 144,** 147, **151,** 156, 157, **160, 161, 162,** 165, 166, 167, 168, **177,** 187, 188, 189, 196, **197**
Wilde, Marjorie, 10, **18**
Prince William of Glouster, **21**
Winnie the Pooh, 126, 127, **131, 146, 162**
Wol, 127
Wood, Lawson, 7, 142, 148, 154, 155, 177
woodpecker, 113

Z
zebra, 107, 167, 172, 174, 175, 190

FRONT COVER: A 1984 pure mohair bear produced in a limited edition of 2,500 pieces. *Photo by Harvey Dresner.*

BACK COVER, TOP: On the left: 18inch (45.7cm) *Beefeater Bear*, plush, 1973-1975; at right: *Beefeater*, No. D60/1, 1985; with mohair bear parts and a jointed head.

BACK COVER, BOTTOM: *Ginger Persian Cat*, 1938.